THE FAULD DISASTER
27 NOVEMBER 1944

THE FAULD DISASTER
27 NOVEMBER 1944

Nick McCamley

FOLLY BOOKS

Folly Books 2015

© Nick McCamley 2015

A catalogue record for this book is available from the British Library.

ISBN 978-0-9928554-3-7

Published by Folly Books Ltd
Monkton Farleigh
BA15 2QP
www.follybooks.co.uk

Designed and typeset by Vicky

Printed and bound in India by Replika Press Pvt Ltd.

Jacket and introductory photographs
Front jacket: Smoke blackened passageway near the Castle Hayes Pillar
Facing title page: The wall sealing the railway tunnel through the Air Ministry barrier
Facing page one: Aerial view of the fauld crater in 1950

PREFACE

On the morning of 27th December 1944 a huge explosion destroyed the RAF's most important underground ammunition depot at Fauld in Staffordshire causing widespread damage to military and civilian property and claiming the lives of seventy people. Within minutes of the explosion wild rumours began to circulate about the cause of the disaster – it was the result of bombardment by German V2 missiles; it was the work of the Irish Republican Army; it was the consequence of sabotage by co-operating Italian Prisoners of War (despite the fact that several Italians lost their lives in the explosion), or that it was caused either by the detonation of American cluster bombs stored underground which had a notorious reputation for instability, or by British Smith gun ammunition which had an equally unenviable record for killing or maiming its unfortunate handlers.

Although the subsequent Court of Inquiry came quickly to a definite conclusion not only as to the root cause of the disaster but also as to the identity of the man whose hand triggered the whole catastrophic chain of events, many writers, either ignorant of the true facts or else intent upon espousing elaborate conspiracy theories, have disregarded the convincingly persuasive evidence and continued their speculations to the present day. The first accurate account of the events at Fauld appeared in an excellent article by John Reed in *After The Battle* magazine in the late 1970s, following the recent release to the National Archive of documents relating to the explosion. It was the belated reading of that article that prompted my first visit to Fauld in 1985 and initiated the subsequent research that provides the background for this current volume.

The perceptive reader will notice that much of the text in this book relating to the RAF reserve ammunition depots and the aftermath of the Fauld explosion first appeared in one of the author's earlier works, *Disasters Underground*, published by Pen & Sword Books in 2004. In the light of more recent research some amendments and corrections, both minor and major, have been made to this earlier work and some sections of excessive detail have been removed completely where they appear irrelevant to the current book, but otherwise it has remained largely unchanged. This approach has been taken, in part, due to the fact that a large proportion of the text consists of verbatim quotations from evidence given at the RAF Court of Inquiry held shortly after the explosion and from the subsequent Coroner's Inquiry and must

thus, of course, stand as they are as part of the public record. The latter part of *Disasters Underground* relates the unfortunate story of the RAF's dalliance with chemical weapons, both home-manufactured mustard gas weapons (which, recent evidence has indicated, were produced in much greater numbers than was at first admitted), and German *Tabun* nerve-gas bombs which were brought to the UK in the immediate post-war years in the mistaken hope that they might find utility should this country become involved in a major conflict with the Soviet Union. Much of this is peripheral to the current work and has been omitted, although brief mention is made of the facilities provided at Bowes Moor for the storage of RAF mustard gas bombs. The storage and later disposal of the German *Tabun* bombs, under *Operation Sandcastle*, also gets a brief mention but only in so far as the ill-fated bomb store at Llanberis was involved as a temporary transit depot for the bombs as they made their way to more permanent quarters on the bleak and remote coastal airfield at Llandwrog. Readers with a special interest in Britain's chemical warfare programme might wish to read *Disasters Underground* and the author's *Secret History of Chemical Warfare*, both published by Pen & Sword Books.

It will also be noted that the introductory section of this book makes mention of the various underground facilities in the Corsham area of north Wiltshire, a subterranean complex engineered by the War Office in the inter-war years within a network of abandoned underground stone quarries. The intention was to use these sites, collectively known as Central Ammunition Depot Corsham, to house the entire war reserve of ammunition for the British army, but logistic failures on the part of the Air Ministry led to some of these sites being seconded, either temporarily or permanently, to the RAF for bomb and small-arms storage. The history of the Corsham depots is recounted in detail in the author's *Secret Underground Cities* (Folly Books, 2014) and *Second World War Secret Bunkers* (Folly Books, 2010). Much of the information in those books relating to the RAF utilisation of the Corsham quarries is reproduced here and I must apologise for the repetition, but the Corsham connection was so pivotal to the early development of RAF munitions storage policy that it cannot be overlooked.

Most historians or industrial archaeologists write from one or both of two perspectives: their books are based either, (if their work is to be of any consequence), upon the arduous sifting, sorting, analysis and extrapolation of information from primary sources found in obscure and dusty archives, or else they are based upon personal experience, groundwork and physical investigation. My own approach, like that of many others, is an attempted amalgamation of both. My first book, *Secret Underground Cities*, Describes in detail the varied underground wartime facilities in the Corsham area and goes on to cover other underground military sites across the United Kingdom in rather less detail. The reason for the disparity in depth of coverage is that, through chance, I had access to a huge volume of archive material relating to the Corsham area *and* I had physical access to most of the Corsham establishments; I had owned Monkton Farleigh Quarry (Central Ammunition Depot Corsham, Sub-Depot No.3) for almost ten years and through my association with that quarry I was given access, via sympathetic staff at the government's Property Services Agency, to the other, hitherto rather secret, underground depots in the Corsham area. All of these sites were fairly intact and, although some had been adapted for other Cold War purposes, were very much still in their wartime condition. It was, therefore, enlightening to be able to see in the flesh, so to speak, what one had previously only read about in official documents. What is often obscure in the written description becomes glaringly obvious when inspected in corporeal form. This was a luxury unavailable at the time in respect of any of the RAF depots other than Llanberis - hence the relatively shallow descriptions, which were based entirely upon documentary evidence.

In the intervening years however, even since the publication of *Disasters Underground* in 2004, hitherto unknown plans and engineer's drawings have come to light, more documents have been released into the public domain, more and better archive photographs have been unearthed and, most important of all, several of these sites have become, at least briefly, more accessible. To stand at the severed end of one of the storage tunnels at Llanberis and imagine being choked by dust as the rest of the depot collapses around you with thousands of bombs cascading from the shattered floor above, or standing at the door of 'A' Group Office in the Fauld depot and imagining yourself – as Foreman Salt described in his evidence at the Court of Inquiry into the disaster there – being blown bodily through the doorway by the force of the explosion, brings history to life and adds a vital spark to the bland documentary description.

This book would have been impossible without the help of so many people that it is difficult to know where to begin in offering my gratitude. Thanks must go first, as always, to the late Fred Allen, for without his fabulous collection of original documents, drawings, glass plate negatives and contemporary photographs, the story of Britain's subterranean wartime heritage would have been lost forever. From 1936 Fred was in charge of most of the underground construction in the Corsham area and, with great good fortune, was involved jointly with Eric Bryant from the Air Ministry in adapting certain of the Corsham quarries for RAF usage. From the very start, Fred was aware of the historic importance of the work he was involved with and ensured that, without any specific official sanction, any documents, plans or photographs of any significance that either passed over his desk in the course of his work, or could be cadged from Mr Bryant, were safely squirreled away for posterity rather than be destroyed. I also have to thank Peter Yarbrough, who accompanied me on my first visit to Fauld in 1985 which sparked my enthusiasm for further investigation, and to Bradley Wyatt with whom I first discovered the secrets of Chilmark. Bradley, together with Jake Boardley, also deserve credit for practical assistance in many other fields, about which I will say no more. Primarily, however, I must offer my gratitude to Bruce Maskery, for without his help in so many ways this book could never have been written. It is only due to Bruce's enthusiasm, meticulous planning and eye for detail that the gathering of much of the material for this book was made possible.

The photographs herein originate from many sources; most of the archive photographs are from the late Fred Allen's fabulous collection, other than the image on P121 and the panoramic image on P124/5 which are reproduced courtesy of the National Media Museum/Science & Society Picture Library. The ever-dependable Nick Catford provided several of the contemporary photographs of Llanberis and elsewhere, and I have to give a very special thanks indeed to Paul Thompson and Mark Rivron who provided a number of the stunning underground images of Fauld.

Nick McCamley

Monkton Farleigh
January 2015

CONTENTS

Chapter 1

INTRODUCTION

At 11.13 am, Greenwich Mean Time on the morning of 27 November 1944, geophysicists in Casablanca noticed a sudden peak register on the recording chart of their seismograph, indicating a significant earth tremor somewhere in the northern hemisphere. Seconds earlier Squadron Leader Anness, the officer temporarily in charge of the huge underground RAF bomb store at Fauld, near Burton-on-Trent in the midland region of England, watched in horror as the hillside above his underground depot rose bodily before his eyes, broke asunder in a searing fireball and erupted in a towering pillar of flame and debris, a quarter of a mile in diameter, rising two-thousand feet into the air before opening out into a mushroom cloud of smoke, rock debris and white-hot unexploded bombs that, minutes later, rained down upon the surrounding villages and farms, bursting in the air as they fell or exploding on impact with the ground.

The explosion, at the time the most powerful single explosion the world had ever witnessed, was the result of the sympathetic detonation of 4,000 tons of high-explosive bombs stored in galleries ninety feet below the fields of Upper Castle Hayes farm on the outskirts of the small Staffordshire village of Fauld. The initial blast initiated a catastrophic chain of events resulting in widespread destruction and the loss of seventy military and civilian lives, many of them far beyond the immediate boundary of the RAF facility. The crater left by the explosion, once one hundred feet deep and almost a quarter of a mile in diameter but now a little reduced by seventy years' erosion and weathering, is still a prominent feature on current Ordnance Survey maps and is clearly visible on satellite imagery.

Just minutes after the explosion speculation as to its cause began and, despite a conclusive RAF Court of Inquiry finding and a subsequent civilian Coroner's Inquest which, as far as the boundaries of its competency allowed, established a broadly similar course of events, public perception of what happened on that day is still confused. Many of the more outlandish suggestions that have circulated and gained currency in the intervening seventy or so years have gained traction over the decades having, perhaps, a more dramatic or conspiratorial appeal than the evidence supports.

This book is an attempt to set the story straight. Without the risk of prematurely revealing the conclusion, we can say at this point that the immediate cause of the disaster was the carelessness of one low-ranking airman who used the wrong tools in the wrong place performing a relatively routine task he had undertaken many times before. The root cause, however, stretches back much further, back to the mid-1930s when the RAF was making its first tentative preparations for the war which, by then, seemed to all those who were interested in such things, despairingly inevitable.

From the outset, as far as resources were concerned, the RAF always appeared to be on the back-foot. It was last on the list of the three fighting services in the allocation of secure underground storage space for its reserve stocks of ammunition and had to make do with facilities that, by comparison with those of the Admiralty and War Office, were severely inadequate. As the war progressed the role of the RAF expanded beyond that ever envisaged at the outset and, with the Battle of Britain won, and with its previously defensive role turning to one of offence, its bomb storage capacity and ammunition maintenance manpower were stretched to breaking point. Inevitably, corners were cut, safe storage limits were exceeded, explosives handling precautions were relaxed and often, as familiarity led to complacency, ignored entirely. It was this disregard of proper safety procedures and absence of vigilant oversight that was pinpointed as the ultimate cause of the disaster. The relaxation in vigilance identified generally throughout the RAF was recognised by the Court of Inquiry which commented that:

There are obviously mitigating circumstances during wartime when urgency is a keynote, manpower is of poorer quality and quantity, and more work is expected of a unit than that for which it is designed. Some relaxations can be made with safety and there must have been a tendency to extend relaxation locally owing to 'familiarity breeding contempt'.

However, despite recognition of the endemic nature of the conditions that led to the explosion, the hierarchical command structure of the RAF ordained that one individual must shoulder the blame, and that person was Squadron Leader Lionel Anness who, by ill fortune, unexpectedly found himself in temporary charge of the depot on the morning of the explosion. Judged by the standards of today the verdict against Squadron Leader Anness appears somewhat harsh and, indeed, up until the day he died, on active service in South Africa in May 1953 at the age of 47, he continued to argue his innocence, even so far as to exercise his right as a commissioned officer to petition his case to the King.

In order to fully understand and explain the circumstances that culminated in the catastrophe of 27th November 1944, this book is divided into three sections. The first gives an overview of the evolution of RAF ammunition storage policy during the decade leading up to the Fauld disaster while the second section describes in more detail the series of Reserve Ammunition Depots constructed between 1935 and 1941 and describes also a few examples of the later, temporary woodland bomb stores and airfield bomb dumps. The third section describes the construction, and day-to-day operation of the Fauld depot, culminating in a detailed account of the explosion and its immediate aftermath, drawn largely from the surviving records of the Court of Inquiry and the subsequent Coroner's Inquest.

Chapter 2

INTER-WAR PLANS

The fragility of the peace that briefly bound the nations of northern Europe following the armistice of 1918 was exposed following the rise to power of Adolf Hitler as Chancellor of Germany. In 1934 it became obvious to military strategists in Britain and elsewhere that another European conflict, to settle the unfinished business of the Great War, was inevitable and from the summer of that year, despite the overt pretence of appeasement, preparations for war began. With little other data upon which to make predictions, the War Office assumed the coming war would be much the same as the last and began to put in place provisions for a prolonged and largely static artillery and infantry affair. Thus, in June 1934, they began planning for the vast underground Central Ammunition Depot at Corsham in Wiltshire which, at that early stage, was expected to supply all the ammunition that the British Army would require in the forthcoming conflict. At much the same time the Admiralty, always keen to engage upon new construction on a monumental scale as befitted its self-proclaimed role as the Senior Service, also began to prepare for war.

By 1936 the RAF was still very much the junior partner in Britain's military triumvirate, although there was a tangible feeling in the air that things were perhaps about to change. Air Ministry calculations indicated that storage would be required for a war reserve of 98,000 tons of bombs consisting principally of 82,000 tons of 250 lb and 500 lb HE bombs and 16,000 tons of incendiaries. Based upon War Office experience, (because they had no corresponding experience of their own) the RAF decided that this storage capacity should take the form of a series of heavily protected underground depots each with a capacity of 10,000 tons, later rising to 30,000 tons. The War Office storage criteria sprang from the findings of an Army Council committee convened in June 1919 to 'Consider the Revisions of the Regulations for Magazines and Care of War Materiels' that sought to identify the shortcomings that led to a number of serious explosions at ammunition depots in France towards the end of the Great War. The committee found that the weapons most vulnerable to enemy bombardment were not high explosive shells, shrapnel, illuminating rounds and other similar thick-cased classes of shell, but propellant

charges, cased cordite, mortar shell and other thin-cased rounds. It was found that thick-cased shells were immune from the effects of a very close near-miss and were similarly immune, except in the most extreme circumstances, to sympathetic detonation. The mass detonation of such ammunition could, however, be initiated by the superheating effect of an extensive cordite fire nearby. Experiments indicated that the most catastrophic chain of events might be started by hot fragments of an enemy bomb penetrating the thin case of a trench mortar, the detonation of which would cause the destruction of similar ammunition in the same magazine, fragments from which might ignite cordite stored elsewhere in the dump, generating large conflagrations the heat from which would then cause the explosion of HE shell and so on. In the light of these conclusions the Air Ministry decided that it was imperative that the large reserve ammunition stocks currently contemplated, all of which consisted of either highly inflammable incendiary bombs or thin-cased HE bombs with a relatively high filling to gross weight ratio must be stored in completely bomb-proof underground magazines.

Planning for the underground depots proceeded in accordance with the overall policy agreed towards the end of 1936; i.e. a total weight of 98,000 tons of incendiaries and HE of which only 48,000 tons of the latter would be filled. The bulk of the HE component would consist, as we have seen, of 250 lb and 500 lb GP bombs, and dispersal, safety distances within the stores, transport and handling procedures were based on these assumptions. Again, belatedly following the War Office example, the Air Ministry sought out existing disused underground mines suitable for conversion, but found the task a troubling one, for the War Office had already bought the best in the early 1930s and what remained was marginal. Without the luxury and freedom of time adequately to plan, the Air Ministry again slavishly followed the War Office construction techniques and it was at this point that the seeds of future failure were sown.

The first difficulties have already been hinted at above. Over the ten-year period from 1934 until the end of the war army ammunition had tended to get smaller. When the War Office Central Ammunition

Depot at Corsham received its first stocks, transferred in haste from the existing, highly vulnerable depots at Woolwich and elsewhere, it consisted, for the greater part, of huge 9.2" and 12" howitzer shells weighing 290 lb and 750 lb each respectively, and shells for the 18" railway gun, each weighing well over a ton and requiring a two-hundredweight cordite charge to propel it to its target. All of these massive projectiles required special handling facilities that were particularly difficult to provide in the restricted underground areas, yet none were fired in anger during the Second World War (few were even practice-fired), and all made a final, melancholy journey to the bottom of the Irish Sea in the early 1950s. Thereafter, and for the rest of the war, the staple turnover of the underground depots consisted of 25-pounder shells packed four to a box, ammunition for the 4.5" and 5" field gun, 6 pounder and 17 pounder anti-tank rounds and, in by far the greater numbers, 3.7" anti-aircraft rounds. The important thing about all those weapons listed above, and the army's other weapons — anti-tank mines, grenades, mortars and small-arms ammunition — is that they were all a one-man-lift, easily stacked and manoeuvred, and ideal for transport by conveyor belt which was by far the best-suited system for underground use. So, although by

Above: The type of ammunition the conservative-minded War Office initially thought would be required for the next war with Germany. 18-inch howitzer projectiles, manufactured for a railway gun brought into use at the very end of the First World War but never fired in anger. Rounds for the gun were stored at Woolwich Arsenal until 1936 after which they were transferred to Corsham. Obviously obsolete even then, they remained in store there until 1964 when they were unceremoniously dumped in the Irish Sea.

Left: High-explosive rounds for the 9.2" howitzer, another of the guns that were largely obsolescent by 1939. Most of the few remaining in service were abandoned at Dunkirk, those still remaining in mainland Britain were quickly rigged-up as coastal anti-invasion weapons but there is little record of their use, even for training purposes, after the summer of 1942.

Above: The red-brick building is the weapons charging unit of the Forward Filling Depot at Lord's Bridge. The corrugated asbestos structure behind is the empty weapons and container store. The circular structure in the foreground, which could be mistaken for the top of a mustard gas bulk storage tank, is in fact a fire-fighting water reservoir.

Right: The chemical weapons charging building at Little Heath Forward Filling Depot.

Right: Storage buildings at Lord's Bridge FFD.

to be stored had already been made and it had also been confirmed that, for reasons of security and logistic convenience, these weapons should be stored in three underground depots, one each in southern, central and northern England. Under the Air Ministry plan, as finally revised in 1938, the three underground reserve depots would supply ammunition to five, later increased to eight, above-ground forward depots or 'Air Ammunition Parks'. The forward depots were to be located in the 'bomber zone' of eastern England at locations convenient to serve groups of between three and seventeen airfields within a radius of about twenty-five miles. They were to consist of open traversed storage compounds with a nominal capacity of one thousand tons, or approximately one week's consumption by the airfields they were designed to service. Although it was intended that construction should begin immediately the Air Ammunition Parks were war contingency establishments and would be neither stocked nor manned until war was declared.

During the first eighteen months of the war the initial scheme developed and expanded rapidly. The five original Air Ammunition Parks became eight, and under operational wartime conditions their nominal capacities were quickly exceeded. To alleviate the situation

the peacetime regulations specifying safety distances were abolished, allowing concentrations of explosives unthinkable under normal conditions. The authorized capacity of most of the Air Ammunition Parks was increased from 1,000 tons to 10,000 tons and to increase their capacity still further extensions were constructed and searches made for suitable locations for additional satellite sites. In July 1941 the whole organization of RAF ammunition supply was overhauled. The Air Ammunition Parks were renamed 'Forward Ammunition Depots' (FADs) and an additional series of smaller depots known as Advanced Ammunition Parks or AAPs, with nominal capacities of 500-1,000 tons, were constructed to supply the relatively light demands of fighter and coastal command stations.

Forward Ammunition Depots

Forward Ammunition Depots built later in the war, from 1942 onwards, bore little resemblance to those constructed during 1939/40, which were much more compact and heavily engineered. The earlier depots were all variations on a standard design. All were located close to trunk railway lines and had standard-gauge sidings serving the main weapons storage areas. Typically, the widely dispersed storage facilities consisted of an enclosed component store, four enclosed incendiary stores protected by earth traverses and two or more groups of open-topped, reinforced concrete HE storage magazines, each seventy-two feet square, built in pairs. Each magazine was designed to hold fifty-six tons of bombs and it was calculated that the combination of concrete walls and earth traversing would ensure that, in the event of an accidental explosion of the entire contents of one magazine, the blast would be deflected upwards and would not affect adjoining cells. By 1943, however, such was the pressure upon No.42 Group (the RAF administrative unit in overall charge of ammunition supply) that individual magazines typically held some 600 tons of bombs, more than ten times their design capacity.

Normally a standard 'group' would consist of two pairs of magazines, (a total of four 56-ton cells) intersected by a railway loading platform and surrounded by loop roads with lorry loading facilities. Provision was made for the addition of an extra cell to each pair of magazines, which would thus form a 'group' of six cells. Two groups of six-cell HE magazines were provided at Lord's Bridge FAD in Cambridgeshire, while Brafferton had only one four-cell group, Norton Disney three four-cell groups and Eynsham in Oxfordshire had two four-cell HE groups, together with three incendiary magazines. Facilities at all sites were increased continually throughout the war to meet the ever-increasing weapon loads of bomber command.

The mid-war depots, by contrast, were field storage sites with only the minimum of permanent buildings. The storage areas were typically concealed within large areas of woodland and the individual storage buildings or bomb-stacks were widely dispersed. South Witham FAD in Lincolnshire, for example, was hidden within the 500 acres of Morkery Woods which formed part of the Stocken Hall

Principal Forward Ammunition Depots			
First series			
36 MU	Snodland	11 Group Fighter Command	Opened 9/7/40 Replaced Staple Halt AAP which had opened 25/5/40. Subsequently reduced to AAP status.
91 MU	Southburn	4 Group Bomber Command South	Opened 1/11/39
92 MU	Brafferton	4 Group Bomber Command North	Opened 1/11/39
93 MU	Norton Disney	5 Group Bomber Command	Opened 1/11/39
94 MU	Barnham	2 & 3 Group Bomber Command	Opened 1/11/39
95 MU	Lord's Bridge	2 & 3 Group Bomber Command	Opened 16/11/39
96 MU	Eynsham	South Midlands OTUs	Opened 1/6/40
97 MU	Staple Halt	11 Group Fighter Command	Opened 25/4/40, Closed 9/7/40
98 MU	Mawcarse	All units in Scotland	Opened 1/5/40
Second Series			
100 MU	South Witham	1 Group Fighter Command	Opened 7/42
231 MU	Hockering	2 Group Bomber Command	Opened 1/1/43

Below: A contemporary aerial view of Brafferton Forward Ammunition Depot. Although abandoned and disused for decades a few of the buildings still survive and the outline of the roadways are still discernible amongst the trees and undergrowth.

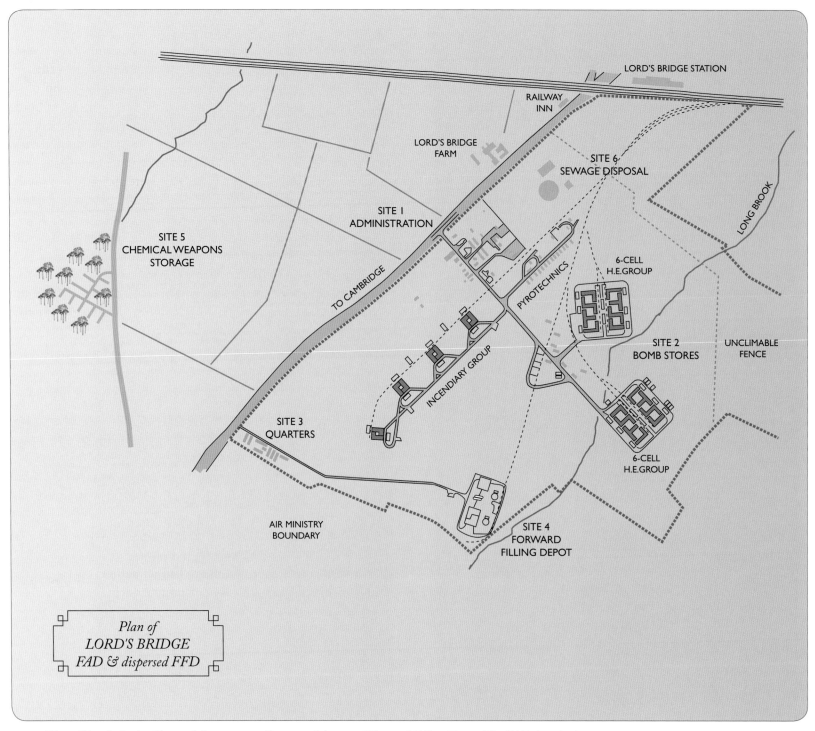

LORD'S BRIDGE STATION

RAILWAY INN

LORD'S BRIDGE FARM

SITE 6
SEWAGE DISPOSAL

SITE 1
ADMINISTRATION

SITE 5
CHEMICAL WEAPONS
STORAGE

TO CAMBRIDGE

PYROTECHNICS

6-CELL
H.E.GROUP

LONG BROOK

SITE 2
BOMB STORES

UNCLIMABLE
FENCE

INCENDIARY GROUP

SITE 3
QUARTERS

6-CELL
H.E.GROUP

AIR MINISTRY
BOUNDARY

SITE 4
FORWARD
FILLING DEPOT

Plan of
LORD'S BRIDGE
FAD & dispersed FFD

Above: Plan of Lord's Bridge Forward Ammunition Depot and dispersed Forward Filling Depot. The FAD, beside the Cambridge Road, is now home to the Mullard Radio Astronomy Observatory. All trace of the rail link to the site is long gone. The FFD, a short distance to the west, was accessed from Comberton Road.

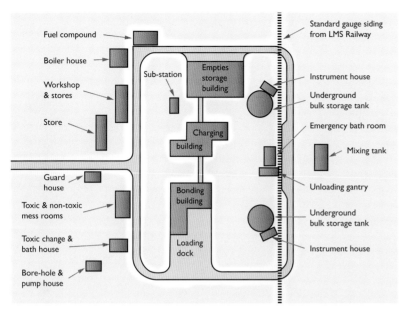

Above: Typical layout of a chemical weapons Forward Filling Depot. The empty storage building, charging house and bonding building are connected by covered ways.

Above: A preserved example of the Smith gun and limber. The cheap, flimsy construction of this weapon is clearly evident.

estate, bounded on the west by the Great North Road and to the north by Morkery Lane. As a safety precaution no HE bombs were stored within 400 yards of the main road or Stocken Hall. By the summer of 1942 Nissen huts, the RAF's favoured temporary storage buildings, were in short supply so at South Witham a range of other prefabricated storage sheds were employed. Six hundred tons of small arms ammunition was stacked in ten 'Handcraft' huts, and a further twenty-eight Handcrafts were used for pyrotechnics. Components and category 'X' explosives were stored in two groups of three 'Iris' huts. Interspersed among these were twenty-two groups of open-storage HE bomb dumps each holding 400 tons of bombs.

Three more Handcraft huts, in a remote corner of the woods, were filled with 3" smooth-bore ammunition for the awful Smith gun and quietly forgotten about. The Smith gun was a hastily cobbled together home defence weapon designed by a Mr Smith, chief engineer of the Trianco Engineering Company, makers of tinplate toys. It was in service as a Home Guard and RAP airfield defence weapon by June 1941 and quickly gained an unenviable reputation. Fuses fitted to the early batches of High Explosive shell were so sensitive and unreliable that even the official handbook was forced to admit that they had 'a reputation for lack of safety'. One Home Guard Officer went further, stating quite bluntly that the Smith gun had 'a terrifying reputation for killing its crew'.

The Forward Ammunition Depot established in March 1942 at Hockering in Norfolk was arranged in a similar manner. Existing 'rides' through Hockering Wood were widened to nine feet and metalled to take the weight of ammunition lorries, but otherwise little else was done to alter the natural camouflage, instructions to the RAF Works Directorate stressing that trees and other features are to be retained as far as possible.

Hockering, like South Witham, had an authorized capacity of 8,400 tons of HE bombs, 840 tons of incendiaries in huts and stacking areas for small arms ammunition amounting to 40,000 square feet, as well as a few huts for components, tail assemblies and special stores. Three sheds for the storage of ammunition for the reviled Smith gun were built in open country, well away from the main site, beside one of the many country lanes in the vicinity that were closed to the public except for pass-holding agricultural workers. A small technical site was established about one mile north-east of the woods beyond Heath Farm. Hockering was the last of the major FADs to be commissioned and delays in its construction caused concern during the autumn of 1942 as its capacity was desperately required to supply bombs to Swanton Morley in support of the Circus and

Right: A demonstration of the Smith gun in action, for the benefit of Winston Churchill. Once tipped over into its firing position, one road-wheel of the gun became a traversing platform while the other acted as a fairly ineffective shield. Note the tow-hook attached to the end of the smooth-bore barrel. One of the design features of the Smith gun was that it was light enough to be towed by an Austin Seven motor car.

Ramrod operations mounted by Bostons and Mitchells of No.226 Squadron. Hockering finally opened five months behind schedule in January 1943.

At other mid-war FADs the storage areas were more widely dispersed. At Earsham near Bungay, for example, accommodation for HE bombs was provided in woodland south-east of Banham Road to the north of the village, but other weapon types were stored in roadside stacks in a number of highly dispersed locations south and east of Earsham Hall.

Throughout the war many of the Forward Ammunition Depots changed their status to reflect the fluctuating demands on the various bomber or fighter groups they served. Until the end of the Battle of Britain fighter stations in No.11 Group were supplied primarily by a rather vulnerable and unsatisfactory FAD at Staple Halt in east Kent. In 1941 this depot was closed and its function taken over by a newly formed unit further north on the Medway estuary which, like most depots established during the war, took maximum advantage of the existing topography. Established as an Air Ammunition Park and then reclassified as a FAD, 36 MU, officially named Snodland but actually located in the nearby village of Halling on the north bank of Medway, made use of a series of worked-out chalk quarries associated with Lee's Lime Works, one of many cement factories that had been the staple industry of the immediate area for over a century. Chalk reserves in the hills bordering both banks of the river had been worked so intensively that the original topology of the land is hard to define. Most of the chalk downs running west from Strood to Snodland consist of tiers of gaping white gashes cascading down to the valley floor with each level joined to the one below by tramways on steep incline planes. In places the public roads weave around the quarry edges and below the roads numerous tunnels once carried the cement company tramways from pit to pit. Following a survey in June 1940 South Hill and Houlder quarries, high above Halling village and very prominent from the air, were somewhat inexplicably chosen by Maintenance Command as the site for No.11 Group's ammunition depot. South Hill quarry lies at the very top of Chapel Hill in an area known locally as Mount Ephraim and has the appearance of a white volcano hollowed in the hilltop. Access for the ammunition lorries was via a spiral concrete roadway laid by the RAF. An even more bizarre feature of 36 MU Snodland is that an adjoining quarry, 100 feet below vertically but within grenade-throwing distance laterally, was used throughout the war by the local Home Guard, and after February 1943 also by the regular home defence units and by the RAF, as a practice firing ground. Ample evidence of this wartime use can still be found today. Narrow-gauge tramway trucks abandoned in the quarry when the works closed in the early 1920s are riddled with bullet and cannon shell holes, and among the more recent undergrowth the floor of the quarry, which extends over several acres, are hundreds of discarded sticky-bombs, the Home Guard weapon of last resort against invading German Panzers.

The shortcomings of the site must soon have become apparent, for in May 1942 a new storage depot, 64 MU, was formed at Newdigate to take over the central role of ammunition supply to No.11 Group. In July Snodland was reduced to the status of a Maintenance Sub Unit (MSU) under Newdigate and its importance thereafter declined. Evidence that the RAF's apprehension rergarding the vulnerability of the Snodland depot was well founded came on 29 January 1944 when several bombs were dropped in the quarry, destroying 400 tons of incendiaries. A second raid four weeks later did less serious damage. Clearance began in July 1945 and by February of the following year Snodland, with its parent station at Newdigate, was finally closed and most of the buildings removed or demolished.

Locating the reserve depots

Searches throughout England in 1936 and the early months of 1937 for underground sites for the main reserve depots initially proved fruitless. With the assistance of staff from the Geological Survey, the Mines Department and from a number of mining and quarrying companies, over one hundred sites were identified and surveyed, but none met the rigorous Air Ministry criteria. Most of those that were suitable had already been snapped up two or three years earlier by the War Office and those that remained failed because they were either too small, too wet, had insufficient head cover to assure safety, were too distant from suitable railway connections or too close to existing active quarry workings. There was a brief competition between the Air Ministry and the War Office for Acorn Bank gypsum mine near Temple Sowerby in Westmorland (now Cumbria) until a survey showed that the quarry was liable to severe winter flooding. Similar friction arose between the Admiralty and the Air Ministry over Beer Quarry near Seaton in Devon; after an initial investigation the Admiralty pronounced the somewhat prominent site too vulnerable

to bombardment, an assessment with which the Air Ministry reluctantly concurred. Having succeeded in the bluff and seen off the men from the Air Ministry, the Admiralty immediately retracted its objections and acquired rights over the quarry a few days later.

Charged after 1937 with the task of maintaining ever increasing stocks of anti-aircraft ammunition for the Air Defence of Great Britain, the War Office continued to seek out underground accommodation at the expense of the RAF, a situation exemplified in a memorandum to Southern Command urging officers there to investigate, and if possible acquire, the show-caves at Cheddar *'because if we do not then the RAF most certainly will'.*

Eventually, in the summer of 1936 adequate, although not ideal, underground sites were found in southern and central England for two of the three proposed underground reserve depots. It was clearly evident, however, that the War Office had already monopolized all the most promising underground real estate then available and what was left for the RAF was very much in the second division.

For the southern depot a recently disused limestone quarry at Chilmark near Wilton in Wiltshire that had once provided stone for the construction of Salisbury cathedral was selected. In the Midlands region the Air Ministry selected a partially disused alabaster mine at Fauld, a few miles north of Burton-upon-Trent, owned by Peter Ford's plasterboard company. Ford's mine extended below several hundred acres of Staffordshire countryside and the area selected for conversion to a bomb store lay approximately four hundred yards east of the company's active working area. In view of the urgency of the situation the rules regarding the proximity of operational quarry workings, that would otherwise have precluded the use of Ford's mine, were disregarded.

Unable to find any suitable underground sites in the north Midlands the Air Ministry was compelled to fall back on the less favoured option of building an 'artificial' underground depot by constructing a series of concrete storage chambers in the bottom of a deep open quarry and backfilling up to ground level with forty feet of waste stone. Suitable disused limestone quarries were plentiful in the Buxton area of Derbyshire, which had the twin advantages of being geographically well situated and provided with good railway connections. Sorrow Quarry at Harpur Hill, just to the south of Buxton, was purchased from ICI in July 1938 and construction work began immediately. Shortly afterwards, in response to the increasing demand for storage, a slate quarry and 350 acres of adjoining land near Llanberis in North Wales was purchased and preparations got

Above: The overgrown remains of one of the stacking areas at 36 MU Snodland in Kent. Here the floor of the terraced chalk quarry was levelled and the bombs and small-arms ammunition stacked in the open. A spiral roadway winds around the chalk hill in the background, terminating in a further stacking area in a bowl-shaped quarry in the very top of the hill.

Right: One of the very few surviving structures at 36 MU Snodland. There is little evidence in the form of concrete bases, etc, of any other permanent buildings on site.

under way for a second 'artificial' underground depot broadly similar to that at Harpur Hill. Much later, in April 1941, it was proposed to establish a fifth underground reserve depot in Linley Cavern, an abandoned limestone mine near Aldridge in Staffordshire. Early investigation indicated that the quarry had a long history of instability and frequent flooding. Conditions at Linley were marginal at best and despite the expenditure of over £1,000,000 on reconstruction it was found impossible to make the quarry safe and it was subsequently abandoned.

By October 1941 the Air Ministry estimated that within eighteen months No.42 Group would need to provide storage for a reserve of 632,300 tons of bombs. The existing reserve depots had a capacity of only 158,000 tons and the prospect of finding suitable accommodation for the balance of 474,000 tons in the immediate future seemed bleak. Even as they struggled to overcome the current shortfall their problem was compounded by the catastrophic collapse of the underground depot at Llanberis due to structural failure in January 1942 and the subsequent precautionary evacuation of Harpur Hill, which was built in a similar way and, it was thought, might similarly collapse.

An immediate search was made for even marginally suitable underground sites, although it was realized, as a Maintenance Command minute reveals, that 'disused quarries mines and caves in the land are in great demand'. An examination of Bradbar Quarry near Gifthock proved disappointing. On arrival the inspection team found the quarry partially flooded, subsiding and at risk from gas infiltration from a nearby coal seam. As a last resort Pretoria mine at Bakewell and Clearwell Caves in the Forest of Dean were inspected, but neither were at all suitable. By this time, though, with German air attacks upon the mainland diminishing to little more than occasional nuisance raids, there was a growing realization that the huge underground depots planned in the 1930s were something of an expensive, inconvenient anachronism. The reserves were simply no longer vulnerable to attack by air, and the original system of operation by which all new stocks were routed from the factories and docks by a rigidly fixed route to the airfields via the reserve depots and FADs was abandoned. Under the new system most supplies were transferred directly from the factories and docks to the FADs, and on occasions, during periods of particularly high demand, straight to the airfield bomb dumps. The reserve depots, particularly the main underground sites, gradually became dumping grounds for obsolete weapons, holding points for large overseas issues, and centres for the

Above: Outline plan showing the locations of the most important RAF ammunition depots used during the Second World War.

Bomb store

Keevil Airfield: A typical early Type 'D' bomb store.

Left: Aerial view of the airfield showing location of the bomb store. Although initially planned as a fighter Operational Training Unit the airfield was built as a bomber OTU. Ultimately, however, it was used as neither and began life in Army Co-operation Command. Until 1944, when it was used for glider towing for operation Overlord, it saw little use other than as a dispatch and testing site for Spitfires manufactured at a dispersed factory in Trowbridge and assembled in a MAP hangar on the airfield.

Below left: Brick abutments to the somewhat eroded earth mounds around a couple of bomb storage bays.

Below right: Concrete ramp adjacent to the inner circuit road where bombs were unloaded from delivery lorries into the storage bays.

Above: A bomb storage bay viewed from the bomb-trolley circuit. A series of three storage bays can be seen in the background of this photograph.

Right: These iron rings, set into the front of the lorry unloading ramp, were used to secure ropes employed to 'trammel', or roll heavy bombs in a safe and secure manner off the beds of the lorries and down the concrete ramps into the bomb storage bays.

Right: Aerial view of Bowes Moor chemical weapons storage site. The wartime layout of roadways and building is still quite evident although the topography around the communal site in the south-west corner has changed dramatically. Bowes station and the railway line have been swept away and replaced by the new alignment of the A66 trunk road.

Below: A plan of the Bowes Moor depot showing the distribution of the various types of weapon throughout the site.

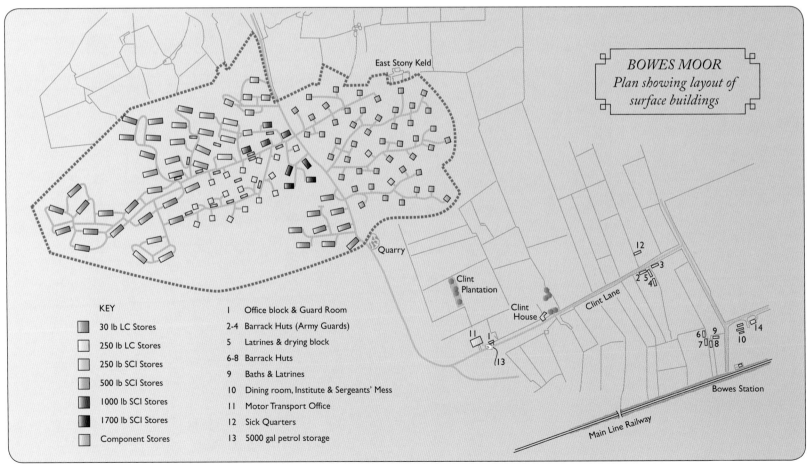

East Stony Keld

BOWES MOOR
Plan showing layout of surface buildings

Quarry

Clint Plantation

Clint House

Clint Lane

Bowes Station

Main Line Railway

KEY

- 30 lb LC Stores
- 250 lb LC Stores
- 250 lb SCI Stores
- 500 lb SCI Stores
- 1000 lb SCI Stores
- 1700 lb SCI Stores
- Component Stores

1   Office block & Guard Room

2-4 Barrack Huts (Army Guards)

5   Latrines & drying block

6-8 Barrack Huts

9   Baths & Latrines

10 Dining room, Institute & Sergeants' Mess

11 Motor Transport Office

12 Sick Quarters

13 5000 gal petrol storage

repair, maintenance and upgrading of unserviceable stock.

Quickly established and cheaply constructed field storage depots which were flexible in operation and elastic in size were seen as the immediate solution to No.42 Group's difficulties and within a short time three locations for such depots were identified at Longparish in Hampshire, Wortley in Yorkshire and Gisburn in Yorkshire. Meanwhile, the Llanberis collapse had drawn attention to the potentially awful consequences that might have occurred had the depot contained poison gas bombs. This was no irrational fear because the lower floor of the almost identical 'artificial' underground depot at Harpur Hill had been designated in June 1940 as the main location for handling chemical weapons. By the following summer doubts were already surfacing regarding the wisdom of storing large quantities of chemical weapons underground and it was decided to establish a dedicated reserve depot on the surface in a remote location in northern England to take over Harpur Hill's chemical weapons

role. The site chosen was Bowes Moor to the south-west of Barnard Castle in County Durham. The first mustard gas bombs arrived at Bowes Moor on 8 December 1941 with receipts accelerating markedly after the Llanberis collapse. The development and demise of each of the main reserve depots is detailed in the pages that follow, but first it is necessary to explain the measures taken to overcome the immediate shortfall in storage capacity that arose between 1936 and 1941 while the new depots were under construction, and to examine the temporary role played by the War Office quarries at Corsham in meeting this deficit.

Below: In March 1945 Bowes Moor became the central disposal point for the RAF's chemical weapons stockpile. Disposal was initially accomplished by filling the existing storage sheds to capacity and then igniting the whole lot with incendiaries. This process proved too time consuming and ultimately resort was made to deep sea dumping. Although reported as cleared of chemical weapons in July 1946 doubt over the site's safety has remained.

Above: The site remains littered with the concrete bases of buildings destroyed by fire during the mustard gas disposal programme of 1945.

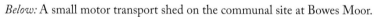

Below: A small motor transport shed on the communal site at Bowes Moor.

Below: One of several Stanton shelters that survive on the communal site.

Chapter 3

RIDGE & CORSHAM QUARRIES

Ridge Quarry & the RAF reserve depots

The immediate result of the Air Ministry's dilatory decision-making and the War Office's conservative preparations was that shortly before Munich the Army found itself in possession of four immensely sophisticated underground reserve storage depots at Corsham that would ultimately cost some £4.4 million to construct but had virtually no shot nor shell to store in them, while the RAF had almost the entire output of the explosive chemical industry bearing down upon it but with precious little storage space to hand.

As an interim measure the War Office was approached with the request that some of the quarry space under development at Corsham should be temporarily allocated to the RAF until the new Army weapons programme got properly under way. The outcome was that in November 1936 the RAF was granted the exclusive use of Ridge Quarry, the smallest of the four quarries that comprised Central Ammunition Depot (CAD) Corsham, which was then approaching completion. Some time later a substantial part of Eastlays Quarry was also seconded to the RAF to supplement the Ridge holding.

Development of the Corsham quarries by the War Office had begun in July 1935 when preliminary work began on the adaptation of the relatively small, nine-acre Ridge Quarry at Neston near Corsham as a temporary ammunition store. Simultaneously, clearance of approximately two million tons of waste stone debris had begun from the fifty-acre maze of tunnels and chambers that formed Tunnel Quarry, an abandoned Bath stone quarry lying just to the north of Brunel's Box railway tunnel on the main Bristol to London line near Corsham. This was to become the most important of the series of permanent underground depots that was to comprise

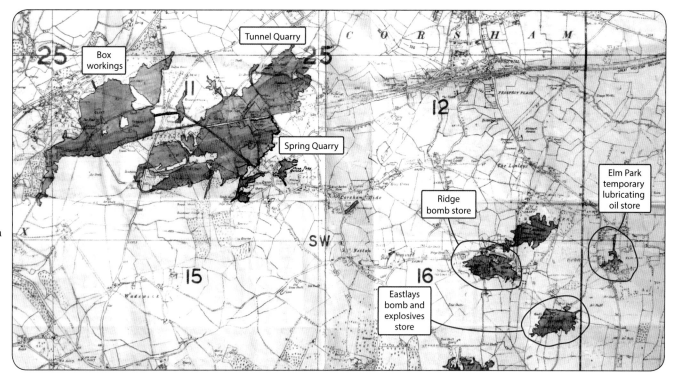

Right: A detail from a War Office plan of the Corsham area of north Wiltshire showing the underground areas utilised by various government and military organisations for storage and other purposes. Those areas occupied by the RAF have been highlighted.

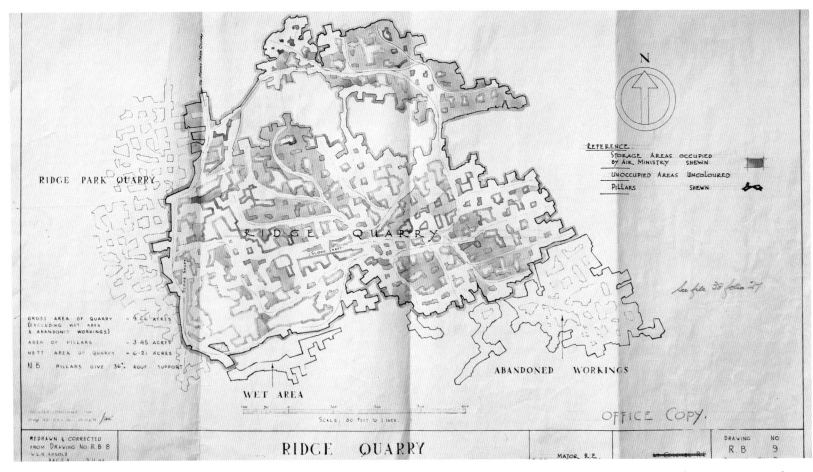

RIDGE PARK QUARRY

RIDGE QUARRY

GROSS AREA OF QUARRY
(EXCLUDING WET AREA
& ABANDONED WORKINGS) = 9.66 ACRES
AREA OF PILLARS = 3.45 ACRES
NETT AREA OF QUARRY = 6.21 ACRES
N.B. PILLARS GIVE 36% ROOF SUPPORT

WET AREA

ABANDONED WORKINGS

REFERENCE
STORAGE AREAS OCCUPIED
BY AIR MINISTRY SHEWN
UNOCCUPIED AREAS UNCOLOURED
PILLARS SHEWN

SCALE, 80 FEET TO 1 INCH.

OFFICE COPY.

RIDGE QUARRY

REDRAWN & CORRECTED FROM DRAWING No. R.B.8

DRAWING No R.B 9

Above: Although built as a War Office depot Ridge Quarry was occupied throughout the Second World War by the RAF. As the war progressed large stocks of obsolete bombs, mostly of American manufacture and with a questionable safety record, had accumulated at Ridge. This plan, drawn up in August 1945, shows the location of this dubious stockpile within the quarry.

the Corsham Central Ammunition Depot. It was intended that Ridge would perform a transitory function only until the much larger depots nearby were completed some four years hence.

Shortly after developments began at Corsham it was made clear that Ridge Quarry must be ready to receive stocks of explosives by the end of December 1936 and, given this precondition, there was an acceptance that the heavy civil engineering works initially proposed would necessarily be abandoned. Ridge had been one of the very few underground locations used for the storage of high explosives during the First World War and the mine had altered little since being vacated by the Ministry of Munitions in 1922, but it still proved necessary to remove a total of 96,000 tons of stone debris to provide sufficient storage space. All the raised stacking areas constructed in the Great War were removed and the floors rolled and levelled. The already comprehensive two-foot-gauge railway system was extended to serve all the storage bays, and an existing steam winch at the head of the access shaft was overhauled and provided with a new boiler. Because the 1:3 gradient put a considerable load on the winding

plant a standby electric hauling engine was installed in case of a breakdown of the primary set.

At the bottom of the main slope shaft the rails served a primary reception and marshalling area. Nearby an old vertical ventilation shaft was adapted for winding by the installation of a pair of counterbalanced electric lifts running in wooden guides. This was a primitive affair with a poor loading capacity, capable of handling only one third of the throughput of the slope shaft.

Underground, the mine is crossed by a major slip-fault, with the result that one half of the workings is about 20 feet lower than the other. Two sloping haulageways were driven to connect the upper and lower sections; to enable wagons to be drawn up these inclines two steam winches were installed, adapted to operate on compressed air supplied by compressors housed on the surface. Generally, however, loaded trucks were manoeuvred manually throughout the level areas of the quarry.

Some months after stacking had begun a construction programme was initiated, designed to produce a layout of storage areas more regular than the random pattern of existing pillars. It was planned to reinforce the stone pillars by corseting them with concrete, making them rectangular in section with straight haulageways between. Concreting began early in 1938 on fifteen pillars and a length of perimeter wall in the south-east corner of the quarry, but this operation was permanently suspended a few months later. The cost of the work and the quantity of materials consumed were much greater than anticipated and were out of proportion with the benefits obtained. The unfinished concrete reinforcing can still be seen in varying degrees of completion in the quarry today and illustrates the constructional techniques used in the larger and more sophisticated of the Corsham depots. A second slope shaft, the steeply graded West Ridge incline, was reopened on 12 February 1942 to improve access to the lower level of the mine and provide space for a further

1,500 tons of weaponry. The underground access tunnel linking this shaft to the new storage bays passed through an area of treacherous roof formation that required substantial support to ensure safety.

Ridge Quarry was allocated to the Air Ministry in November, 1936, under the command of Squadron Leader F. R. Lines, and was designated a sub-unit of the Altrincham small-arms depot. Control of ammunition and support supplies became the responsibility of RAF Maintenance Command following its formation in March 1938, at which time Altrincham became No. 2 Maintenance Unit (2 MU) and Ridge Quarry No.2 Maintenance Sub-Unit (2 MSU). The following spring separate Groups were formed within the Command for specific functions, ammunition, fuel and oxygen being the remit of No.42 Group. The total capacity of Ridge Quarry was 13,000 tons, of which the RAF at first required about 5,000 tons to store 500 lb and 250 lb GP bombs. By the outbreak of war RAF stocks at Ridge had expanded to 11,569 tons, including 4,000 tons of bulk TNT. At that time the RAOC retained a small area to store 2,000 tons of bulk explosive for Army use.

During the early months of the war Ridge Quarry was used as a

Right: A lorry loaded with RAF bombs, probably transshipped from Beanacre Sidings, being unloaded at the top of No.1 loading platform at Ridge Quarry in the early years of the Second World War.

Above: An example of the unfinished concreting reinforcement in Ridge Quarry, a consequence of the RAF taking occupation of the depot before construction was completed.

temporary holding point for bulk explosives and as a long-term store for obsolete GP bombs returned from various active airfields via the Pulham depot. A typical week in September saw the receipt of twenty-two tons of raw TNT from the ICI works and the dispatch of four tons to the Thames Ammunition Company at Erith in Kent. The following month there began an appreciable increase in the inward flow of surplus bombs with 1,245 tons arriving in the first two weeks. A record 210 tons was transported underground in less than twelve hours on 7 November, but this continuous use overtaxed the aged steam winch which failed at 6 pm. Ninety minutes later the standby electric unit was coaxed into motion; this sufficed barely adequately until 8 pm when the more powerful steam winch was brought back into action, following hasty repairs.

January 1940 saw a reorganization of No. 42 Group, resulting in the recently opened Chilmark reserve depot becoming parent to Ridge Quarry, which was re-designated No. 11 MSU. Conditions underground were becoming congested due to the large influx of obsolete material which was accumulating with no immediate prospect of disposal; a problem made more acute by the RAOC insistence that they be allowed to store rather more than the agreed amount of Army TNT in the quarry. The situation eased at the beginning of May when calling-forward instructions were received for a shipment of 5,000 250 lb GP bombs destined for No. 4 Base Ammunition Depot in the Middle East. The whole of this consignment was dispatched from Ridge, where labourers were employed on overtime breaking down stacks and placing bombs on end beside the narrow-gauge railway ready for loading.

Large issues continued throughout July and the early part of August, the space vacated being filled by huge quantities of imported TNT from the United States and Canada, and eight tons of French manufacture and dubious nature hurriedly recovered from the continent. Administrative responsibility for all Air Ministry bulk explosives stored at Corsham was transferred to the RAOC in January 1941 and independent accounts of receipts and issues disappear from the record book from that date.

The spring of 1941 saw increasing deliveries of munitions from the United States under the terms of the Lend Lease Act of 11 March. Turnover of bombs at Ridge Quarry increased dramatically and a two-shift system was introduced in an effort to increase the daily rate to 400 tons. In preparation for the expected German invasion Ridge received 3,000 hand grenades from Tunnel Quarry on 22 August for issue to airfields and depots in the south-west within the next

few days. Delivery also began at this time of tens of thousands of rounds for the Smith gun, although it is unlikely that stocks were retained for long periods. 27,000 rounds were issued to airfields in the southern counties early in December, and further stocks were received early the following year, 1,750 practice rounds arriving from Chorley Ordnance Factory at the end of February, followed by 19,000 high explosive rounds from Aycliffe on 10 March.

Operations became hectic at Ridge early in March 1942, following the sudden and catastrophic collapse of the artificial underground depot at Llanberis and the subsequent precautionary clearance of Harpur Hill. Evacuation of bombs from the surviving section of Llanberis began on 9 March and continued until 28 April when the last bomb was recovered. A total of 8,230 tons of ammunition was recovered in this exercise, nearly 2,000 tons of which was dispatched to Ridge Quarry. Between 30 March and 16 May a total of 15,676 tons of bombs and other ammunition was evacuated from Harpur Hill as a precautionary measure; of these just 650 tons were transferred to Ridge Quarry.

Once the abnormal activity resulting from the Llanberis accident had subsided, Ridge fell into a busy routine through the rest of 1942 and into the following summer. The average turnover amounted to balanced receipts and issues of about 2,000 tons each month. Receipts normally consisted of 500 lb bombs from the Risley and Swynnerton filling factories, 250 pdrs from Glascoed and a few 1,000 lb bombs from Ruddington.

During the early months of 1944 stock levels increased at Ridge to a peak of 31,563 tons, and in March preparations for the invasion of Europe began. During April and May the RAF dropped more than 200,000 tons of bombs as a direct preliminary to Operation Overlord. The contribution to this effort made by Ridge Quarry amounted to 7,744 tons in April and a massive 14,294 tons in May.

Eastlays Quarry

Construction began at Eastlays in July 1936. Development of this site and the nearby Ridge Quarry was intended to progress in parallel with that at the principal War Office underground storage site at Tunnel Quarry, but the urgent need for premature storage disrupted this plan at an early stage. Most of the labour force was withdrawn in the autumn and concentrated at Ridge Quarry which had to be completed to a minimum standard for occupation by the Air Ministry by December. Urgent work was also needed at Tunnel

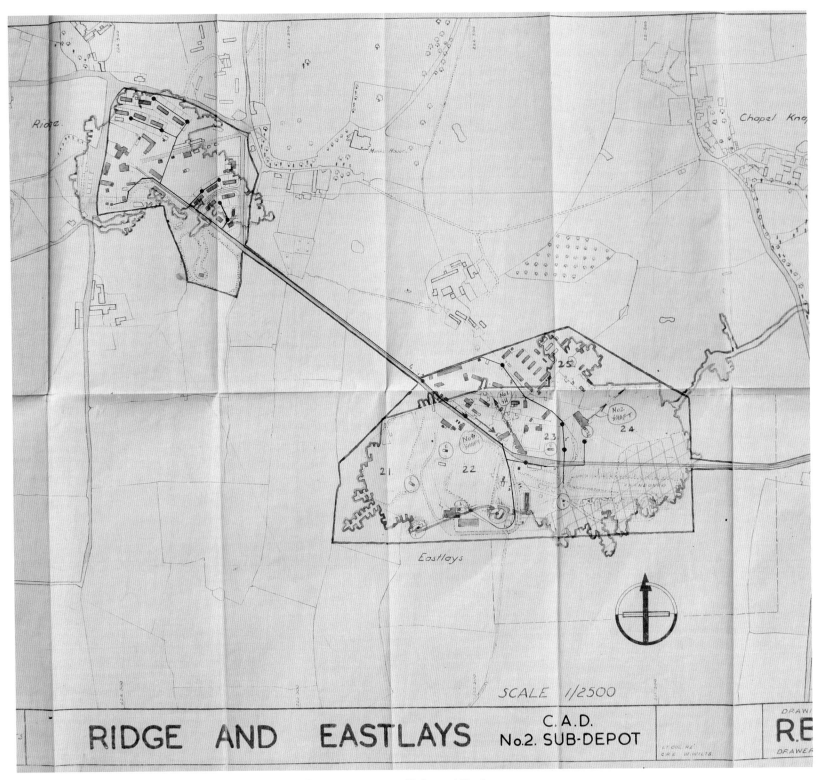

Above: Fred Allen's original water colour drawing of the surface arrangements at Ridge and Eastlays.

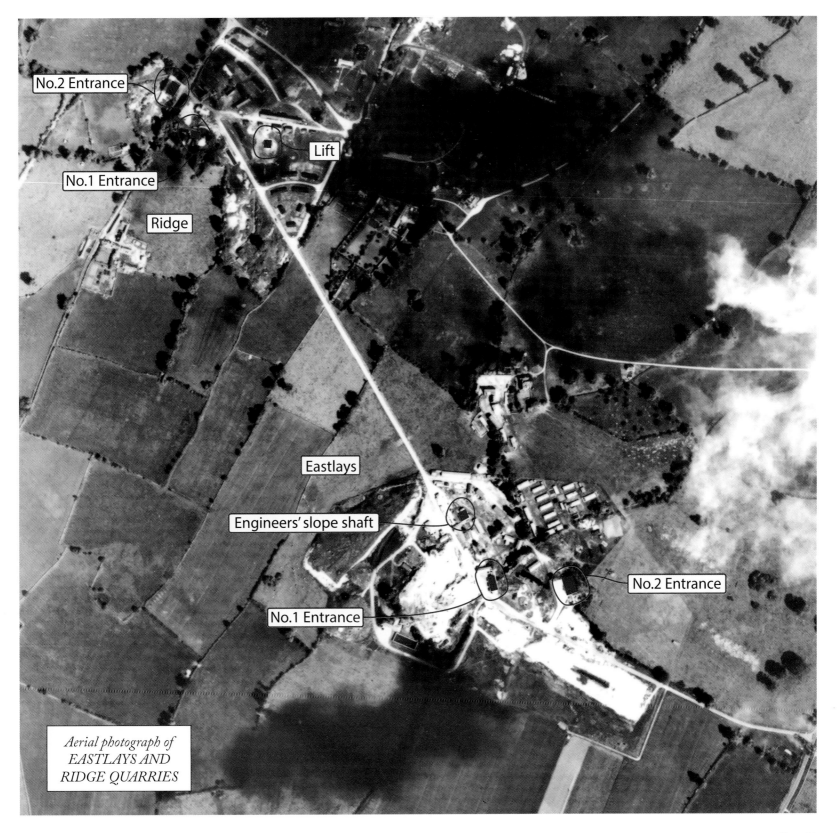

No.2 Entrance

No.1 Entrance

Ridge

Lift

Eastlays

Engineers' slope shaft

No.1 Entrance

No.2 Entrance

Aerial photograph of
EASTLAYS AND
RIDGE QUARRIES

Quarry to finish the first storage district there by July 1938 to meet a War Office deadline, resulting in a further transfer of labour and equipment from Eastlays.

Although it was originally intended that Eastlays should store a mixed inventory of Army field ammunition similar to those at Tunnel Quarry and Monkton Farleigh, agreements reached with the Ministry of Supply in 1939 and with the RAF in 1940 resulted in a radical change of plan. In October 1940 Wing Commander Lines visited Corsham to discuss the storage of Air Ministry bulk explosives and was subsequently granted the use of one complete district at Eastlays for this purpose. Later the RAF occupied a second district as a bomb store to supplement its existing holding at Ridge Quarry. It was agreed that non-phosphorous incendiaries could be stored underground safely and that all such stocks would he transferred from the Altrincham depot, as would surplus stocks from the RAF reserve depots at Fauld, Chilmark and Harpur Hill.

Building work in the HE magazine, known as No.21 District, was not finished until the late autumn of 1939 and until that time TNT scheduled for storage at Eastlays was held under less than ideal conditions at Ridge Quarry. The first stocks were accepted into Eastlays early in January 1940 at which time the RAOC agreed to transfer all of its remaining storage space at Ridge to the RAF. Heavy inward movements of explosive and delays in the completion of the cordite store in No.22 District meant that the Army was unable to keep to this agreement, and on 15 January the Commanding Ordnance Officer (COO) requested space for a further 1,000 tons of TNT at Ridge. The RAF complained about the monopolization of the Ridge Quarry winding shaft by the RAOC, which was engaged in an urgent shipment of TNT to Bombay. Meanwhile the temporary inability of the RAF to receive stock at Ridge created congestion farther down the supply chain and within two days thirty-two truck loads of obsolete bombs despatched from the overstocked and unsuitable RAF small-arms depot at Pulham had accumulated at Thingley Sidings and more were on their way.

By the spring of 1940 Districts 21 and 22 were fully occupied by the RAF and turning over 2,000 tons of bulk explosive weekly. When completed in October 1940 No.23 District was handed over to the RAF under an agreement to store Air Ministry TNT negotiated a few weeks earlier. Two months later the newly completed No.24 District was also allocated to the RAF to store high-explosive and incendiary bombs. The first stock receipts were made on 15 January when 50,000 incendiary bombs were received from the reserve depots

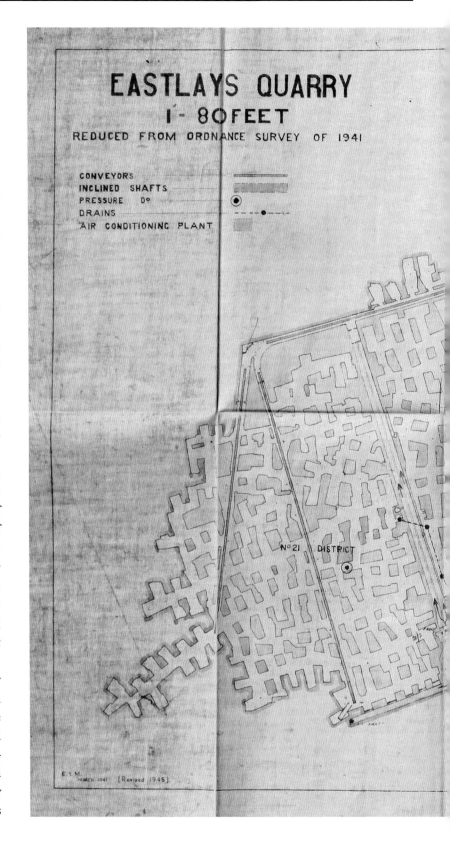

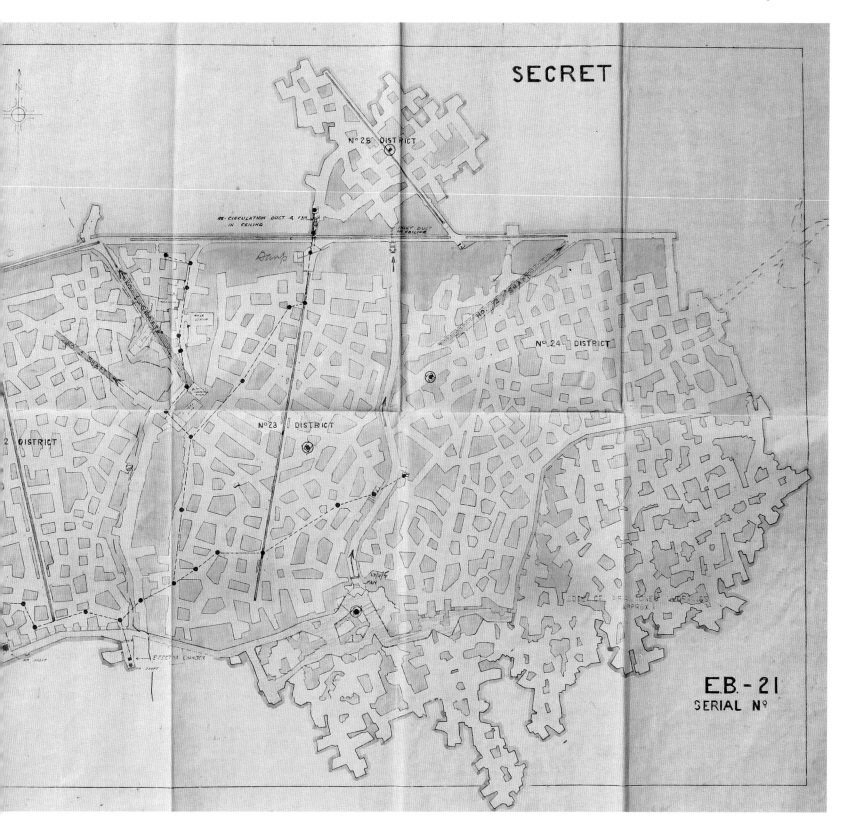

SECRET

N° 25 DISTRICT

RE-CIRCULATION DUCT & FAN
IN CEILING

INLET DUCT
IN CEILING

N° 24 DISTRICT

N° 23 DISTRICT

DISTRICT

FAN

EJECTOR CHAMBER

E.B.- 21
SERIAL N°

Above: A view of the aftermath of the May 1944 runaway at Eastlays. This is the view from the main haulageway looking in to the No.24 District bomb store.

Right: Seen from inside the bomb store, the damage appears somewhat more severe.

at Altrincham and Chilmark.

For transportation underground the Air Ministry preferred Ransome Rapier electric tractors, similar to those used to move heavy shells at Tunnel Quarry, in combination with castor-steering dual-purpose trucks suitable for use on both smooth surfaces and narrow-gauge tracks. Trucks full of bombs were lowered down the No.2 slope shaft by an electric winch in trains of three to be picked up at the bottom by the electric tractors. The massively proportioned No.2 surface loading platform was completed in February 1941. A four-ton electric winch was positioned clear of the shaft top, arranged so that its hand-brake was mechanically interlocked with detent dogs at the top of the slope in such a way that the dogs were raised when the drum was not under the control of the operator. This system

was supposed to prevent wagons being accidentally jolted into the shaft while loading, which it accomplished quite successfully, but it could not prevent trucks breaking away from the winch cable once they were in the shaft. This is exactly what happened during the afternoon of Monday, 8 May 1944. Three trucks loaded with 500 lb bombs became detached near the top of the shaft, careered down the incline, scraped around the corner at the bottom and continued at great speed for a further twenty-five yards before smashing through the reinforced blast doors into No.24 District. Many of the bombs were thrown a further thirty feet into the bomb stacks, disrupting these and creating more havoc. Surprisingly, no bombs were seriously damaged and there were no injuries, but the district doors were buckled beyond repair.

Eastlays in operation —1939 to D-Day

Although Eastlays was designed for operation as an integrated whole with loading and transport arrangements planned for utmost flexibility, this was not the case for most of the war years. There were effectively two separate users with distinctly different material handling and storage requirements. The differences were such that should a breakdown occur in the No. 2 slope shaft which was dedicated to movement of heavy RAF bombs then there was no viable alternative means of access, the No. 1 slope shaft operated by the RAOC being equipped with conveyors and quite unsuitable for such bulky loads.

Notwithstanding these difficulties, the depot muddled along reasonably well under joint masters until 1944. During the early days of the war receipts of British-manufactured TNT into No. 21 District amounted to only about twenty tons per week, but by the spring of the following year this increased enormously due to the flow of imports from Canada and consignments from the United States, now freely available following the repeal of the Neutrality Act in November. Within a year the depot held over 12,000 tons of TNT

Above right: American-made 1100lb HE bombs being stacked on dunnage in the bomb store at Eastlays. Markings on these bombs indicated that they were manufactured in September and October 1939. These weapons were supplied under the Lend-Lease arrangement and the photographs of them in-situ at Eastlays were used for publicity purposes in the United States.

Right: American 1000lb GP (General Purpose) high-explosive bombs stacked in bay number 863 at Eastlays.

Right: American-made 250lb GP bombs being stacked in Eastlays. Most of these bombs appear to have been manufactured in 1939 and by the time this publicity photograph was taken in November 1944 they were clearly obsolete. It is probable that this image is posed and that the bombs have been removed from the stack to give an impression of activity.

Left: Boxed raw TNT from the Tennessee Powder Company in store at Eastlays. A total of some 40,000 tons of TNT from various sources were stored in Districts 21, 22 and 23 at Eastlays. Mixed with RDX, manufactured at the Royal Ordnance Factory at Puriton near Bridgwater in Somerset, which was constructed in 1939, the TNT stockpile from Eastlays was used as the explosive content for many of the larger sizes of RAF bombs produced in filling factories in South Wales and Herefordshire.

Right: The rather overgrown, heavily protected shaft-top building for the engineers' slope shaft. This is the only shaft head building at Eastlays that has remained unaltered since the Second World War. The flimsy wood and steel structure above No.1 shaft collapsed in the mid-1970s while No.2 shaft, seen below, has undergone considerable alteration in recent years.

Left: Following the reincarnation of Eastlays Quarry as a bonded wine store in 1985 many alterations have been made to the above ground structures. A modern lorry loading dock incorporating administrative offices has been built at the head of No.1 shaft while here, at No.2 shaft, the massive concrete blockhouse has been considerably extended. To the right-centre of this view the front of the loading dock, which formerly consisted of loading bay doors set back beneath an overall concrete canopy, has been infilled with a new steel frontage, while a completely new corrugated steel extension has been erected to the left of the original building.

on behalf of the Ministry of Supply in Nos. 21 and 25 Districts, and a further 4,000 tons of TNT on Air Ministry account in No. 23 District. Meanwhile receipts of cordite for both the Air Ministry and War Office had started in No. 22 District, the first consignment arriving from the British Manufacturing & Research Company of Grantham on 25 August.

Management of the increased capacity now available to the Air Ministry required more RAF inspection and clerical personnel than their hard-pressed resources could offer. These difficulties were resolved towards the end of January 1941 when it was agreed that the RAOC would henceforth vouch for all RAF explosives held at Ridge and Eastlays and a month later, on 24 February, the RAOC Inspection Ordnance Officer agreed to supervise inspection of all RAF ammunition in the Corsham depots, all the necessary gauges being transferred on 14 March. The rationalization was completed in May when the COO Corsham took responsibility for the entire RAF inventory held in the CAD.

The monthly turnover of high explosive bombs was in excess of 2,000 tons until July when it dropped temporarily to about half that volume. A provisional allocation of storage capacity was made at this time which allowed the RAF to maintain 21,000 tons of assorted bombs at Ridge and Eastlays, and not more than 4,000 tons of TNT in No.23 District. These limits were soon exceeded and by August 1942, the total holding of Air Ministry TNT at the two depots was well over 43,000 tons, together with 28,000 tons of bombs.

The second half of 1942 was a period of intense activity at Eastlays, with a particularly heavy turnover of bulk TNT. At the beginning of July the total stock amounted to 39,000 tons and this was increasing daily due to the huge imports of Lend-Lease material from the United States. During just four days, ending 16 July, 693 tons of American TNT was received by rail via the Beanacre Sidings. Three weeks later, following unprecedented demands from the filling factories, there were very large issues of explosives from Nos. 21 and 22 Districts and the Ordnance staff reported that there was now plenty of spare room in these districts. The influx of bulk explosive accelerated again in November when the first 7,000 packages of Canadian TNT arrived. Large imports from this source continued throughout November and December, and by Christmas the depot was nearing capacity with space left for only 2,500 tons of TNT and 1,500 tons of cordite.

While these heavy movements of explosives were stretching the capacity of No. 1 slope shaft, an equally prodigious weight of American 250 lb, 500 lb and 1,100 lb HE bombs was putting a similar strain on No. 2 shaft. American-made small-arms ammunition was also arriving in significant quantities. Most of this, along with some dubious home-produced ammunition for the notorious Smith gun, was stacked in the bomb store. Consolidation of the odd Air Ministry items currently stored in disparate sub-depots of the CAD was put in hand at this time, and to this end during October and November fifty lorry-loads of incendiary bombs were transferred to No. 24 District from Monkton Farleigh, where they had lain in temporary surface accommodation since the start of the war.

Co-operation between the RAOC and RAF continued smoothly until the weeks approaching D-Day, when the increasing turnover of War Office stock proved too great to be dealt with without the full capacity of the Eastlays depot. It was resolved in April 1944 that the Air Ministry would give up their Eastlays holding, although implementation of this decision was deferred for several weeks. Arrangements were accordingly made to transfer all RAF stock to other storage within No. 42 Group, the labour and transport for this task being provided by the Army. On 19 June Eastlays was designated a shuttle depot for incoming War Office ammunition as Tunnel and Monkton Farleigh could no longer cope with the increased volume of traffic. The RAF vacated No. 24 District and within ten days it was filled to capacity with 11,000 tons of 5.25" and 6" shell, thus easing congestion at Tunnel Quarry. From the beginning of June all issues of RAF bombs to Forward Ammunition Depots normally supplied by No. 11 MU were made from Eastlays, the small residual stock being transferred to Ridge Quarry on 22 June.

A few weeks after the RAF relinquished the bomb store the Ministry of Supply gave up Districts 23 and 25, freeing space for a further 13,000 tons of field ammunition. In August Nos. 21 and 22 Districts were also cleared of high explosives, increasing the storage capacity available to the RAOC to 45,000 tons. Alternative underground accommodation had been found for the 4,000 tons of MOS high explosives at yet another Bath stone quarry at Hayes Wood, near the village of Limpley Stoke border.

Beanacre Sidings

During the first year of operations all deliveries of RAF bombs to the underground store at Ridge Quarry were made by lorry from the pre-war stone-loading dock at Corsham station, but following the opening of the War Office interchange yard at Thingley Junction

Above: These two buildings, a three-bay motor transport shed and an adjoining corrugated steel structure are all that remain at Beanacre. The former railway siding is now occupied by the access road to Beanacre high-voltage switching station which covers much of the earlier RAF storage site.

in 1937 rail interchange operations were concentrated there and the importance of the small yard at Corsham declined. Meanwhile, with the prospect of a two-fold increase in ammunition traffic following the commissioning of their second underground storage depot at Eastlays, the War Office took steps to establish a more conveniently sited rail yard nearby at Beanacre on the Thingley to Bradford Junction loop line. Treasury consent to purchase the necessary six and a half acres of land was given on 6 September 1938 and construction started soon after. Although built at War Office expense, the sidings were used almost exclusively by the RAF for transshipment of bombs and high explosives destined for the Eastlays/Ridge complex.

Occupation of the Beanacre site proved to be operationally advantageous to the RAF and in August 1941 Squadron Leader Creighton from No. 42 Group visited the sidings with Colonel Allen, Commanding Ordnance Officer from CAD Corsham, to investigate the possibility of establishing an RAF component store on land immediately north of the sidings. Accommodation was desperately needed for fuses, strikers and bomb-pistols for which there was no suitable provision at Ridge or Eastlays, and which were accumulating in excessive numbers at Altrincham. Within three months a few temporary storage sheds were in use and construction of a permanent

examination laboratory was nearing completion. Even while work was in hand on the component store the Air Ministry was drawing up more expansive plans for a 10,000-ton pyrotechnic store which would see the existing development extend north and west to include an extensive standard-gauge railway system with a reverse spur serving six bomb-proof magazines. The rationale behind this plan is outlined in correspondence between Air Vice Marshall Edmonds from Maintenance Command and the Commanding Ordnance Officer at Corsham, in which Edmonds explains that:

> *It will be recalled that the original intention of Eastlays was to provide a universal holding of explosives which would be used to supply RAF units operating with the Expeditionary Force in France. to meet this requirement an overground storage site was contemplated at Beanacre and a layout has been prepared by the Air Ministry and agreed by this Headquarters. It is understood that the construction on this site is still [in December 1940] awaiting Treasury approval.*

A small amount of preliminary groundwork was completed but in March 1941 the scheme was abandoned and all work stopped, only to be revived three months later. Aware of the strain that would be put upon the already critically overstretched reserve storage capacity of No. 42 Group following the arrival of the USAAF in the United Kingdom, and aware that few if any suitable underground sites remained, the Air Ministry initiated a search of southern England for large areas of woodland that might provide adequate cover for bombs in open storage. In June 1941 it was proposed that, because of the excellent rail link already available and its proximity to the existing RAF establishments at Eastlays, Daniel's Wood near Beanacre should be developed as a 20,000 ton HE store. A survey of the area was made and detailed plans prepared showing a narrow-gauge rail link from Beanacre sidings crossing the main road north of the railway and connecting with three concentric rings of narrow-gauge tracks serving thirty storage sheds in the woods. Very little groundwork was completed, however, before this plan, like its predecessor, was abandoned in July 1942. Surviving records indicate that plans for the Beanacre depot were overtaken by a much larger-scale scheme to utilize the greater part of Harewood Forest near Longparish in Hampshire as a second-generation, 40,000 ton reserve ammunition depot.

Longparish

No. 202 MU Longparish was developed as a major, 40,000 ton Reserve Depot and the principal source of ammunition supply for the 2nd Tactical Air Force. Longparish was created just as the RAF's disillusionment with underground storage was at its zenith and the need for ever more storage capacity was at its peak. Air attacks by the Luftwaffe had faded into insignificance leaving little justification for the complexity and expense of deep underground storage; cheaply and quickly constructed field storage depots with bombs stacked by the thousands with no more cover than that offered by deciduous woodland seemed to offer the perfect solution, so in the spring of 1942 searches were instituted for suitable woods and forest.

The east end of Harewood Forest in the vicinity of Longparish recommended itself immediately. Strategically well placed to serve the growing number of RAF bases in southern England that were to become pivotal to the war effort as the RAF's role became increasingly proactive in the final years of the war, the dense, ancient woodland offered excellent camouflage and had excellent rail connections. As part of an unsuccessful project to provide improved communication with Southampton in direct competition with the Great Western Railway, the London & South Western Railway had, in the early 1880s, built a loop-line from Hurstbourne to Fullerton, skimming the south of the forest. The line, however, was never financially viable and in May 1934 track on the northern section was lifted from

Longparish to the junction with the main line at Hurstbourne. The stub-end of the line from Fullerton to Longparish via Wherwell was retained, though it carried little traffic other than the occasional freight train transporting forest products from a works at Longparish.

The railway proved invaluable to the RAF and during the summer and early autumn of 1942 the sidings at Longparish were realigned and extended to serve the new ammunition interchange yard being built just to the north of the station. Construction of the administrative and domestic site was also well advanced by this time and contractors were at work laying mile upon mile of concrete roadways through the forest to carry the fleet of lorries that would service the depot. Initially bomb storage was confined to the eastern section of the forest, but between October 1942, when the depot opened, and the end of the war the roadways and storage sheds were gradually extended until they reached the western extremity of the woodland beside the Clatford to Wherwell road south of Andover.

No. 202 MU ceased to exist as an operational unit in May 1955 and the last train left the yard at Longparish carrying the residue of the RAF inventory on 28 May 1956. Almost fifty years on there is still considerable evidence of the RAF presence in and around the forest. The railway yard and main administration site have in recent years been submerged in a new business park development although a few older buildings survive to remind one of the area's wartime provenance. Throughout the forest the wartime concrete roadways survive intact, their complex patterns of chords and curves at each of the dozens of crossroads in the woods — more like railway junctions than road intersections — appearing bizarre now in their overgrown sylvan setting. A few of the brick-ended, curved asbestos storage sheds also survive among the trees, retained once for forestry purposes but now largely abandoned. They, like the smattering of huge, circular static water tanks, are most numerous in the west of the forest near Wherwell.

Clearing up at Corsham

Although desperate for short-term storage capacity at the end of the war in Europe, officers from No. 42 Group voiced their reservations in June 1945 about using the Corsham depots due to the fact that they were only really suitable for bombs of 500 lb or less and that the inclined shafts limited turnover to a maximum of 400 tons per day. The limited potential of Ridge Quarry for storage over extended peacetime periods, deficient as it was in ventilation or air-

Left: Plan showing the location of RAF Longparish and its associated rail loading facility.

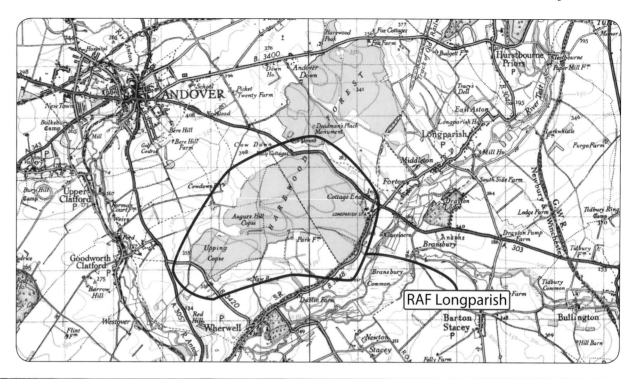

RAF Longparish

Below: There is little evidence of the wartime RAF occupation of Harewood Forest other than the regular grid pattern of concrete roads hidden amongst the trees. This group of three huts located on the northern perimeter of Upping Copse close to Keeper's Cottage is an interesting survival.

Above: The exact function of this building is unknown, although it is situated in what was the depot's main administrative area at the entrance to the site on the Andover to Wherwell road.

Left: A detailed front view of one of the three huts at the Keeper's Cottage site in Upping Copse.

Opposite above: Numerous corrugated asbestos shelters similar to this example were scattered throughout the woodland; most are now gone and those few that survive have been adapted for various forestry purposes.

Opposite below: An example of the wartime, concrete-lined corrugated steel fire-fighting water tanks that can be found distributed throughout the forest.

conditioning equipment, had been questioned a year earlier following an inspection by the Air Ministry Director General of Equipment. Noting the poor condition there of a large stock of bulk TNT packed in wooden cases, he commented that:

> *Storage conditions at that unit appear to be unsuitable for the prolonged storage of wooden items. Destruction of 2,000 boxes was recently recommended in view of an advanced state of decomposition due to wet-rot peculiar to the storage conditions at Corsham.*

In February 1945, a further inspection revealed that 6,000 500 lb bombs of US manufacture stored in the lower section of Ridge were in a very unstable condition and that the wooden dunnage upon which they were stacked was rotting away. It was feared that, should the bombs be disturbed, the dunnage could collapse and initiate an explosion. The most dangerous of these bombs were removed to the Pembrey filling factory to be broken down over the next five months.

A number of airfields, redundant following the end of hostilities, were absorbed by No. 42 Group as concentration points for surplus bombs from active airfields, pending arrangements for disposal. Charlton Horethorne in Somerset was one such airfield, which acted as an overflow for 11 MU Chilmark until the end of 1947. Long Newnton airfield in Gloucestershire was also absorbed by No. 42 Group, being taken under the wing of Chilmark in July 1945. Stocks earmarked for disposal at Ridge Quarry were regularly sent by lorry to Long Newnton, over 100 tons of bombs being dispatched at the end of May 1948, followed by a further 445 bombs a week later. Most were eventually deep-sea dumped via Barry Docks.

The remaining stock of 7,249 tons of High Explosive bombs, together with a small inventory of non-explosive items such as bomb-tails, parachutes and packing cases, was finally struck off charge at Ridge Quarry and transferred to Chilmark on 4 January 1949. The RAF did, however, maintain an interest in the quarry throughout the early 1950s during the evolution of its future weapons policy. For a while it was thought that an increased storage requirement for conventional ammunition would be needed and in October 1950 it was suggested that Ridge should be retained temporarily as the best subsidiary underground site until a viable alternative could be found.

Chapter 4

CHILMARK QUARRY

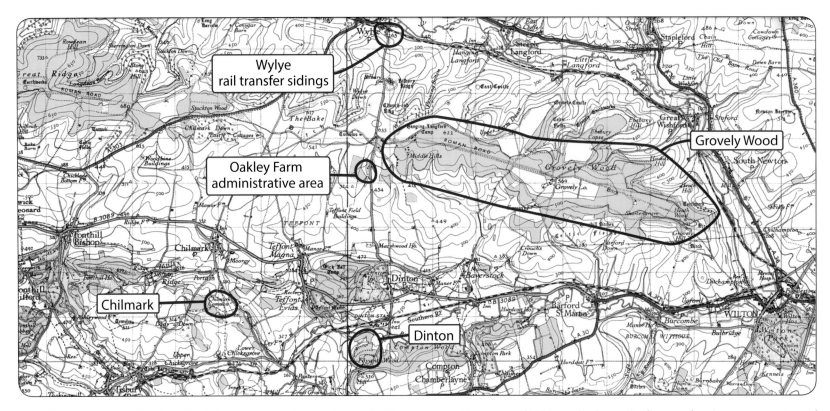

The first step taken by the Air Ministry towards locating suitable sites for their proposed reserve depots was to follow the proven example of the War Office and investigate the limestone quarries of north Wiltshire. There was much logic in this decision as the RAF was, by late 1936, already in what it hoped would be only temporary occupation of the War Office quarry at Ridge, near Corsham, and was also storing 4,000 tons of incendiaries under an informal local agreement at Monkton Farleigh Mine, a much larger War Office underground depot nearby. By this time, however, there was little hope of finding anything suitable in the immediate area of Corsham, but the attention of the Air Ministry investigators was directed some thirty miles south to the Nadder valley between Wilton and Tisbury where similar limestone quarries had recently been abandoned. During the thirteenth century quarries at Chilmark, a small village

ten miles west of Wilton, had supplied stone for the construction of Salisbury cathedral and in the nineteenth century new underground quarries had been opened to supply more stone for its restoration. The quarries struggled through bad times in the nineteen-twenties and early thirties, but, having run at a loss for several years the owner, Mr Gethings, finally closed them down in 1935, citing the increasing use of concrete as the cause of their demise. Following a complete survey, the quarries and 350 acres of surrounding land were purchased by the Air Ministry on 11 June 1936 and preliminary underground engineering works began the following month.

The RAF underground real estate consisted of two separate quarries to the west and east of a lane running north from Ham Cross to Chilmark village. To the west the eleven-acre Chilmark Quarry lay beneath Chilmark Common with the smaller and less significant Teffont Quarry to the east. The surface land encompassed the common and extended eastwards to Dinton village with, at Ham Cross, the Southern Railway main line as its southern border. Here, following negotiations with the railway company, construction work began in October 1936 on a new half-mile-long spur from the main line to serve a group of RAF interchange sidings and transit sheds. Engineering works on this short length of track were heavy, including a deep cutting, one over-bridge and two under-bridges. The Ham Cross sidings were officially opened in September 1938 and as the site developed, the standard-gauge railway system was extended further into the depot, the trackwork eventually extending to over two and a half miles.

Construction of the main underground store proceeded quickly, allowing the first consignment of bombs to be received on 10 May 1937. All railway movements were made via Dinton station until the depot's own sidings at Ham Cross were completed in the following autumn. Much of the engineering technique employed in the conversion of Chilmark Quarry was copied from that employed by the War Office at Corsham where conditions were broadly similar. At Chilmark, however, the quarry industry and the quarry infrastructure were on a much smaller scale. Whereas the Corsham area boasted several hundred acres of underground workings potentially suitable for government use, Chilmark had less than twenty acres, and little more than half of that proved ultimately to be viable. Unlike quarries in which the abandoned galleries could be up to thirty feet in height and choked with waste stone debris, headroom in Chilmark Quarry was a very convenient ten feet or so, the floor was relatively level and there was little clearance required. A further advantage of Chilmark was that, although overhead cover near the entrances was shallow and caused some problems with overall stability, the roof in the deeper sections was very sound and consequently the existing support pillars were widely spaced and in sound condition. No major concrete reinforcement was required and where additional roof support was erected it took the form of simple upright steel girders topped by short spurs to spread the load. The main entrance to the quarry is somewhat deceptive as, due to the badly fractured rock on

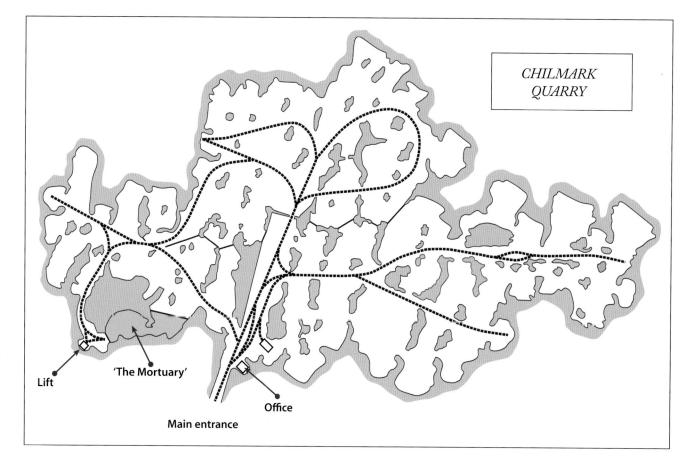

Right: Outline plan of the main underground bomb store at Chilmark showing the arrangement of the internal narrow-gauge railway system and the relative positions of the entrance tunnel and lift shaft.

CHILMARK QUARRY

Lift · '**The Mortuary**' · **Office** · **Main entrance**

the hillside edge, it was heavily reinforced and consists of a concrete arched tunnel that gives the impression that the entire quarry might be similarly engineered. Once through the fractured strata, however, the concrete gives way to the natural rock formation that has been little altered since quarrying ceased.

Transport within the quarry was by means of a two-foot-gauge railway, using specially designed wagons made by Hudsons Ltd, hauled by diminutive electric locomotives. A single line entered the quarry and inside, beyond the concrete entrance tunnel, split into three loops where wagons bearing consignments of ammunition for receipt or issue could be sorted. Beyond this assembly area long headings ran off to the south and north to serve the storage bays. For ease of reference and record-keeping the eleven-acre quarry was divided into six colour-coded areas, each of which was subdivided into nine or ten storage bays.

As August 1939 drew to a close Britain was weighed down by a great foreboding. Most people in the country and in government knew by then that war was inevitable, many were convinced that it would start within weeks if not days and they thought that the opening move would be an annihilating aerial attack by clouds of German bombers on London and military bases in southern England. On 22

Below: Gates securing the main bomb store at Chilmark. The large stop-valve in the foreground is part of the fire-fighting water main.

August a crisis alert was issued by the Air Ministry and at Chilmark four NCOs and thirty-two soldiers from the Dorset Regiment were detailed to act as a guard force to repel a possible parachute attack. Meanwhile urgent action was taken by RAF staff working alongside soldiers of the Dorset Regiment, civilian labourers and Southern Railway personnel to camouflage the entire depot, working fourteen-hour shifts to complete the work by the end of the month. Working in conjunction with civil engineers from the Southern Railway, the Air Ministry Works Directorate at Chilmark developed a method for producing pre-aged green concrete that was so successful that its implementation became general. Chilmark's southerly location made it the most vulnerable of all the reserve depots and it suffered a disproportionately high number of attacks by the Luftwaffe, though

Below: A view along the access tunnel looking into the depot from the gates.

Above: Immediately inside the gates there is a pair of heavy steel blast doors. In the latter years of the depot's operational life these doors were, under normal conditions, left open with the gates securely locked in order to enable the free circulation of air throughout the depot to counter the risk of the accumulation of radon.

Above: The entrance gates seen from the inbye end of the main entrance tunnel. Most of the storage areas consist of natural stone walls and ceiling, largely unsupported, but the entrance tunnel runs through an area of shallow, faulted rock on the hillside edge and it was found necessary to reinforce this section with an arched concrete lining.

Left: The reception area inside the bomb store. The inner end of the access tunnel can be seen to the right of the quarry office with the railway route to the east side of the workings curving away to the left.

Left: The triangular junction immediately outside the entrance to the lift-shaft and emergency exit. The spur in the foreground, which continues behind the photographer's position, leads to the 'mortuary'. There, bombs condemned after inspection would be stored remote from the main stock until they were transferred to the surface via the lift for subsequent repair or disposal.

Below: Interior view of the lift cage. The turntable in the floor is necessary due to the orientation of the landing in the surface building, which is at a right-angle to the lower lift landing. Access to an emergency escape ladder is through a door in the back of the lift cage.

no serious damage was done. Raids continued intermittently through 1940 and 1941, the potentially most serious incident occurring in March 1941 when a badly damaged JU88 fell on the Dinton sub-site and exploded, setting fire to undergrowth close to an incendiary magazine. One crew member successfully evaded capture, three were detained immediately and one was caught several days later.

Although the 15,000-20,000 ton capacity of the quarry seemed adequate when its development was first proposed in 1936 it was far from adequate by 1939. Site plans prepared by the Works Directorate in November 1937 show sixteen semi-underground incendiary magazines on high ground above the quarry close to the edge of Moses Wood. By September 1939 these had been supplemented by a further ten similar buildings and a large number of other sundry storage buildings in the valley closer to the main administrative site. Meanwhile the depot had already taken control of four more distant sub-sites at Worthy Down, Ruislip and Hawkinge, although the latter site, which was used only for the storage of tail assemblies, was

Right: This typical view of the underground workings at Chilmark, like the larger image overleaf, shows the general structure of the quarry. One of the most noticeable features is the wide expanse of unsupported roof and, in comparison with the much larger depots in the Corsham area constructed in a similar rock formation, the minimal use of additional roof supports in the form of vertical steel girders. The red and white hatching on the left-hand pillar denotes a fire-point with warning lamp and siren. When the depot was operational fire extinguishers and sand buckets would have stood against the white rectangle at ground level.

Left: This massive, horizontal sliding blast door secures the lift shaft and mortuary from the main depot. As well as obstructing the blast wave from the detonation of an enemy bomb near the lift-top building this door would also have offered protection to the main magazine from the accidental detonation of a suspect bomb stored in the mortuary.

EXIT ➔

Above: Like all the other RAF reserve depots, Chilmark has a group of semi-underground pyrotechnic storage bunkers; these are situated on a loop road a little to the north of the main underground storage area.

Right: The interior of the pyrotechnic bunker the entrance to which is illustrated above. Notice the heavily reinforced concrete roof and the ventilation trunking running along the rear wall. A branch crosses the width of the building and is connected to an external inlet adjacent to the bunker's No.2 door.

Above: Another example of the semi-underground pyrotechnic bunkers at Chilmark. Here we see the external cowling for the ventilation ducting and the switchgear for lighting in the storage area which, as a safety precaution, is positioned outside the danger area.

Right: The military police guardhouse on the pyrotechnics site. The change in colour of the brickwork and tiles on the left-hand wing of the building suggests that it was considerably extended at some time in its life. Abandoned for some twenty years when this photograph was taken, the building remains in remarkably good condition and still retains its striking, blue enamel 'Police Office' sign.

closed down when the war began and its remaining stocks transferred to the parent depot.

Dinton

While these small additions were being made to Chilmark's inventory of remote sub-sites much larger works were in hand nearer home. Ground clearance had begun in August 1939 in preparation for an extensive range of semi-underground magazines on land east of the main depot near Dinton village, just to the east of Chilmark. All the magazines and other storage buildings at Dinton were served by a network of narrow-gauge rails that connected to an independent main-line interchange yard at Dinton station. Up until the mid-1990s the little trains of Chilmark could often be seen trundling along the pavement beside the public road that ran through the depot before crossing the road at an ungated level crossing to enter a series of sidings at the quarry entrance. Over the years a wide range of standard and narrow-gauge motive power and rolling stock has found employment at the depot including a series of 44 horsepower

Below: The narrow-gauge locomotive shed at Dinton, a photograph taken after the narrow-gauge rails had been removed. This is building number 35 on the plan opposite.

Ruston & Hornsby diesel locomotives purchased in 1940 and three 50 horsepower Baguley-Drewry battery electric locomotives for use in the quarries. The early Rustons were replaced in the 1960s by four 65 horsepower Baguley-Drewrys. Standard gauge locomotives included a 1939 Fowler, rebuilt in 1961 and a 150 horsepower Drewry. Among the more obscure rolling stock at Chilmark were six specially adapted mines rescue wagons, a two-ton passenger coach (the sole function of which was to ferry important official visitors around the site), and two fire-tenders. The latter formed an emergency fire fighting train and were permanently attached to Ruston & Hornsby locomotive number AMW 165 which was painted fire-engine red and fitted with a gleaming brass bell.

Grovely Wood

Chilmark continued to expand throughout the war, both at its main site and by the absorption of remote sub-units that were gradually brought under its control. The creation of a new site at Redbrook in the Forest of Dean and the absorption of Ridge and Eastlays quarries

Below: The military police guardhouse at the south entrance to the Dinton site. This is building number 37 on the plan opposite.

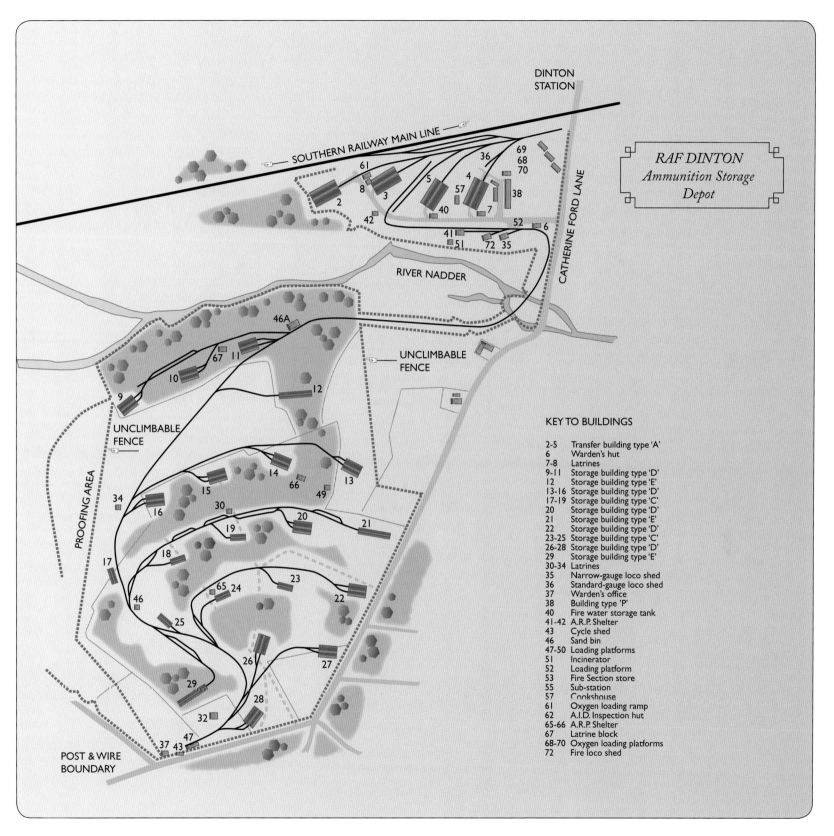

DINTON
STATION

SOUTHERN RAILWAY MAIN LINE

RIVER NADDER

CATHERINE FORD LANE

UNCLIMBABLE
FENCE

UNCLIMBABLE
FENCE

PROOFING AREA

POST & WIRE
BOUNDARY

RAF DINTON
*Ammunition Storage
Depot*

KEY TO BUILDINGS

2-5	Transfer building type 'A'
6	Warden's hut
7-8	Latrines
9-11	Storage building type 'D'
12	Storage building type 'E'
13-16	Storage building type 'D'
17-19	Storage building type 'C'
20	Storage building type 'D'
21	Storage building type 'E'
22	Storage building type 'D'
23-25	Storage building type 'C'
26-28	Storage building type 'D'
29	Storage building type 'E'
30-34	Latrines
35	Narrow-gauge loco shed
36	Standard-gauge loco shed
37	Warden's office
38	Building type 'P'
40	Fire water storage tank
41-42	A.R.P. Shelter
43	Cycle shed
46	Sand bin
47-50	Loading platforms
51	Incinerator
52	Loading platform
53	Fire Section store
55	Sub-station
57	Cookshouse
61	Oxygen loading ramp
62	A.I.D. Inspection hut
65-66	A.R.P. Shelter
67	Latrine block
68-70	Oxygen loading platforms
72	Fire loco shed

at Corsham in 1940 are examples of the latter process, while the development of the large surface store at Grovely Wood in 1941 is typical of the former.

Under increased pressure to find suitable storage capacity for the estimated 400,000 tons of bombs that could not be accommodated in the two reserve depots still fully functional after the collapse of Llanberis, No. 42 Group agreed, with some reluctance, to follow the War Office example and opt for limited roadside stacking and widely dispersed surface storage in woodland. In late June 1941, staff from 11 MU inspected Grovely Wood, an area of dense, ancient woodland extending over some twelve square miles of the Wiltshire downs on a high plateau bordered by the rivers Wylye and Nadder, approximately five miles north-east of the unit's main underground site and railhead at Chilmark. Initially it was intended that only Pitt's Covert, a relatively small area of the woods at the east end of the forest would be utilized. This was conveniently close to a well-made road that gave direct access to the Great Western Railway at Wylye four miles away, where, somewhat oddly, the Southern Railway Company was given a contract to construct new sidings for the RAF.

Work in Pitt's Covert advanced quickly as space was cleared among the trees for a regular but inconspicuous pattern of roadways,

some metalled and others simply overlain with woodchips, beside which a variety of hard-standings and Laing huts were constructed. Stacking began as soon as the concrete was set and by the end of September seven large Laing huts were filled with pyrotechnic stores and eight others were nearly so. The Grovely Wood sub-site was classified as complete at the end of the year but shortly afterwards what was to prove to be just the first of a series of eastward extensions was authorized. By mid-summer there was in excess of 25,000 tons of ordnance secreted among the trees, the management of which required a staff somewhat larger than that employed at the main site at Chilmark. Towards the end of June Grovely Wood was re-designated as a reserve depot in its own right in preparation for its transfer to the USAAF on 14 August. A new headquarters and accommodation site for the newly arrived US staff was constructed to the west of the depot, adjacent to the Wylye to Dinton road on the site of Oakley Farm. The headquarters site consisted of a dozen or so Nissen huts distributed among a small roadside copse, while the airmen's quarters, consisting of thirty-two barrack blocks with

Below: A surviving group of USAAF huts on the Oakley Farm administrative site at Grovely Wood.

Right: This large corrugated steel shed at Oakley Farm was, up until the mid-1990s, filled with ex-RAF radio equipment, aircraft instrumentation and other components, apparently abandoned there.

Below: From the Wylye to Dinton road the USAAF administrative camp site looks remarkably intact and still retains something of its wartime atmosphere. The domestic site, consisting of thirty-two barrack blocks and associated buildings, built further back from the road in Thickthorn Copse, has been almost completely cleared in recent years to make way for an extensive chicken rearing unit.

Left: In amongst the trees of Grovely Wood bombs and other types of ammunition were stored beneath lightweight shelters on concrete bases, or merely stacked on levelled ground and covered with tarpaulins to offer some protection from the weather. Here and there, a few concrete bases can still be found, rapidly disappearing beneath the undergrowth.

Right: The main ammunition railhead for the Grovely Wood depot was at Wylye station on the Westbury to Salisbury line. Three new sidings were opened there in August 1943 to cope with the increased traffic, the existing up refuge siding was extended and an additional down siding laid adjacent to a pre-war timber loading bank. In preparation for this extended layout the signalbox at Wylye was rebuilt a few months earlier. The transfer yard closed and all the sidings were removed by 1951 but a number of features remained until a few years ago including a Stanton shelter (seen here in the foreground covered in brambles and undergrowth), and the two-bay motor transport shed and Nissen general storage building immediately behind it.

associated ablutions, were more closely spaced but better concealed within a dense blackthorn thicket known as Thickthorn Copse. The arrival of the United States 8th Air Force imposed a fresh burden on No. 42 Group as urgent demands were made for storage sites for the vast quantities of American ordnance arriving in Britain.

Initially the Air Ministry offered the underground reserve depot at Linley which, due to increasingly frequent roof falls and the imminent risk of flooding, was still unfinished and virtually abandoned. This site was quickly rejected by the USAAF which accepted instead Grovely Woods and 220 MU at Wortley, near Penistone in Yorkshire, which was a sprawling open storage site consisting of some twenty miles of roadside storage with a nominal capacity of 25,000 tons. Within weeks several other RAF depots were transferred to the USAAF, including Barnham, which was extended in the 1950s to allow the storage of atomic bombs; and the Forward Ammunition Depots at Lord's Bridge, Braybrooke near Market Harborough, Earsham and

Below: As demand for storage space at Grovely Wood increased, the depot expanded to include a number of old tracks across the downs, including Ox Drove, seen here, which was concreted over and had ammunition stacking bays constructed at regular intervals where bombs were stored under tarpaulins.

Sharnbrook. Later, new depots were constructed for the USAAF at Bures, seven miles north-west of Colchester, and at Melchbourne Park, where an additional sub-site at Riseley was developed, along with several others elsewhere in eastern England, for the storage of chemical weapons.

With the USAAF in control of Grovely Wood turnover increased significantly and by early 1944 was regularly in excess of 13,000 tons per month. The depot was quickly reaching saturation with several hundred Laing huts and open stacks thickly clustered among the trees throughout the western and central sections of the wood. So great was the congestion that during January the decision was taken to develop the last remaining area of virgin woodland, known as the Broad Drive, at the far eastern end of Grovely Wood, despite the fact that access from the Wylye railhead involved a nine-mile journey, most of which was along poorly made, steep woodland tracks. To alleviate the transport difficulties, an existing cattle-loading dock at Great Wishford station, four miles east of the main transfer depot at Wylye, was pressed into service as a supplementary railhead to serve the depot's western extension.

The capacity of the USAAF munitions depots in southern England reached a peak during the build-up to D-Day. At Grovely Wood the demand was met by the increased use of roadside storage on the wide verges of numerous secondary roads leading west towards Wincanton, and by the construction of new roadways for the storage of bombs under field conditions on the open downs north of Teffont Magna. Running west from the main camp site for two miles, a virtually disused and undistinguishable ancient trackway known as the Ox Drove was relaid in concrete with wide turning circles every few hundred yards beside which concrete hard-standings were built for stacking bombs. With so much natural cover available elsewhere the reasoning behind the reconstruction of this road and the laying of another completely new concrete road running north from a point midway between the villages of Chilmark and Teffont Magna is unfathomable. Both roads — straight white concrete scars crossing a hilltop ridge in a region of otherwise unobtrusive, narrow winding lanes are blindingly conspicuous from the air.

Grovely Wood continued under American occupation until June 1946 when it was transferred back to No. 42 Group. In October 1948 it was scheduled for clearance and finally closed on 30 November 1949. All the storage buildings in the woods were dismantled leaving only an assortment of concrete bases among the trees but the domestic camp was sold intact and many of the buildings still survive.

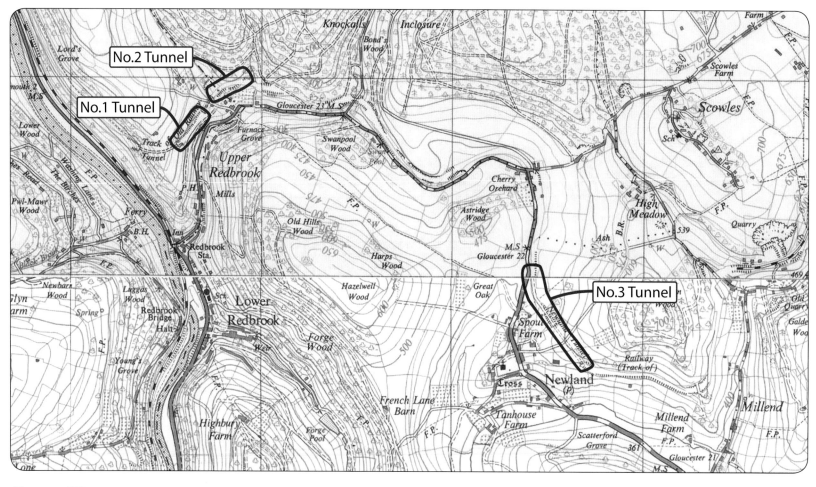

Forest of Dean

The fall of France in the spring of 1940, as we have seen, changed every aspect of No. 42 Group's forward planning, which had previously been based on the assumption that active fighter and bomber units would be concentrated in the east and south-east of England with training, supply and maintenance units in the west and south-west. The inevitable consequence of the events of May 1940 was that active RAF units would flood into the south and west, the status of most of the existing airfields would change and many new bomber, and more importantly fighter, airfields would be built. All of these would require a robust ammunition supply chain that currently did not exist. No. 42 Group immediately instituted a search for suitable locations for a minimum of two new Air Ammunition Parks, led by Wing Commander Lines and Squadron Leader Anness who, on 1 July, reported that they had found an ideal location for the most urgently needed depot in the Forest of Dean. The site consisted of

three disused railway tunnels between the villages of Redbrook and Newland on the alignment of the old GWR Monmouth to Coleford line that had been closed in 1917. The rationale that prompted the search for and selection of this site is clearly explained in the following letter from Air Vice Marshal Edmonds, Commanding Officer of Maintenance Command, to the Air Ministry in September 1940:

I have the honour to say that the supply of ammunition to units in South Wales and the South West of England has been under consideration. Prior to the German occupation of France it was considered unlikely that any stations in these areas would be used for operational purposes other than coastal reconnaissance. Consequently the supply of the small quantities of ammunition required did not present any particular problem and they were based directly on the ammunition depots at Fauld and Chilmark.

Since the German occupation of northern France the situation has changed. Stations in South Wales and the west country are being used by fighter squadrons, many new aerodromes are being opened up in these areas for army co-operation and there are indications that bomber and fighter squadrons may be required to operate from south-western stations in the event of invasion or operations in Eire.

In any of these circumstances it is considered that the distances involved between these stations and Fauld or Chilmark are far too long to ensure a reliable flow of ammunition. Furthermore detail issues to a large number of units is beyond the capacity of an ammunition depot. Issues have to be made by rail and it will be appreciated that a number of small issues despatched in this manner are liable seriously to interfere with the main function of the depot in despatching bulk trains to ammunition parks and to meet other emergencies.

It is therefore recommended that an Air Ammunition Park be opened now in South Wales to relieve Fauld and Chilmark of some of its detail issues to operational stations in this area and the mid-south-west. This will also provide a holding which will be available to meet any of the contingencies envisaged above. Further, it is considered that a small Air Ammunition Park should be sited and prepared in Cornwall. Present issues do not justify opening such a unit at the present time but if more fighter squadrons are moved into this area or army co-operation requirements appear likely to increase, the preparation of a plan of opening a Park within forty-eight hours is regarded as essential.

With this end in view a reconnaissance has been made of a very favourable site near Monmouth consisting of three railway tunnels. It is proposed that part of this storage should be used as an Air Ammunition Park and the remainder as a depository for tail units and the doubtful ammunition and explosives which have been received from French appropriations and captured Italian shipping.

It is therefore requested that approval may be given:

- For the formation of an Air Ammunition Park in South Wales.
- For the acquisition and preparation of the disused tunnels at. Redbrook and Newland for item (one) above and for use as an explosive depository.
- For the selection and preparation of a site in Cornwall for a small Air Ammunition Park which can be opened if required within forty-eight hours.

It should be noted that the tunnels are in excellent order, naturally camouflaged, and could be adapted for storage of explosives at a comparatively small cost. It would therefore be appreciated if very early action could be taken to requisition the site and approval given to proceed with the works services required. After approval has been given to the proposals a detailed estimate of the works services will be obtained and submitted should the total expenditure involved exceed my power.

C. H. K. Edmonds
Air Vice Marshal
Commanding Maintenance Command 5/9/1940

The proposed depot in Cornwall was eventually established at Lansalon clay pit in Ruddlemore, north of St Austell in October. Previously a slate quarry at Quarry Wood about one mile south of St. Neot in Cornwall had been inspected but despite the one hundred feet of overhead cover available it was found unsuitable. Minor works were begun at Ruddlemore and continued at a desultory rate, the site not being completed until September 1942. Designated 230 MU, the depot was parented by RAF St. Eval but was never properly operational and the few surviving records indicate that no weapons were ever stored there.

Unlike the Cornish depot, Newland was required with some urgency, although progress there too was far from brisk. Air Vice Marshal Edmonds' submission to the Air Ministry was the result of a positive assessment made by Wing Commander Worthington on 29 August 1940 following a detailed inspection of the tunnels and the surrounding area. Drawings for the conversion work were prepared in September but were not approved by the Air Ministry until 29 November when a grant of £4,500 was authorized for the completion of the project. A month later, on 31 December, a conference was held at Redbrook to organize contracts and building work was finally completed on 19 May when the depot opened as No 56 MU. The unit lost its independence in May 1942 when it was absorbed by Chilmark and became No 11 SMU Newland.

Accommodation at Newland consisted of three brick-lined railway tunnels with a maximum headroom of sixteen feet six inches and a width of twelve feet six inches. Tunnel No.1, known as Newland tunnel, lies due north of the village after which it was named. A straight bore with a length of 825 feet it was by far the most suitable of the three tunnels and, due to its eminent suitability, had already been earmarked by the National Museum of Wales for the safekeeping of the Welsh national treasures during the conflict. The negotiations that resulted in the museum relinquishing its claim may have been a partial cause of the project's long gestation through the winter of 1940. Access was readily available via an existing trackway from the village. The 700-foot-long No. 2 Tunnel, near Redbrook

Left: The east end of No.1 tunnel at Redbrook. This is the longer of the two tunnels at Redbrook and is built on a pronounced curve. It is accessible from beside an unmade track to the north of the B4231 a little to the east of the Monmouth Tramway bridge of 1812 which crosses the road on the outskirts of Redbrook. The tunnel was on the alignment of the Monmouth to Coleford railway, which opened in 1883 and closed on 1st January 1917.

Opposite: A close view of the tunnel portal. The wall and gate are wartime features, the lintel of the entrance being just high enough to admit a narrow-gauge locomotive used to propel wagons in this and No.2 tunnel. The reinforced concrete ledge on the right-hand side is all that remains of the roof of a guardhouse that once stood at this location.

village, lies just south of Jordan's Barn Farm and has a sharply curved formation which made handling of bombs particularly awkward. A short distance to the south, tunnel No. 3 is just 200 feet long and lies at the far end of a shallow cutting. The north end of No. 2 tunnel and the south end of No. 3, which faced each other in Coleford cutting, were bricked-up, leaving entrances just large enough to admit the narrow-gauge trucks that ran on Decauville track linking the two tunnels. Between them in a shallow section of the cutting a road transport loading dock was erected adjacent to an existing right of way. The far ends of each tunnel were blocked by brickwork and fitted with emergency escape doors provided, like the active portals, with sentry boxes for the military police. Similar arrangements were made at Newland tunnel with Decauville track serving the underground store and feeding a loading dock near the lane to the village. Extensive building work was avoided and while rudimentary electric lighting was installed in the tunnels at very little cost, the greater part of the £4,500 budget was absorbed by the railway track and rolling stock. In an area of recent industrial decline the RAF had little need to build new domestic or administrative accommodation for both Redbrook and Newland were rich in abandoned but serviceable buildings. Administrative offices were established in the disused railway station

at Newland while further accommodation was requisitioned at the west end of the site in an old brewery adjacent to Upper Redbrook station.

Once operations got under way in the Forest of Dean it was quickly realized that the tunnels, like Rowthorne and Butterton in the north midlands, were not well suited to the storage of large bombs or even the ubiquitous 250 lb and 500 lb types. Fears about the difficulty of handling such material in the confines of the railway tunnels led to the immediate abandonment of the proposal to use the smaller tunnel for the storage of suspect foreign weapons and explosives and in May 1941, just weeks after the depot opened, orders were issued that no foreign bombs were to be stored other than those of American origin.

Complaints about the facilities at Newland continued after its absorption by Chilmark and a report issued in December 1943 described the depot as 'cumbersome and inefficient' and recommended its closure. With the pressure on No. 42 Group to provide storage still intense, abandonment was not possible and the depot struggled on through the rest of the war, although used only, until January 1944 at least, as a depository for obsolete bombs. Indeed, from as early as June 1941 Group Headquarters had sought to increase capacity

Above: The west portal of the shorter No.2 tunnel at Redbrook.

Left: This flameproof bulkhead light fitting, attached high on the wall a few yards from the entrance to No.2 tunnel, is one of the few wartime features still evident. Elsewhere in the tunnel a few cable hangers have survived and it is possible to see where other lamps were fitted.

Opposite: Inside No.2 tunnel. While under RAF occupation a raised concrete platform was built along the left-hand side with a narrow-gauge railway to the right. Steel bomb racks were erected on the platform and several of the bolts which attached them to the tunnel wall can be seen projecting from the stonework. The lamp fitting described above can be seen attached to the wall on the upper right of this photograph.

Left: This small transfer shed stands in a shallow cutting midway between the two tunnels at Redbrook. The narrow-gauge railway passed to the left, behind the shed, and there was road access, and a lorry-loading platform, now heavily overgrown, on the right-hand side.

in the Forest of Dean, looking first at Clearwell Cave as a possible underground store, although this proved quite unsuitable, and then at Blakeney Walk, Lower Soudley and Russell's Enclosure as sites for surface expansion. Unfortunately it was soon found that the War Office was already in possession of all three locations, with Russell's Enclosure being used as what was, during the post-war years, to be exposed as the most notoriously mismanaged of all the Army's chemical weapons dumps. Like the Air Ministry, the War Office had also recognized the strategic importance of the Forest of Dean.

Moseley Green Tunnel

Following upon the acquisition of the tunnels at Redbrook in September 1940, the RAF also took possession in the following month of the 503-yard Moseley Green tunnel on the Forest of Dean Mineral Loop, which ran between Tufts Junction and Drybrook Road Junction, serving the needs of a number of financially decrepit collieries. RAF occupation of the tunnel severed the Mineral Loop south of Russell's Enclosure, causing much friction with the War Office. Eventually, the War Office prevailed and on 23 November 1943 the RAF relinquished Moseley Green tunnel and the rails of

the Mineral Loop were relaid in order to provide a southern access to the Acorn Patch ammunition sidings serving the chemical weapons storage facility in Russell's Enclosure.

The Air Ministry made a second foray into the Forest of Dean in January 1944 in search of sites for temporary roadside dumps to cope with the rapid build-up of stock in preparation for D-Day. Once again the Blakeney Walk and Lower Soudley area was inspected and this time the search was more successful. At the end of August the tunnels and the various roadside holdings amounted to some 2,000 tons of bombs and small arms ammunition, but thereafter the stocks dwindled. Although the cessation of the war led to a huge and immediate stockpile of surplus ammunition, including returned stock from remote theatres of war and of new production from the factories resulting from the momentum of industry, RAF Newland was to have no direct role in its disposal. By this time the country was littered with redundant airfields whose wartime roles had ended and many of these were pressed into service as huge open storage dumps for these surpluses. Once again re-designated 56 MU, RAF Newland and the remnants of its stockholdings were transferred to Rhoose airfield in South Wales, leading to the final closure of the Forest of Dean depot in December 1945.

Euroclydon Tunnel

Although unconnected with the RAF activity in the Forest, it is worth mentioning the occupation of Euroclydon tunnel by the Admiralty for weapons ordnance storage during the Second World War for reasons of completeness. Shortly after the outbreak of war in September 1939 the Admiralty took possession of Euroclydon tunnel (also known as Hawthorn tunnel) which lies just to the north of Drybrook on the former Mitcheldean Road & Forest of Dean Junction Railway. Construction of the line was completed by the Great Western Railway in the early 1880s but it was never opened for traffic and the track north of Drybrook, including that through the tunnel, was subsequently lifted.

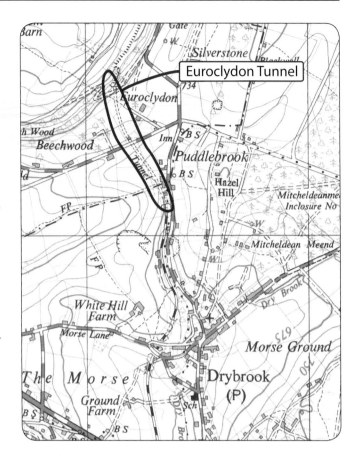

Following its acquisition by the Admiralty, the existing standard-gauge line was extended from its terminus at Drybrook Quarry, several hundred yards to the south, up to the tunnel mouth. A narrow-gauge line was then laid through the tunnel on the east and a raised concrete stacking platform built against the western wall. Palisade fences were erected to create secure compounds at both portals. At the south end a transfer shed was constructed and fitted with a pair of one-ton hand operated cranes. Three old railway carriages were adapted to provide office accommodation and a concrete and brick guard's lodge built. Later, a large corrugated-iron inspection laboratory was constructed a short distance from the tunnel's north portal. Admiralty occupation came to an end on 27 May 1949 and most of the infrastructure, which was temporary in nature, was removed.

Above: The south portal of Euroclydon tunnel seen from the end of the former Admiralty yard. During the Admiralty's tenure an extension of the standard-gauge branch line ran from Drybrook quarry to the south, up to the portal of the tunnel. A narrow-gauge line ran through the tunnel and parallel to the main line through the length of the transfer yard. The Admiralty transfer shed once stood in the middle of this view with the standard-gauge line to the right and the narrow-gauge, with a short loop line going around the loading bay, to the left of the building.

Right: The post-war history of Euroclydon tunnel is somewhat complex. This wall and door, approximately 100 feet inside the south end, although appearing to be of wartime vintage, is a feature of an abortive attempt to incorporate the tunnel into a tourist venture more recently. The narrow-gauge track seen on the right is definitely a relic of this more recent venture.

Opposite: The main gates and remains of the steel palisade boundary fence that once surrounded the Admiralty yard. Until the 1980s a concrete guard hut stood just inside the gate.

Chapter 5

HARPUR HILL & LLANBERIS

The search for a suitable quarry, mine or cave for the northern area having proved abortive the RAF was compelled to consider its less-favoured option of building an 'artificial' underground reserve depot. The criteria to be met were broadly similar to those that determined the suitability of the two depots that were already under construction, and indeed the 'artificial' option made the choice of location somewhat easier, even though the cost would inevitably be much higher. It was necessary for the location to be remote, for reasons of safety and security; it had to be difficult to pinpoint from the air and it had to be close to a suitable railway line adjacent to which interchange sidings and a marshalling yard could be established. Ideally there should be sufficient land available nearby upon which to build a large number of widely-spaced semi-underground incendiary and pyrotechnic magazines. The land should be flat enough to allow all the major buildings on the site to be connected by narrow-gauge railways.

Harpur Hill

Sorrow Quarry, one of many worked-out open quarries on the high ground of Harpur Hill south of Buxton in Derbyshire, was operated in the years following the First World War by the Buxton Limestone Firm and in the 1930s by its successor, ICI Ltd, proved an ideal location despite its altitude. Just one of a large number of seemingly abandoned quarries in a broad landscape of industrial semi-dereliction, Sorrow Quarry was already well camouflaged and, furthermore, due to its high Pennine position, was for many months of the year enshrouded in mist.

The Air Ministry met some opposition to its plans for Harpur Hill, encouraged by the Duke of Devonshire who objected to such a development close to the fading spa town of Buxton, but the exercise of compulsory powers overcame these difficulties enabling the Air Ministry to take possession of the quarry towards the end of 1938. By the following March site clearance was well in hand and drawings prepared for the underground facility. A detailed survey indicated that Sorrow Quarry would be a difficult development. The quarry

varied in depth between sixty and seventy-eight feet with the floor falling away sharply to the north side, and took the awkward form of an elongated 'S', approximately 400 feet long and eighty feet wide.

Initially it was hoped that by blasting away rock at each end of the quarry a more rectangular form could be achieved enabling a simple concrete structure consisting of seven identical, arched tunnels abutting one another and running the length of the quarry to be completed quite rapidly. It soon became obvious, however, that the amount of rock that would have to be moved was prodigious, so the plans were altered and the tunnels made to conform to the existing outline of the quarry. This created a number of engineering difficulties, not the least that the arches of the outermost tunnels could no longer spring from the quarry walls but would instead have to take up shapes that, to the uninitiated eye, appear to defy the laws of physics, springing instead from massive concrete abutments at quarry floor level. The geometry of the arches became so complex at the two positions where the quarry curved that flat slabs were substituted for the conventional arched roofs of the tunnels at these points. A similar flat-slab roof was applied to the west railway access tunnel. An important original specification for the underground depot was that there should be two main entrances and that a standard-gauge railway line should run right through the depot in order that loading and unloading could take place under cover, and that if one entrance was rendered unusable through accident or enemy action then an emergency route should still be available. Unfortunately the amended plan did not allow for this and, although two entrances were still provided, through-running was not possible as access via the west entrance involved negotiating an awkward head-shunt which could accommodate only a few wagons.

The design finalized by the Air Ministry Works Directorate was for a single-storey structure with walls sixteen feet high to the springing of the arches, which allowed for an overhead cover to existing ground level of forty-two feet. This backfill would consist of small limestone waste interspersed with larger boulders which, it was hoped, would act as 'bomb-bursters'. The central tunnel was occupied

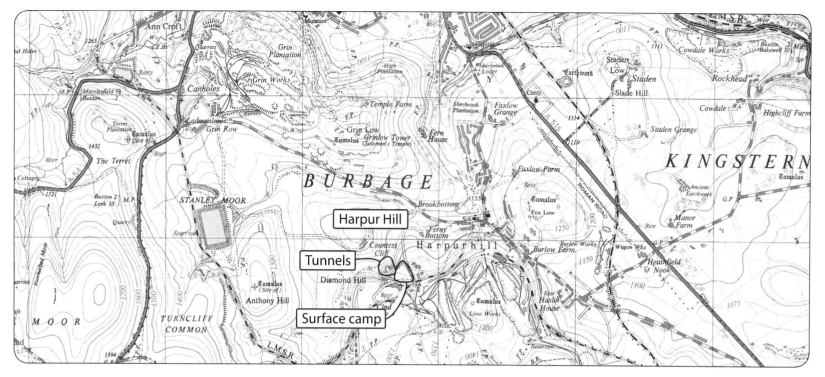

by the standard-gauge railway and its unloading platforms with three storage tunnels to each side. Access to these was obtained by means of arched openings in the lateral walls at ninety-foot intervals. Owing to the natural slope of the quarry floor it was possible to incorporate a lower, basement level below the two most easterly tunnels. Two electric lifts and an inclined ramp gave access to the lower level. Movement of the lifts during normal usage also acted as air-pumps, proving quite adequately to ventilate the basement area without the need for circulating fans or other complicated or expensive plant. Much thought had been given during the early stages of planning to the need for air-conditioning and ventilation of the main floor of the depot, but it was decided that as bombs, unlike artillery ammunition, were not particularly susceptible to deterioration when stored under conditions of high humidity and fluctuating temperatures, such measures were not necessary. Normal operation of the depot and the movement of trains within the depot would, it was calculated, produce adequate ingress and circulation of fresh air. It was, however, realized that while this might hold true during wartime when stocks turned over rapidly, it might not be so in peacetime when bombs might be in store for years if not decades. The Air Ministry was concerned that account should be taken of this as Harpur Hill was classified as a permanent depot with an undefined but assured post-war role. In anticipation of future requirements it was decided to

include in the original construction a wide concrete ventilation duct spanning the width of the depot with openings into the roof of each tunnel. No plant was to be installed, but foundations were cast for an induction fan and associated switch gear should there be a future requirement.

Once the detailed plans were accepted and financial authority granted, a contract was agreed with Alfred McAlpine for the construction of the tunnels and for the first batch of twenty-five dispersed pyrotechnic magazines on land to the south of the main site and for sundry technical and headquarters buildings and associated railway works. Work proceeded throughout the winter of 1939/40 under atrocious conditions of almost continuous rainfall which held up work for days on end, but it was nevertheless hoped that stockpiling could begin in April 1940. Heavy snowfall blocked all road and rail connections to the site from 27 January until 9 February and the first train to get through after that date carrying building materials was derailed when the track beneath it sank into the mud. Work on the pyrotechnic magazines was suspended briefly after workmen preparing the foundations unearthed a number of suspicious objects that were at first thought to be discarded mustard gas shells. Inquiries subsequently revealed that the area had been used as an experimental range during the First World War for testing new patterns of mortar bombs and, although activities at that time were

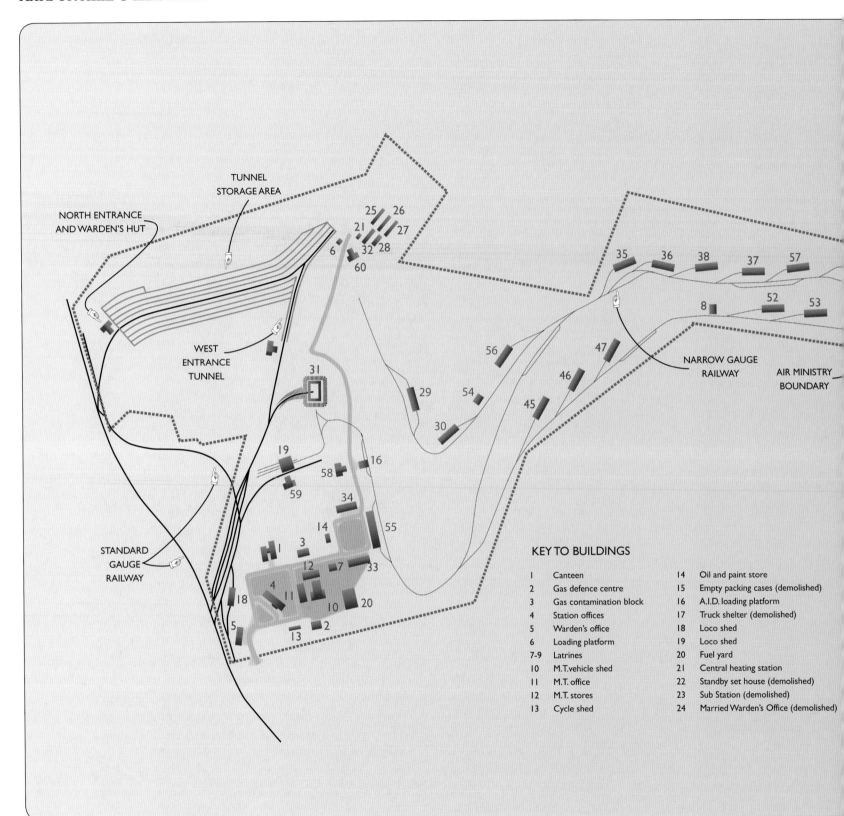

TUNNEL
STORAGE AREA

NORTH ENTRANCE
AND WARDEN'S HUT

WEST
ENTRANCE
TUNNEL

STANDARD
GAUGE
RAILWAY

NARROW GAUGE
RAILWAY

AIR MINISTRY
BOUNDARY

KEY TO BUILDINGS

1	Canteen	14	Oil and paint store
2	Gas defence centre	15	Empty packing cases (demolished)
3	Gas contamination block	16	A.I.D. loading platform
4	Station offices	17	Truck shelter (demolished)
5	Warden's office	18	Loco shed
6	Loading platform	19	Loco shed
7-9	Latrines	20	Fuel yard
10	M.T. vehicle shed	21	Central heating station
11	M.T. office	22	Standby set house (demolished)
12	M.T. stores	23	Sub Station (demolished)
13	Cycle shed	24	Married Warden's Office (demolished)

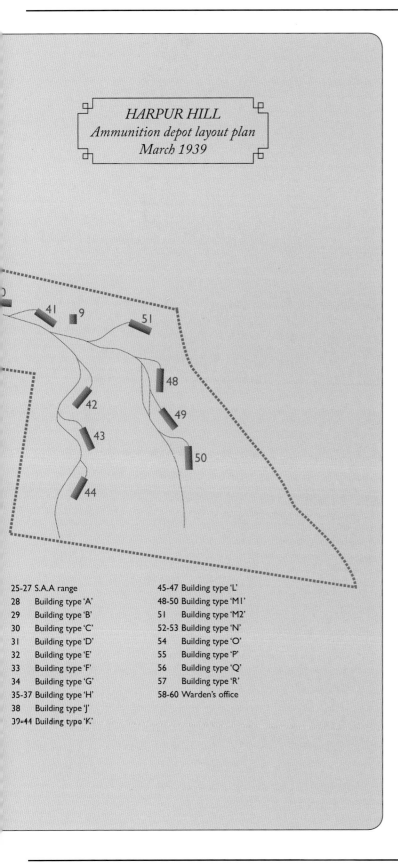

25-27 S.A.A range	45-47 Building type 'L'
28 Building type 'A'	48-50 Building type 'M1'
29 Building type 'B'	51 Building type 'M2'
30 Building type 'C'	52-53 Building type 'N'
31 Building type 'D'	54 Building type 'O'
32 Building type 'E'	55 Building type 'P'
33 Building type 'F'	56 Building type 'Q'
34 Building type 'G'	57 Building type 'R'
35-37 Building type 'H'	58-60 Warden's office
38 Building type 'J'	
39-44 Building type 'K'	

poorly documented, analysis of the recovered weapons showed that the majority were filled with sand and thus quite safe. Similar weapons were unearthed in the post-war years when an extension to the nearby Safety in Mines Research Laboratory was under construction.

As a result of the increasingly bleak events in France during the early months of 1940 it was decided to commission the depot in an unfinished state and the first train load of bombs entered the depot via the north portal on 20 March. Unfortunately this proved to be a false start. On the inward journey the train of box vans just cleared the concrete lintel of the tunnel, which was exactly and inexplicably twelve feet above rail level rather than the standard railway loading gauge of thirteen feet six inches. Unloading proceeded without a hitch, but on the outward journey the roof of the leading empty wagon fouled the lintel and it became jammed in the entrance, trapping the whole train inside the tunnel. Then it was realized that the wagons, each unburdened of some ten tons of cargo, had risen three inches on their springs. Urgent effort was now required to lower the trackbed throughout the depot, a task made more difficult by the fact that in many places where the floor of the quarry had been uneven mass concrete had been used to bring it up to a consistent level and much of this now had to be cut away.

Although the depot became operational in March 1940, much remained to be done at Harpur Hill, particularly to render the site less visible to aerial surveillance after the fall of France and the German occupation of airfields near the channel coast. An RAF reconnaissance flight in June revealed how conspicuous the new works were from the air. All building work on the tunnels had been completed two months previously, but no effort had yet been made to backfill the quarry above the new concrete arches. The protection and camouflage offered by this backfill was, of course, the key element of the design and its omission, at this crucial period of the war, was of grave concern to the Air Ministry. Urgent orders were issued on 4 June for the immediate covering of the arches to a minimum depth of two feet by the end of the following day and to a depth of twenty feet by 5 July. It was hoped that the full forty-two feet of overhead cover would be completed by the end of July, but progress remained slow and the Air Ministry was prompted in October to write a caustic letter to No. 42 Group demanding that the job should be given utmost priority. Surveillance by the RAF also revealed how conspicuous and vulnerable were the trains of railway trucks accumulating at Harpur Hill on what was otherwise an apparently derelict site. Subsequently orders were issued to ensure that trains delivering bombs to the depot arrived at dusk and that those not processed and disposed of overnight should be shunted into the tunnels during daylight hours. Wagons that

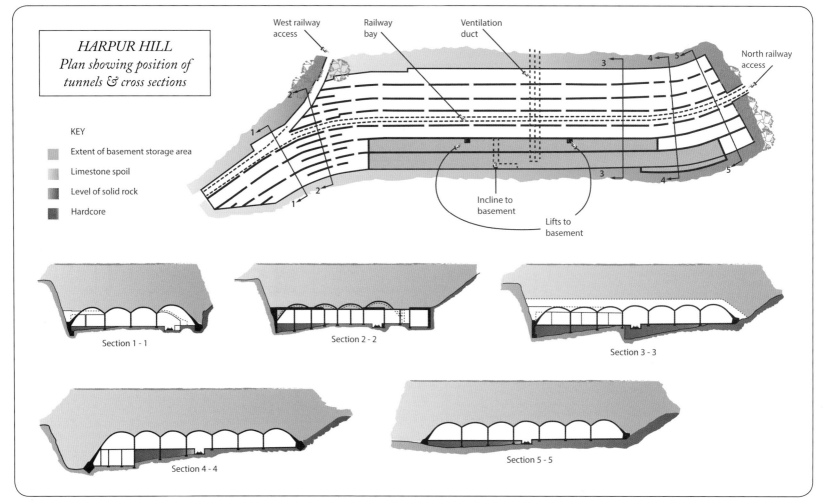

HARPUR HILL
*Plan showing position of
tunnels & cross sections*

West railway access

Railway bay

Ventilation duct

North railway access

KEY

Extent of basement storage area

Limestone spoil

Level of solid rock

Hardcore

Incline to basement

Lifts to basement

Section 1 - 1

Section 2 - 2

Section 3 - 3

Section 4 - 4

Section 5 - 5

could not be accommodated underground were to be shunted at least one mile away from the depot. In the spring, with invasion now an imminent possibility, there was a keen awareness of the risks of sabotage and subversion. Based upon unfounded allegations of fifth-column activity at a major underground defence construction site in Corsham being built, like Harpur Hill, by Alfred McAlpine Ltd, an undercover MI5 investigation was made of the activities of the Irish labourers employed at the Derbyshire depot. Unable to employ English labourers due to the conscription of most eligible men into the services, McAlpine was compelled to fall back upon its traditional source of labour, the legendary 'Mayo men' — Irish labourers who were descendants in habit and inclination, if not by natural lineage, of the hard-drinking, hard-living navvies whose manual labour built the railways of nineteenth century Britain. Groundless allegations were made that the Irishmen were all militant nationalists out to foment trouble and, due to the absence of travel restrictions to and

from neutral Ireland, were free to return to their homeland at any time, taking the secrets of Britain's military preparations with them.

There were good reasons why the security services should be sensitive about Harpur Hill in the spring of 1940. As a result of a decision taken in early April the depot had been designated as the RAF's main storage depot for chemical weapons and early in June huge quantities of mustard gas bombs arrived by train from the docks at Fowey in Cornwall, having been evacuated from northern France by the British Expeditionary Force just before Dunkirk. Just a few weeks earlier it had not been expected that significant stocks of RAF chemical weapons would be forthcoming for several months, so the basement area of Harpur Hill, which was the section of the depot allocated to the storage of such weapons, was adapted temporarily for the storage of tail units until suitable surface accommodation was completed. Alterations made at that time included the installation of a conveyor belt on the inclined ramp to the basement. Storage

Right: This view of the interior of the Harpur Hill depot shows a section of the main railway heading and was probably taken following closure in the 1960s when the site was briefly adapted for mushroom cultivation. It appears that the railway heading is being infilled between the platforms. Note the flameproof switchgear on the walls to operate lights inside the storage magazines.

In the background an overhead crane, used to load and unload heavy bombs on and off the standard-gauge railway trucks spans the track. Nearby there is a hand-operated fire-bell attached to the wall.

of non-explosive material in such costly and secure accommodation when space for priority material was so scarce seems inexplicable, particularly as it was completely contrary to the strategic plan for keeping balanced stocks at all ammunition depots. An Air Ministry minute of 12 April acknowledged this discrepancy, but went on to authorize further unconventional procedures, including the use of pyrotechnic magazines at Harpur Hill for the stowage of incendiary bombs, although it gloomily accepted that these would inevitably be required for pyrotechnics due from the factories during the summer.

It was hoped that eventually some 300,000 square feet of storage space could be found at Harpur Hill or its satellites for chemical weapons storage and to meet this requirement, the Air Ministry, in December 1940, acquired a disused railway tunnel at Butterton, five miles east of Leek in Derbyshire. A year later a second railway tunnel at Rowthorne was acquired to provide an additional 5,000 tons capacity. Unlike Butterton, where just £500 was spent on conversion, works services at Rowthorne were quite expensive at £3,500 and included the erection of a new block wall at the north end of the

tunnel and the laying of an extensive network of Decauville track. Railway tunnels did not provide ideal storage conditions and by December 1943 officers at Rowthorne were complaining that the increasing size of the weapons they had to handle was making operations there excessively cumbersome. Similar problems were already being felt at Butterton and at other adapted railway tunnel stores in the Forest of Dean. Rowthorne was eventually cleared and abandoned on 15 April 1946.

Hopes that Harpur Hill, the third of the great underground reserve depots built in the notionally safe zone west of a line joining Edinburgh and Southampton, might satisfy all future storage needs were dashed even before building got under way. By the early months of 1939, just as preliminary works for Harpur Hill began, it was quite obvious that the supply of weapons to the RAF was outpacing the provision of secure storage at an exponential rate. In an attempt to reduce this discrepancy to more manageable levels a fourth depot was proposed and, in late spring, the eyes of the Air Ministry turned towards the bleak slate district of north Wales.

Above: Two of the many semi-underground pyrotechnic magazines that are widely dispersed across the moorland to the east of the main underground storage tunnels at Harpur Hill. The buildings to the left of the fence are difficult to identify with any certainty, but may be building No.58, the warden's hut, and No.16 the Ammunition Inspectorate loading platform.

Left: A close view of the main entrance to pyrotechnic magazine No.48, located at the far east end of the site.

Opposite above: The north railway access to the Harpur Hill tunnels. When this photograph was taken in 1988 the bomb storage tunnels had recently been taken over by the transport and logistics firm Christian Salvesen, who used it as a high security warehousing facility. The railway entrance was adapted to serve as a lorry loading dock. Note the RAF warden's hut to the left of the entrance, which is a standard design that appears at all the reserve ammunition depots.

Opposite below: The west railway entrance and derelict warden's hut in 1988.

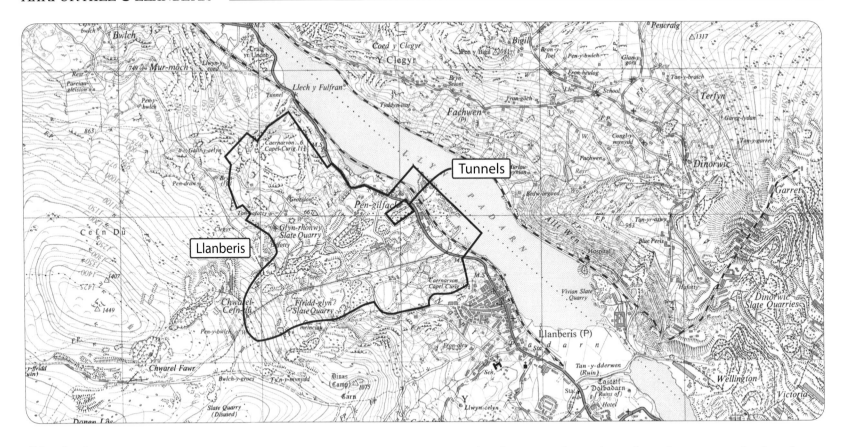

Llanberis

Having spent most of the summer developing plans for the fourth reserve ammunition depot that was now desperately needed, the Air Ministry considered the scheme to locate this at Llanberis in the Snowdon mountains sufficiently advanced to submit it to the Treasury for provisional financial approval on 18 August 1939. An adequately deep, disused slate quarry had been identified at a site just to the west of the town, south of Llyn Padarn and conveniently close to the London Midland & Scottish Railway Company's Llanberis branch, which offered reasonably direct communication with the docks at Liverpool via Caernarvon, Bangor and Chester. The quarry, together with 300 acres of surrounding land consisting almost entirely of waste slate heaps, could he purchased for £20,000 and, in the absence of more detailed estimates, the total cost including all building and railway works, was expected to be £470,000. Of this sum £340,000 was allocated to the construction in reinforced concrete of a two-storey high-explosive store with a nominal capacity of 18,000 tons, similar in all essential features to that recently completed at Harpur Hill. This cost equated to £19 per ton of HE bombs stored,

a similar figure to that achieved at the converted-mine depots already in use. The balance of £110,000 was required to finance the construction of an extensive range of earth-mounded and traversed surface buildings for tail units, detonators, fuzes, etc, and for the necessary service installations, administrative buildings, canteens and staff accommodation. The Treasury response was welcome and rapid. Exercising new powers acquired at the outbreak of war, the immediate requisition of all the land required at Llanberis was authorized, although it was soon realized that, due to the extensive engineering works involved on the site, it was unlikely that post-war reinstatement to the owners would be possible. Arrangements were therefore put in place to purchase the freehold, although this was delayed for over eighteen months.

Within the boundary of the Air Ministry property seven large, abandoned open slate quarries lay in tiers down the hillside. Each was approximately one hundred feet deep and the largest were some three hundred feet in diameter and horribly vertiginous. At the very bottom of each quarry narrow drainage tunnels joined it to the pit below, draining-off seepage water into Lake Padarn. Once cleared of debris, it was discovered that the natural base of the lowest quarry was at the same level as the LMS branch line to Llanberis which followed the southern edge of the lake and it was this quarry that the Ministry selected for conversion.

Its symmetrical rectangular shape enabled the Air Ministry Works Directorate architects to draw up a straightforward layout consisting of two layers of seven parallel tunnels each 470 feet long and approximately twenty-five feet wide with two further half-length tunnels at the innermost end where the quarry was somewhat wider. One full-length tunnel was built to a larger cross section to accommodate a railway siding for standard-gauge wagons. The lower floor had a nine-inch-thick flat concrete ceiling which also served as the floor for the upper level, supported on lateral division walls augmented by a single row of slender reinforced concrete pillars along the centre of each tunnel. Headroom on the lower level was eleven feet, while on the upper floor the nine-foot-high vertical walls supported segmental arched roofs of nine-inch concrete without additional central support pillars. All the lateral support walls on both floors were pierced by wide openings at forty-foot centres to enable the free movement of stores and personnel. Access between floors was by means of three equally spaced three-ton electric goods lifts built by Etchells, Congdon and Muir of Manchester. A single, open concrete stairway at the innermost end of the depot was the only pedestrian route between floors. With the only connection between the storage tunnels and the open air being a standard-gauge railway adit and a smaller tunnel for narrow-gauge trucks, access for workers underground was inadequate under normal conditions and treacherous in emergency. With a view to improving safety, an old drainage adit at the back of the quarry was adapted as an emergency escape route by laying a false floor over the watercourse, which had to be retained because it drained away water from quarries higher up the mountainside. This arrangement was, however, far from adequate as the emergency escape tunnel simply led into the very bottom of a 100-foot-deep, sheer-sided quarry with no immediate means of ascending to ground level, a shortcoming that was vividly highlighted just a few months after the depot opened.

A construction contract was agreed with John Mowlem Ltd in September 1939 and building work started briskly, but by the following spring things were beginning to go wrong. Much against the recommendation of No. 42 Group headquarters, the Air Ministry announced in April that 'in view of the extensive new operational programme Llanberis cannot be placed on the WBA priority list'. What this meant in practice was that the project was to be, at least in the short term, starved of finance, manpower and materials. Mowlem's were asked to economize in the quantities of cement used in load-bearing concrete, and serious reductions were ordered in the previously specified thicknesses of load-bearing components. The floor and ceiling slab that separated the upper and lower levels of the depot, for example, were reduced in thickness from the original thirty inches to just nine inches or less. Building work continued through the summer and autumn of 1940, but had still not reached first-floor level by the end of October. Perturbed at the logistic limitations of the existing design, officers from No. 42 Group visiting the construction site that month suggested that an independent access point for road vehicles should be made into the upper floor level where structural work was about to begin. Implementation of this scheme would have been relatively easy, given the hillside location, but was turned down by the Air Ministry on account of its cost. Eventually, at the beginning of June 1941 building and fitting out was complete and the depot was handed over to No. 42 Group, although a large number of Mowlem's men were still on site completing the job of backfilling the quarry with forty feet depth of loosely packed slate debris above the tunnels.

As originally constructed, a single, standard-gauge siding entered the lower level of the underground depot through a short tunnel that burrowed beneath the main Caernarvon to Llanberis road which skirted the edge of the mountains along the banks of Llyn Padarn. Inside the depot this line branched into two adjacent sidings running the length of the second full-length tunnel from the western perimeter of the quarry. Since the start of operations staff at Llanberis had questioned the necessity for two main-line railway sidings within the depot. With just a minimum of forethought, the designers had presumed that this arrangement would effectively double the handling capacity that would have been available from a single siding, but this proved not to be the case. With two adjacent lines it was possible only to unload trains from one side, and whereas wagons in the east siding could conveniently discharge their cargoes for transfer to six adjacent storage tunnels, the western siding served only one storage area, and only the lower floor of that, as the three lifts, which the only means of accessing the upper floor, were all east of the railway. This unfortunate arrangement had two further consequences, one merely inconvenient, the other catastrophic. In order to accommodate two rail lines it was necessary to increase the width of the bay in which they ran by some fifty percent above the width of the adjacent storage tunnels and, although the designers were confident that by also increasing the thickness of the floor-slab of the

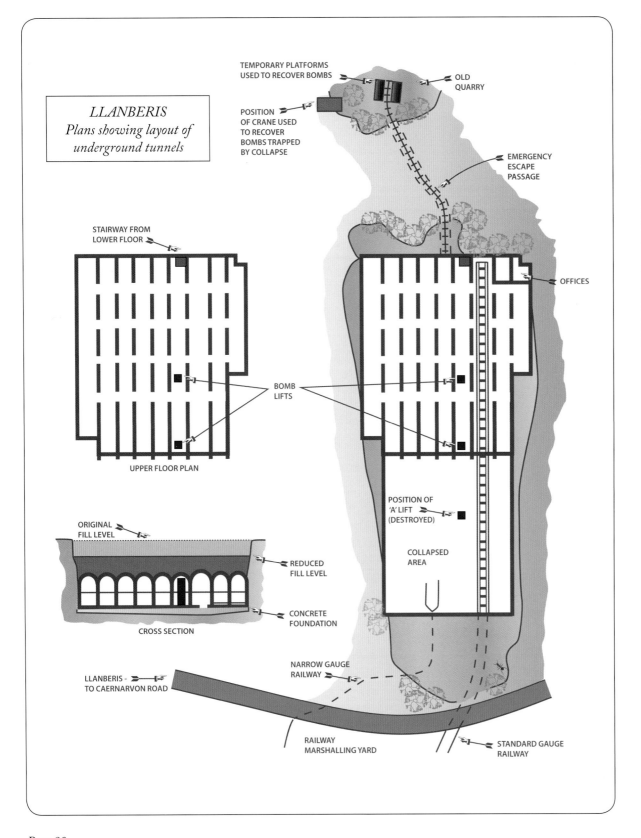

LLANBERIS
Plans showing layout of
underground tunnels

TEMPORARY PLATFORMS
USED TO RECOVER BOMBS

OLD
QUARRY

POSITION
OF CRANE USED
TO RECOVER
BOMBS TRAPPED
BY COLLAPSE

EMERGENCY
ESCAPE
PASSAGE

STAIRWAY FROM
LOWER FLOOR

OFFICES

BOMB
LIFTS

UPPER FLOOR PLAN

POSITION OF
'A' LIFT
(DESTROYED)

ORIGINAL
FILL LEVEL

REDUCED
FILL LEVEL

COLLAPSED
AREA

CONCRETE
FOUNDATION

CROSS SECTION

LLANBERIS -
TO CAERNARVON ROAD

NARROW GAUGE
RAILWAY

RAILWAY
MARSHALLING YARD

STANDARD GAUGE
RAILWAY

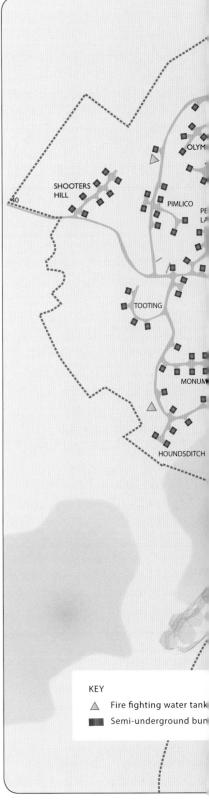

OLYM

SHOOTERS
HILL

40

PIMLICO

PE
LA

TOOTING

MONUM

HOUNDSDITCH

KEY

△ Fire fighting water tank

■ Semi-underground bun

LLANBERIS
*Plan showing layout of
surface buildings*

LMS RAILWAY
CARNARVON & LLANBERIS

INCENDARY AREA

Married
Quarters

STORAGE
TUNNELS

Transfer
Sidings

EMERGENCY
ESCAPE TUNNEL

SEVEN OAKS

BEACHY
HEAD

CAPEL
LLEGYR

SLATE QUARRIES

DISUSED

DEEP

WINDY
RIDGE

HAYMARKET

KEN WOOD

Stores Area

Wharf

OXFORD
STREET

BOX HILL

FINCHLEY

PICCADILLY
CIRCUS

ROTTEN
ROW

Motor Transport
& Works Services Area

CASTLE

LEITH
HILL

RUBBLE
STANDINGS

EARLS
COURT

INCENDARY AREA

ELEPHANT

Right: The construction techniques employed at Harpur Hill and Llanberis were broadly similar. Here we see the building work nearing completion at Harpur Hill. The rough profile of the original quarry is quite evident in the background. The arched tops of the storage tunnels can be seen and there appears to be a gap, beneath the wooden trestle, where the overhead concrete duct for the ventilation system will be constructed.

Left: Building work under way at Llanberis. It would seem that the tunnels were completed progressively from one end as it appears that a section of tunnel in the background has already been covered in a layer of slate debris while in the foreground scaffolding and formwork is only just being put in place for the lower floor walls.

upper story this could he accomplished within the limits of safety, it was felt that these safety limits were critically close, particularly as the row of axial support pillars present in the narrower storage tunnels were of necessity absent in the railway tunnel. Strangely, and ultimately disastrously, the huge arched concrete roof of the upper floor was built to the same thickness — a mere nine inches — as that of the adjacent narrower arches. In order to keep the roof span to a minimum the widths of the railway loading platforms east and west of the underground sidings were reduced to such an extent as to render them unworkable. Within weeks of the depot becoming operational it was decided that, despite the prospective cost, it was essential that the eastern siding should be removed and the width of the loading platform significantly extended. It was initially proposed that a temporary wooden platform should be erected over the redundant eastern siding, but, following an inspection by Flight Lieutenant Grasty from No. 42 Group Headquarters on 14 August, a more permanent solution was authorized. This took the form of a new concrete platform extension, the first section coming into use in mid-October and the entire length at the end of November. A noticeable disadvantage of this arrangement was that subsequently more care had to be taken in marshalling trains entering the depot to ensure that wagons containing the largest bombs were positioned below the three, equally spaced, overhead travelling cranes that spanned the tracks.

The Llanberis depot finally opened for business on 2 June 1941 and the first consignment of bombs, consisting of ten railway wagons despatched from the Royal Ordnance Factory at Swynnerton, arrived early the following day. By the end of the month 332 truck loads had been received at the depot, bringing the stock level up to 1,870 tons, or about ten percent of its design capacity. July and August saw further monthly receipts of approximately 2,500 tons, increasing to 3,500 tons in September and nearly 6,000 tons, including the first consignment of 1,000 lb bombs, in October. Although Llanberis appeared to be operating satisfactorily its additional capacity was making little impression on No. 42 Group's enormous storage shortfall. Just one day after the first consignment was accepted at Llanberis in June, representatives of the Air Ministry arrived at the depot to visit a proposed satellite site a few miles distant at Rhiwlas, where it was proposed to erect thirty-five Laing huts to accommodate small arms ammunition and pyrotechnics in order to relieve pressure on the main underground store. With critically limited underground storage capacity available nationally, No. 42 Group gave increased priority to the safe storage of the most vulnerable classes of bombs,

explosives and ammunition. By mid-August all non-explosive stores had been removed from the tunnels at Llanberis into makeshift surface shelters distributed across the hundreds of acres of slate waste surrounding the depot. Meanwhile, a search was under way for further potentially suitable surface stacking grounds along the route of the Welsh Highland Railway, at Meinofferan Quarry and elsewhere.

Below: 500lb high-explosive bombs stacked on the upper floor at Llanberis before the collapse.

Left: Many of the wartime buildings in the rail transfer yard next to Lake Padarn at Llanberis still survive and are now used for light commercial purposes. The large group of buildings at the far end of the yard were the Small Arms Ammunition belt-filling sheds and the building in the right foreground is a latrine block.

Below left: The standard-gauge locomotive shed at Llanberis in 1988. This building still stands and is used as a bus garage.

Below right: The portal of the narrow-gauge railway tunnel which passes beneath the Caernarfon to Llanberis road and links the bomb-storage tunnels to the railway interchange yard.

By early January 1942 a reasonable routine had been established and the depot seemed to be working smoothly, despite Air Force misgivings about the employment of local civilians for much of the manual labour and guard duty. Indeed, labour relations during the previous August had deteriorated so rapidly that the station's Commanding Officer had written to No. 42 Group complaining that the depot was suffering from a shortage of staff and that those men he had 'were all local, Welsh and very nationalistic, more interested in Home Rule than work,' and that in his opinion 'they should be replaced by Service personnel. Likewise the security wardens are all Welsh and are not considered trustworthy. Handling of stock is slow and the locals are disinclined to hard work.' This was not, however, an isolated situation associated exclusively with the perceived problem of Welsh nationalism, for during the early months of 1941 the headquarters of No. 42 Group was awash with complaints about the inadequate manpower available at several important home depots, particularly the other large, underground reserve bomb stores at Fauld and Harpur Hill. The principal and inevitable cause of this difficulty was that the younger, fitter and more capable men had by that time been conscripted into the services, and even within the services the best men seem to have been despatched for duties abroad leaving, predominantly, those less able in body or mind for home defence. Shortages of suitable manpower perhaps had their most profound effects within Anti-Aircraft Command, the home command that seemed always to be granted the lowest of all priorities in the provision of resources. The situation there is sharply highlighted by General Sir Frederick Pile, who led the command through most of the war years. In his memoirs, *Ack-Ack*, Pile records that many of the men allocated to him were quite unsuited for any military duty, let alone the highly technical duties of Anti-Aircraft Command. Out of twenty-five who arrived at a representative battery, one had a withered arm, one was mentally deficient, one had no thumbs, one had a glass eye which fell out whenever he doubled for the guns, and two were in the advanced and more obvious stages of venereal disease.

The first catastrophe

Suddenly, on the morning of 25 January 1942 petty labour difficulties at Llanberis were cast into insignificance. That morning a train of twenty-seven wagons loaded with bombs from the Swynnerton Royal Ordnance Factory was shunted into the underground siding and had just begun unloading when deep, ominous grating sounds were heard above the normal din of metal on metal as bombs were rolled off onto the loading platform. Dust, then heavier lumps of concrete, began to fall from the ceiling above, followed by the appearance of wide lateral cracks that opened up and spread quickly along the length of the tunnel. Fearful for their lives, the men unloading the train ran for safety towards the emergency exit in tunnel 'B' as, within seconds of the first movement occurring, the ceiling broke away from the east wall at a point near No. 1 ammunition lift and collapsed on to the train below, releasing hundreds of bombs from the chamber above which rained down through the void. Devoid of lateral support from the failed floor slab, the walls on either side of the platform quickly folded inwards and crumpled, initiating a terrifying chain reaction. In a slow progressive wave like a collapsing house of cards, tunnel 'A' to the west and all the tunnels east of the railway fell inwards, tipping their high-explosive contents into the mess of twisted steel and concrete below. As the fragile arches of the upper floor gave way the 100,000 tons of slate backfill above poured down, completely burying everything below and filling the quarry with choking dust. Once the dust had settled it was apparent that approximately forty percent of the depot had collapsed and that everything between the northern extremity of the tunnels and No. 2 ammunition lift had been utterly destroyed. It was later calculated that the steel structure of the lift and the extra support offered by the rails of an overhead crane spanning the tracks nearby had arrested the collapse and saved the rest of the depot from absolute disaster. Luckily the depot offices and the portal of the emergency exit were both in relatively undamaged sections of tunnel and all twenty-two men working underground at the time escaped uninjured.

Ammunition in the Llanberis Tunnels at Time of Collapse	
20 lb HE	2
40 lb HE	9,830
250 lb HE	14,965
500 lb HE	46,691
1000 lb HE	420
250 lb AS	420
500 lb AS	1,613
250 lb SAP	32
500 lb SAP	608
25 lb HE	115
250 lb DC	983
Smith gun	23,000 rounds
TNT	40,000 lbs
250 lb practise bomb	200

There was no explosion, and the immediate danger was not from the 75,000 HE bombs trapped amongst the debris but from 23,000 highly unstable rounds of Smith gun ammunition and 18 tons of bulk TNT that were buried there. All deliveries to Llanberis were suspended for several days and when receipts were eventually resumed on 30 January all new HE bombs were routed to the recently completed satellite incendiary store at Rhiwlas. Meanwhile an inspection team from the Air Ministry Works Directorate arrived at Llanberis on 26 January to spend a couple of days making a preliminary assessment of the stability of the remaining structure and to devise a recovery plan. The need to begin a recovery operation as soon as possible was vital because fifteen percent of the RAF's entire stock of HE bombs was sequestered in the wreckage of the tunnels.

The pressing need for progress was, however, offset by a necessary degree of caution due to the presence in the debris of the highly temperamental Smith gun ammunition and a large quantity of raw TNT, and by a lack of any clear evidence of the condition of the other bombs trapped with it. Caution also had to be exercised in order to ensure that evidence regarding the cause of the collapse was not destroyed as it was inevitable that a Court of Inquiry would be required to investigate this. Meanwhile, sixty civilian labourers who previously worked on ammunition movements for the RAF were transferred to John Mowlem Ltd, who were still on site, to begin preparing temporary stacking grounds for recovered bombs.

On 10 February, more than two weeks after the disaster, a thorough investigation of the collapsed area was undertaken by Dr Sands and Dr Rotter from the Ministry of Aircraft Production Ammunition Inspection Directorate, accompanied by Dr Phillips, Dr Payman and Dr Titman from the Safety in Mines Research Department at Buxton. An unlikely hero, Dr Rotter was later to be awarded the George Cross, the highest civilian award for bravery, for a similar role in an infinitely more dangerous recovery task undertaken three years later. On the same day that Dr Rotter began his investigation a Court of Inquiry assembled at the Headquarters of Maintenance Command under the chairmanship of Group Captain Pawdrey. With him sat Mr P. Harris, OBE, the chief engineer of Maintenance Command and Wing Commander Quale, Commanding Officer of No.11 MU Chilmark. Their task was to 'investigate the situation at No.31 MU Llanberis arising from a collapse of the explosives storage and to obtain any evidence to assist in determining the cause of the occurrence.'

After hearing eye-witness accounts, reports from Dr Rotter and his team of investigators, and submissions from the contractors John Mowlem Ltd, the Court of Inquiry submitted its findings to the Air Ministry on 2 March. Deep concern about the building's design had been expressed from many quarters during the construction of the depot, so the findings came as little surprise. The inquiry concluded that the main cause of the collapse was a series of fundamental design faults compounded by poor implementation. It was also agreed that the wrong grade of concrete had been used in construction, a direct result of the Air Ministry's request to John Mowlem Ltd in April 1940 that they should minimize the amount of cement used in load-bearing concrete. Poor workmanship, attributed to the dire shortage of skilled labour available at that point in the war, was also pinpointed as a contributory factor. The inquiry was told, for example, that lateral walls on the upper floor, which should have been perpendicular to those on the bottom floor in order to transmit the overburden load from the arches above to the bedrock below were, in some cases, offset by several inches, thus transforming this load into a shear stress on the upper level floor slab. The Court heard that cracks were noticed in the structure as building work neared completion, but that these were optimistically but erroneously attributed to minor settlement defects rather than a fundamental miscalculation. It later emerged, as we have seen, that similar cracking occurred at Harpur Hill which, in the light of the Llanberis disaster, called for immediate remedial action.

Once the Court of Inquiry had delivered its verdict No. 42 Group was free to begin the recovery process. Access to the collapsed area was only possible via the undamaged sections of tunnel, and the only access to that was through the small emergency exit passage at the south end of the depot. Despite the fact that more than five weeks had passed since the accident still no clear picture of conditions within the collapsed section was available and it was realized that it would be impossible to put together an evacuation plan for that area until the whole of the undamaged section had been cleared of bombs. It was obvious that everything would have to be removed through the small emergency escape passage, so during the first week of March narrow-gauge rails were laid through this tunnel and substantial brick and concrete footings built on the edge of the open quarry into which it led. Once the footings had set, a gantry crane was set up overhanging the quarry and the tedious process of evacuating the bombs could begin. Each had to be manhandled, one at a time, on to a narrow-gauge truck, pushed by hand through the narrow confines of the emergency tunnel, slung in a net and hauled by crane 100 feet to the surface. On

9 March, when the operation began, just two tons of bombs were recovered. The following day this was increased to forty tons, then seventy tons and by the end of the month, as techniques improved with practice, the labour gangs were recovering two hundred tons per day. On 20 April a record 490 tons were recovered and by 28 April, when evacuation of the un-collapsed area was finally completed, a total of 8,230 tons of bombs had been recovered.

On the same day a conference was held at the offices of John Mowlem Ltd to discuss methods of removal of the remaining stores and debris from the collapsed section. Those present included Wing Commander Smith and three other senior officers from No.42 Group, Dr Rotter and his team, Major Doherty and four engineers from John Mowlem Ltd. No record of their discussion has survived, nor any explanation for the delay of fourteen weeks before work finally began at 2.10 pm on 24 July. The task was completed on 22 October when the last of the remaining 6,047 tons of bombs was removed from the wreckage of the tunnels. Searches continued for a further ten days, however, until the Ammunition Inspection Directorate was able to certify the site as free from explosives. Mowlem's were then given possession of the site in order to clear the remaining concrete debris and stabilize the structure while the Air Ministry considered its long-term future. Once clearance was complete it was found that of the 75,000 bombs that had been in the depot at the time of the collapse only 19 were irreparably damaged. Twenty-one of the twenty-seven railway trucks that were unloading at the time of the accident were completely destroyed.

Ripples from the disaster at Llanberis affected the whole of No.42 Group's strategy for the rest of the war. Not only was 20,000 tons of storage capacity lost immediately, but space had to be provided elsewhere for all the ammunition subsequently recovered from the tunnels, for all the bombs evacuated as a precaution from Harpur Hill, and for all those weapons already in the pipeline scheduled for despatch to the two artificial underground depots. We have already seen how the Corsham quarries absorbed a substantial proportion of these stores, and how a number of disused railway tunnels were adapted at short notice to take material from Harpur Hill. It was evident, however, that proper underground protection could not be provided for the majority of the material and that other, less attractive, options would have to be adopted.

The RAF did possess one other small underground site in North Wales, Grange Quarry at Holywell on the Dee estuary, that was under-utilized at the time of the Llanberis disaster. Grange Quarry had been identified just before the war as a potentially suitable location but, after inspection, was declared too inadequate for use as a permanent storage depot. Too small, excessively damp, with a steeply inclined floor and accessible only via a steep winding lane the quarry was nevertheless adopted by No.42 Group in September 1939 as a satellite of 21 MU Fauld for temporary storage until the permanent depots were completed. At the time of the accident Grange Quarry was used only to store a few obsolete weapons for 21 MU and on 1 July 1942 it was transferred to 31 MU Llanberis to absorb some of the recovered bombs. By the following March its deficiencies had become patent and it was again relegated to the storage of obsolete bombs only and was closed a couple of months later. The site was temporarily re-opened in May 1945 to process 500 lb bombs in preparation for the invasion of Europe and was closed permanently at the end of the following year.

Meanwhile, at the main site in Llanberis plans were being prepared for the future operation of the depot. In mid-September 1942 it was decided that the rest of the recovered HE bombs would remain on site and arrangements were made to stack these in the open on the slate heaps that surrounded the depot while the British Runway Company Ltd laid new, permanent stacking bays both on the main site and at Rhiwlas. Eventually a network of roadways was built through the 350 acres of slate heaps on the mountainside above the collapsed tunnels to serve twenty-five groups of storage units, including covered sheds and semi-underground magazines for incendiary bombs and components and open hard-standings for HE bombs. To make identification easy each group was quaintly named after a well known area of London, hence there are incendiary groups with names like 'Oxford Circus', 'Rotten Row' and 'Haymarket' together with HE hard-standings named 'Box Hill' and 'Elephant & Castle'.

John Mowlem Ltd continued work on the wreckage through the autumn and winter of 1942 and eventually completed the task of stabilizing what survived in June 1943, but by that time the fate of the remaining tunnels had been decided. After all the collapsed concrete and other debris was removed from the pit and dumped on the waste heaps higher up the mountainside, Mowlem's engineers were able to trim the ends of the remaining tunnels and insert brick end-walls to seal them from the elements. The entire structure was still considered to be unstable, however, and it was decided to immediately excavate twenty feet of the backfill from above the tunnels to reduce the overhead load and then to infill the majority of the arched openings in the lateral tunnel walls. These openings were pinpointed by the

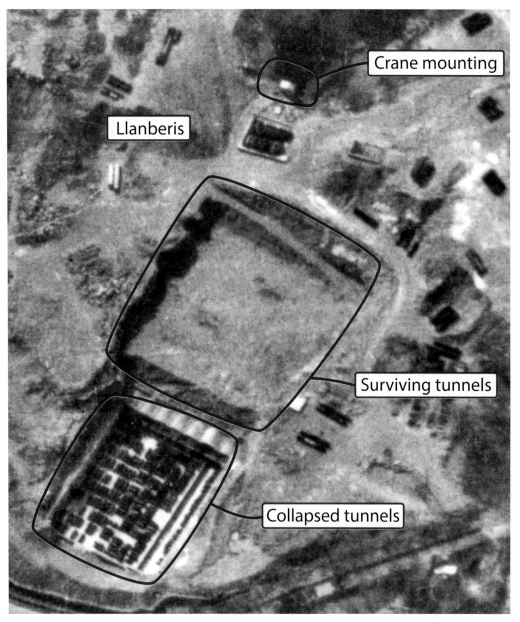

Crane mounting

Llanberis

Surviving tunnels

Collapsed tunnels

Above: Aerial view of Llanberis in April 1947. Small arms ammunition can be seen stacked in the cleared area where the tunnels had collapsed. The ends of the surviving sections of tunnel can be seen emerging from the waste slate laid above them. There is a ramp visible from the surface of this infill, which was used by vehicles employed to reduce the depth of this overburden. Note the numerous piles of ammunition in open storage on the surface, these may be German *Tabun* bombs awaiting transfer to Llandwrog, the last of which were transferred on 13 July 1947.

inquiry as important contributory causes of the initial failure. The few openings retained to allow movement between the tunnels were reinforced with concentric rings of brickwork. Elsewhere, massive brick buttresses were erected to resist any further movement of the most suspect lengths of internal wall.

Both the cost of further reconstruction and questions about the overall requirement for underground protection, given the diminishing risk of German aerial attack, prompted the Air Ministry to comment on 27 November that:

bearing in mind the speed and ease with which storage can be provided overground and that open storage for 20,000 tons HE is already being developed, further expenditure on repair of Llanberis is unjustifiable.

It was evident anyway that No. 42 Group had lost all confidence in the underground structure at Llanberis and on 30 December authority was sought from the Air Ministry to abandon the tunnels. It was suggested that perhaps they could be used for the storage of tail units, packing cases and other non-explosives materials, but this was unacceptable due to the potential risk to personnel working underground.

Eventually, on 25 June 1943, it was agreed that the underground area would be completely abandoned and never again used for storage of any kind, but that the cleared area where the collapse had occurred should be used for the open storage of small arms ammunition. Thus ended the short but dramatic history of the Llanberis tunnels. The remaining surface storage facilities at Llanberis depot was finally closed in 1956, though this was not to be the end of the depot's troubles which, as a result of post-war ineptitude and ignorance, were to haunt the Air Ministry and the Ministry of Defence for a further thirty years.

Repurcusions at Harpur Hill

Immediately after the collapse of Llanberis concerns were raised regarding the stability of the tunnelled storage at Harpur Hill which was

Above: The surviving elements of the Llanberis tunnels in 1990. Originally the tunnels would have extended over the whole of the open area in the foreground, and would have been covered with waste slate debris to the full height of the rock formation seen on the right. The alignment of the collapsed walls can be seen in the concrete foundation.

Right: In the early years of the present century work began on an abortive plan to infill the abandoned tunnels and the open space in front with builders waste. At that time the railway cutting was filled and a small amount of waste brought in, but then, thankfully, the scheme was stopped. It is possible in this view to see how some of the walls on the upper floor were out of alignment with those on the bottom level, one of several factors that contributed to the collapse.

Left: This closer view of the ends of the surviving tunnels illustrates how dangerously thin the upper floor slab and arched roofs were. The specifications for both these features were reduced while construction was under way. The break-up of the concrete around the bottoms of the division walls is also evident in this picture, a consequence of inadequate materials used in construction.

Left: This view shows how the section of tunnel carrying the railway heading was built to a larger scale than the others. This was because as originally built the depot had two parallel sidings throughout the length of the tunnel. It was not until the depot became operational that this arrangement was found to be inefficient, leading to the left-hand siding being removed and replaced by a widened platform.

Below left: The portal of the railway runnel linking the depot to the transfer yard on the far side of the Caernarfon-Llanberis road.

Below right: A narrow-gauge truck, dumped and abandoned in the railway cutting. Note the standard-gauge rails still in-situ.

Above left: The inward end of the railway platform in the tunnels. It was a crack along the centre of this wide expanse of roof that gave the first warning of the collapse.

Above right: This flight of concrete steps on the west side of the railway platform once led up to a group of prefabricated wooden offices.

Left: Bay 'B', the first of the two parallel bottom-floor storage tunnels to the west of the railway platform. This view is looking out towards the open end of the tunnels, taken from the top of the office steps.

Above left: The cage of No.2 lift at rest on the upper floor of the depot. With the drive gear vandalised, the lift's counterweight has caused the cage to rise to the top. (Contrary to popular fiction, when lifts fail they are more likely to ascend rather rapidly, rather than plummet to the bottom of the shaft).

Above right: The wrecked remains of the drive unit and gearbox for No.2 lift.

Left: No. 1 lift at rest on the upper floor. The brick wall immediately behind it marks the end of the surviving section of tunnel. It was believed that it was the presence of the lift that gave sufficient structural stability to prevent the total destruction of the depot, which collapsed progressively from north to south, halting at this point.

Above: A panoramic view of tunnel 'N' (the second to the east of the railway heading), showing the general layout of the tunnels and the brick reinforcement applied to the interconnecting arches following the collapse.

Left: A wider view of the lift on the upper floor of tunnel 'M'. Notice that the archways through the walls of bay M7 have not been reinforced with brickwork.

Right: A view through the interconnecting arches on the upper floor. The red dot and concentric circle on the wall mark the proposed position for a firefighting water pipe that would have pierced the wall at this point. The abandonment of the tunnels after the collapse brought this project to an end.

Far right: Extensive brick reinforcement at the outer end of a lower floor tunnel.

Above: The exit from the emergency escape tunnel. Two brick and concrete loading platforms lie hidden amongst the undergrowth in the foreground. A crane was mounted on the edge of the quarry to lift out the recovered munitions.

Left: The emergency escape tunnel between the bomb store and an old open quarry beyond. Narrow-gauge rails were laid and eventually 75,000 bombs, 23,000 rounds of Smith gun ammunition and 18 tons of raw TNT were extracted from the wreckage of the collapsed depot and extracted via this route.

built on similar principles and to a similar design. After a delay of two weeks, attributable perhaps to the attention of the somewhat traumatized Air Ministry Works Directorate being directed wholly towards the Llanberis problem, an exhaustive structural examination of the Harpur Hill tunnels was ordered. The inspection revealed a number of serious cracks similar to those that had erroneously been dismissed at Llanberis and the level of disquiet caused by their discovery was such that instructions were issued for the immediate removal of the protective backfill over the tunnels to a depth of twenty feet. On 12 February, amid growing concern, it was decided to empty the depot as quickly as possible, and to that end arrangements were put in place to fulfil all upcoming overseas requirements exclusively from Harpur Hill, and also to prepare alternative temporary storage for evacuated material. Three thousand tons of chemical weapons were transferred to Butterton Tunnel, six hundred tons of 250 lb HE bombs were sent to Ridge Quarry and eighteen 1,000 lb bombs despatched to the recently converted Elm Park Quarry near Corsham. Other items were distributed amongst a number of Forward Ammunition Depots. By the end of March 5,634 tons were removed, the remaining 10,042 tons going by midday on 16 May.

The investigation quickly focused on the series of arched openings in the lateral division walls between the tunnels. Detailed examination at both Harpur Hill and among the debris of Llanberis indicated that it was from points around the tops of these arches that cracks spread out into the roof and, at Llanberis, probably initiated the collapse. Unknown to the Works Directorate at that time, the failure of a broadly similar underground depot built by the War Office at Monkton Farleigh near Corsham in May 1940 was attributed to almost identical design failures in a series of arched openings in concrete walls, although at Monkton Farleigh the walls were subject to an overpressure of some seventy tons per square foot. As the various bays were emptied of bombs, action was taken by the Works Directorate to strengthen the tunnels by bricking up half of the arched openings in the concrete walls and shoring those that had to remain open with steel arches. The repairs were finally completed early in April 1943 when the Air Ministry agreed that underground storage of HE bombs and small arms ammunition could resume. Confidence in the structure had been severely shaken, however, and the storage of sensitive items such as Smith gun ammunition, boxed TNT, land-mines and chemical weapons was expressly excluded.

Llanberis: The post war debacle

Although the storage facilities at Llanberis had been decommissioned in 1956 certain activities continued on site for several more years. Four groups of slate pits, some as much as 900 feet in depth, had

Below: Aerial view of the open quarries to the south of the Llanberis depot which were used post-war for the large-scale dumping of redundant munitions.

been used from the mid-1940s up until the time of closure for the disposal of surplus and suspect ammunition, using either the quaintly named 'shaft' technique, which simply involved tipping the unprocessed material down a mine shaft, or by incineration. The latter method involved the construction of steeply inclined steel chutes down the side of the open quarries which fed the material for disposal into rudimentary furnaces at the bottom where it was, theoretically at least, completely consumed. Years later, however, it was discovered that much of the explosive materials despatched for incineration had not been destroyed but had instead lodged on ledges and in crevices on the rock face. The severity of this problem was at first dismissed by the Air Ministry and little or no remedial action was taken until, in the years following the closure of the depot, several civilians were badly injured when tampering with devices recovered from the pits.

Concern both locally and nationally was such that in February 1970 a working party was set up to investigate the problem under the chairmanship of Group Captain Waterkeyn. On 3 March the working party issued a preliminary 'Report on the Inactive RAF Site at Llanberis' which concluded that:

It is apparent from the files and the history of Llanberis that various half-hearted attempts in the past have been made to do something about the whole site but they have generally foundered because of the inherent difficulties and uncertainties.

The working party has been unable to establish with absolute certainty what explosives are or are not in the various pits, but after an examination of the history of the whole site and detailed examination at pit level we have no reason to suspect the presence of particularly dangerous items and we are confident that total clearance of the pits is at least worth the attempt.

From the few available records, the working party had been able to draw up an outline historical timetable of events at Llanberis:

1943: Destruction of obsolete incendiary bombs started.

1944-5: Destruction of unserviceable ammunition on an extensive scale begins.

1955: 31 MU at Llanberis is disbanded and its administration transferred to RAF Llandwrog in connection with the disposal of 71,000 *Tabun* nerve-gas bombs recovered from Germany at the end of the war and stored precariously for a decade in North Wales. Meanwhile, the Llanberis site was retained exclusively for the

disposal of conventional weapons.

1956: In response to local agitation, the Treasury Solicitor advised that: 'the Air Ministry would discharge its duty to use reasonable care to prevent damage or injury by erecting suitable fences and warning notices and by ensuring that such fencing and notices were kept in good and efficient repair.'

1960: It was discovered that the fenced-off areas had been broken into and several items of an explosive nature had been removed. The pits had in fact become a playground for youths from all over North Wales and in 1960 a group of teenagers from Conway had removed a number of detonators from the pit. A sixteen-year-old boy was seriously injured when an item of ordnance exploded in his hand while he was trying to dismantle it.

1961: Fencing repaired and improved with the addition of barbed wire. Later that year the Air Ministry made an astonishingly naïve and ultimately unsuccessful effort to dispose of all its liabilities at Llanberis, which was so absurd that it gave rise to Parliamentary questions. A note of this proposal, penned by an anonymous Air Ministry acronym, survives in the public record as a warning to posterity. It reads:

A question was raised in the House of Commons regarding the sale of RAF Llanberis to the Caernarvonshire County Council. At that time the Board of Trade made a statement that the clearance of explosives would be a dangerous and expensive proposition which would not be justified on financial or land utilization grounds. It was suggested that the County Council should purchase the whole RAF site to promote employment in the area and should accept liability for any accidents caused by the contents of the pits.

1962 : The County Council's refusal to accept the Llanberis depot under any circumstances, let alone by the purchase of all its liabilities, caused little surprise. The Air Ministry then issued two further proposals: the first, that a permanent guard force should be kept on site, was rejected on grounds of cost; the proponent of the second solution, to completely destroy the pits and their contents by bombing them with napalm, thankfully came to his senses before any real damage could be done.

1964-9: It was accepted that the RAF would probably have to retain the pits area in perpetuity. Occasional inspections were made of the fencing and warnings signs but otherwise little else was done to ensure the safety of the site.

The final solution to the Llanberis problem was prompted by events surrounding the investiture of the Prince of Wales at Caernarvon Castle on I July 1969. For some weeks before the investiture the security services had been aware of Welsh Nationalist agitation in the area, with the possibility of some form of terrorist threat. On the strength of these rumours, in June 1969 No. 71 MU Bomb Disposal Flight carried out a reconnaissance of the [RAF Llanberis] site and reported that there was evidence of excavation and sifting of the explosive items in pit area No.4. In view of the known activities of the 'Free Welsh Army' in the area, and of the forthcoming investiture of the Prince of Wales, RAF Valley and the local police were informed.

So, this was the background to the Working Party's initial investigation in early February 1970. This first examination of the site produced results that were not encouraging, and on 12 March Waterkeyn, accompanied by Wing Commander Wood and Lieutenant Colonel Wright of the Royal Engineers, made a hazardous descent on ropes into one of the quarries to make a more thorough examination. What they found there appalled them, but represented, they thought, a containable and soluble problem. Matters were made more difficult by the fact that, in a desultory attempt to make the quarries safe immediately after ammunition disposal ceased, a certain amount of demolition had been done to render the pits inaccessible.

It appeared that, of the four main areas used for ammunition, two could be cleared with relative ease by a small RAF detachment, but the remaining two posed major difficulties. Quarry No.3A, it was thought, could only be cleared effectively by the in-situ demolition of explosive items that lay in the bottom and then by blasting the face of the quarry to dislodge rock that would be bulldozed over the debris to a depth of twenty feet. The latter part of this process caused some trepidation among the members of the investigating team, who noted in their report that: 'to do this it will be necessary to lower a machine such as a D2 or D4 bulldozer down the rock face (210 feet!) on ropes.'

Of Quarry 'C' in No.2 pit area, which was some 900 feet in depth, the working party's report noted that it: 'includes a three acre lake and can be cleared manually by RAF bomb disposal personnel, probably without assistance from the REs. However, an underwater check by a qualified Royal Navy diver is considered essential before the area can be certified clear of dangerous material.'

Towards the end of April the report had found its way to the desk of Air Vice Marshal F.R. Bird, and it did not make appetizing reading. Bird wrote gloomily to the Air Ministry that 'We are guilty at the moment of polluting a large tract of attractive countryside' and acknowledged that decisive action must be taken whatever the prospective cost.

More bad news soon followed. Air Vice Marshal C.N.S. Pringle gave evidence to the working party that: 'A Chief Technical Armaments Officer at RAF Valley made a formal statement to the police at RAF Valley that when he was a SAC fifteen years earlier he had taken part in the dumping of Phosgene gas bombs in a pit at the then 31 MU Llanberis.'

This assertion sparked panic at the Air Ministry because of the possibility that the material the Armament Officer referred to could in fact have been *Tabun* rather than Phosgene. There was little probability that 31 MU would have been involved in the disposal of Phosgene during the period in question, but it was very much involved in Operations *Dismal* and *Sandcastle*, the disposal of German *Tabun* bombs. Almost all of these weapons were deep-sea-dumped from Cairn Ryan, but it was known that a few leakers' were disposed of locally at Llandwrog; the nerve agent being thoroughly incinerated in a burning pit, the remains treated with a neutralizing agent and then buried in situ. It was feared that one or more of these weapons had, without authority, been disposed of at Llanberis.

During the closing months of the Second World War the Allies discovered that Germany had erected a top-secret factory at Dyhernfurth in western Poland capable of a monthly production of 3,000 tons of the deadly nerve gas *Tabun*, along with considerable quantities of the even more lethal nerve agent Sarin. Some 71,000 *Tabun* filled bombs – a total weight of 14,000 tons – had been manufactured at Dyhernfurth and subsequently transferred to an underground storage facility at Krappitz in Upper Silesia. This stockpile was eventually located and after intensive negotiations with the United States government it was agreed that the captured weapons should be taken under British control and transferred to the UK mainland. The selected storage site, chosen for its remote, windswept position in Caernarvon Bay, was the by now disused airfield at Llandwrog near the small, isolated port of Fort Belan.

Operation Dismal, the shipment of bombs to the UK, began in October 1945, each consignment of 500 weapons travelling from Hamburg to Newport docks in South Wales and thence to a temporary storage compound at Llanberis. There, each bomb was examined to assess its condition before transfer to permanent storage in specially built sheds on the disused runways at Llandwrog. During the eight years they were stored at Llandwrog it became increasingly clear the British Government, nor any other Western Power, had any use for them, and meanwhile the bombs deteriorated alarmingly. In January 1955 detailed plans were drawn up for their disposal by deep sea dumping at a point 120 miles north-west of Ireland, beyond the edge of the continental shelf. The disposal process, codenamed *Operation Sandcastle* involved yet another perilous seaborne transfer, this time from Fort Belan aboard adapted Landing Craft to Cairn Ryan in south west Scotland where they were loaded into three ships, SS *Empire Claire*, MV *Voigtland* and SS *Kotka* for scuttling.

A thorough search was made of the remaining records but it was discovered that: 'It would seem that the demolition diaries and all similar records relating to the destruction of explosives at Llanberis have been destroyed and no record can be found giving the total quantity or the types of explosive that have been destroyed.'

Subsequently a great many men who had been involved in both *Operation Sandcastle* and other weapons-disposal programmes at Llanberis were interviewed at length but no other evidence as to either the disposal of *Tabun* or Phosgene came to light. It was assumed that the original assertion was spurious if not malicious and the matter was quietly dropped.

Work began during April in the most accessible of the pits. By 27 May a system of aerial ropeways had been erected to transport materials and 2,240 lbs of explosive and over two tons of explosive debris had been recovered. A bulldozer had been lowered without undue incident into Quarry 3A and work was proceeding satisfactorily there. But a very different story was unfolding in Quarry 'C', where the Navy divers were discovering a growing nightmare below the turgid waters of the lake.

In the murky waters, which were much deeper than had been supposed, they found a vast, ninety-foot-high mountain of unexploded ordnance intermixed with ordnance debris and incendiary slag estimated to weigh some 3,000 tons. Investigation of Quarry 2C, just down the hillside, revealed a similar situation once 20,000,000 gallons of polluted water were pumped out. The clearance task proved prodigious and was finally completed in October 1975. By that time 352 tons of high explosive had been recovered, along with 1,420 tons of explosive components and 85,000 tons of non-explosive ordnance debris. Even after the closure of the recovery programme the RAF was unwilling to certify the area safe of explosives and the pits are still surrounded by security fences and warning signs.

Left: Rows of German *Tabun* bombs laid out on roller conveyors on a purpose-built hardstanding at Fort Belan, a small port adjacent to RAF Llandwrog, awaiting transshipment to Cairn Ryan for deep sea dumping. These bombs were briefly stored and inspected at Llanberis before being transferred to Llandwrog for long-term storage.

Chapter 6

21MU FAULD

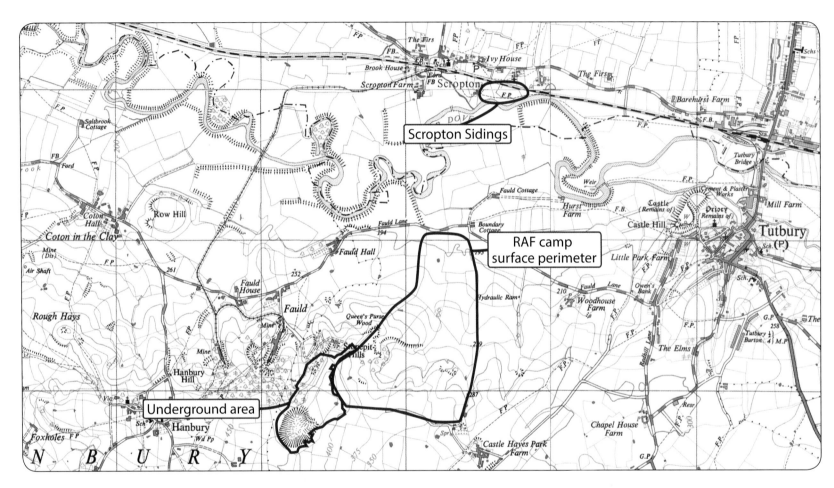

Scropton Sidings

RAF camp
surface perimeter

Underground area

The Fauld disaster

Locating a suitable site for the second and by far the most important of the RAF reserve depots proved difficult due to the strict criteria that had to be met. A site in the Midlands, west of the notional Edinburgh to Southampton line, with a minimum overhead cover of sixty feet and with good railway connections, was difficult to find in a region where the extractive industry to the north and west was predominantly salt and to the south and east predominantly coal. The vacant subterranean real estate left by both these mining industries

was ruled out by both geology and depth. Limestone was quarried in quantity from the Pennines, but here the outcrops were shallow and worked predominantly from the surface in vast open pits.

There was, however, another mineral that occurred only in isolated pockets in Staffordshire which, once extracted, left cavities that fulfilled every requirement. The mineral was calcium sulphate and it was found below the Needwood Forest north-west of Burton-upon-Trent as gypsum, anhydrite and, in its finest form, alabaster. The gypsum seam, which is about fifteen feet in depth, outcrops to the north of this area near the village of Tutbury, after which the seam is named, and then dips to the south-west towards Tatenhill. Apart from the few surface outcrops in the Tutbury area the incline of the seam takes it to an average depth of between sixty and ninety feet below ground. Although the outcroppings have been scratched for over one thousand years and gypsum extracted in a minor commercial way by means of shallow bell-pits for at least three hundred years, underground quarrying began in the mid-nineteenth century with the opening of Draycott mine, which finally closed in 1939. Exploitation of the reserves on an industrial scale, however, began in 1868 when two firms, J.C. Staton & Co and Peter Ford & Sons, established deep-level mines at Fauld to provide raw materials to meet the increasing demand for building plaster. Both companies were amalgamated into the British Plaster & Boards Company in 1936, but the two mines maintained independent operations until 1944, when events beyond the company's control required the construction of a new single shaft that served both sets of workings.

By the time of the amalgamation in 1936 Staton's mine, which lies within the western section of the known reserves, extended to approximately ninety acres, while Ford's mine to the east extended to a contiguous block of forty-eight acres of exhausted workings. A major problem encountered by the gypsum industry in north Staffordshire is that, although the Tutbury sulphate seam is extensive, it is not uniform but consists of discontinuous masses of commercially valuable gypsum separated by troublesome and valueless outcrops of silty mudstones. Early in the twentieth century Ford's hit an area of mudstone as they extended their Fauld Quarry southwards and were compelled to dig a trial heading to discover new reserves of saleable mineral. Trial borings indicated that fresh sources of gypsum lay a little to the south-west of the existing mine, so a half-mile-long underground roadway was dug to connect the western perimeter of the exhausted mine to the new reserves which by 1940 were quarried over an area of some twenty acres.

Ford's surface buildings lay north of the main quarry adit and covered an area of approximately two and a half acres. Here the raw material was ground and treated, after which the bulk was bagged for sale and a certain amount converted into plasterboard. Huge volumes of water were required for these processes and to supply this a large storage reservoir or artificial lake, thirty feet deep and with a surface area of over an acre, was formed by building a dam across a north-flowing stream just south of the factory. The dam consisted of a clay-lined earth bank, thirty feet in height and thirty-five feet deep at its base. Most of the factory's output was despatched by rail from

a goods yard on the LMS line at Scropton, which was connected to the factory by Ford's own three-foot-gauge railway system.

A detailed survey of the old, exhausted workings, which most concerns us in this narrative, shows the gross area of the mine divided into two uneven sections, with thirty-eight acres to the east of a broad barrier of unworked gypsum known as the Castle Hayes Pillar and a further ten acres to the west. Overhead cover, which consists principally of a thin strata of blue lias overtopped to the surface by marl, increases from forty feet at the eastern extremity to ninety feet in the vicinity of the Castle Hayes Pillar. This pillar, which was approximately two hundred feet in width, had been left unworked by the quarrying company in order to afford support for the buildings of Castle Hayes Farm on the surface immediately above it. In the early quarry days the area of mine to the east of the Castle Hayes Pillar had been entered via two separate adits from within Ford's factory boundary and, after quarrying finished there, a third drift was dug to access the gypsum west of the pillar. The original entrances were then barred and gated and an interconnecting roadway known as Ford's Level was dug between the new drift and the old workings to assist ventilation. When all the accessible gypsum immediately west of the pillar was exhausted in the early 1930s the new drift was extended to gain access to the isolated reserves of minerals further south.

The disused workings came to the notice of the Air Ministry in 1937 and caused great excitement because they met almost all the necessary criteria. Following the briefest of surveys the largest part of the mine, consisting of the thirty-eight acres of underground space east of the Castle Hayes Pillar, together with three hundred acres of surface land, was acquired early that year. Initially it was intended that the mine would provide storage for 10,000 tons of high explosive bombs at an estimated cost of £350,000.

Later the HE requirement was increased to 24,000 tons and significant additions were made to the overground facilities, including a large number of semi-underground bunkers and sheds for the storage of pyrotechnics, components and small arms ammunition, which together increased the final cost of the depot to £635,000.

The task of converting the mine for ammunition storage was undertaken by the Air Ministry Works Directorate under the overall control of the structural engineer Mr Eric Bryant who was closely involved with the project throughout the war years and beyond. It was originally intended that the mine would provide accommodation only for HE bombs which did not require particularly sophisticated storage conditions. Construction work was expected to be minimal,

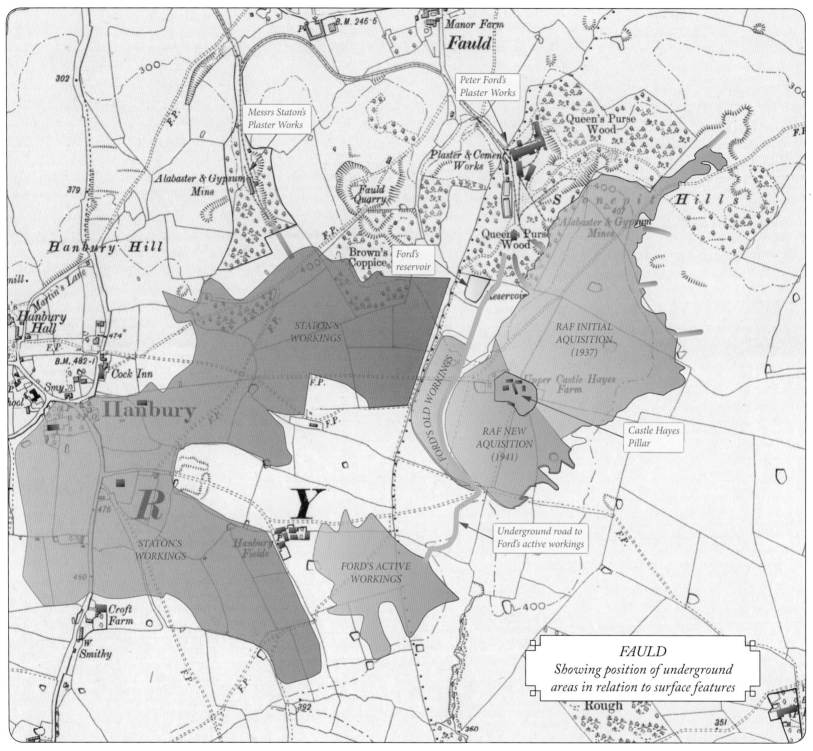

Above: This plan shows the extent of the various underground workings in the Fauld and Hanbury area immediately before the disaster of November 1944. It is important to be aware of the relative positions of the underground roadway leading from Ford's plaster works to their active underground workings, and of the position of the main reservoir, to understand the sequence of events that led up to so many civilian fatalities in the aftermath of the explosion in the RAF depot.

involving just the clearance of a relatively small amount of remaining loose debris, levelling the floor where necessary, laying narrow-gauge railway track and installing basic electric lighting. It was anticipated that a small amount of roof reinforcement would be required, but it was expected that the erection of standard, colliery-pattern rolled-steel arch supports would suffice in the few areas where the stability of the roof was suspect. Towards the middle of 1938 the first of several significant changes was made to the original plan when the Air Ministry authorized the underground storage of incendiaries at Fauld. A few months later it was also decided that detonators could be safely stored underground in an area detached from the other explosive materials. By this time stacking of 500 lb and 250 lb bombs had already begun at the innermost end of the mine up against the Castle Hayes Pillar. At first bombs arrived at the mine entrance by lorry and were unloaded using a temporary loading ramp, to be transported underground on temporary two-foot-gauge track.

Basing their calculations upon the presumption that the area where bombs were already stacked would continue to be used for HE storage in the finished scheme and having already calculated that 10,000 tons of bombs would require a stacking area of approximately twenty-five acres, the Works Directorate was able to produce layout drawings for the new detonator and incendiary storage areas. To provide space for the incendiaries an area of just over seven acres at the north side of the mine was segregated from the HE store by constructing a fifty-foot-thick barrier of rubble and faced block. A small, one-acre heading at the top of the incendiary store was then further segregated by a massive 110-foot-thick barrier to form the detonator store. During 1939 four new entrance tunnels varying in length between 100 feet and 230 feet were constructed by the Air Ministry on the east side of the mine where the land sloped quite sharply down to the valley where building work was already well advanced on the surface camp. Two entrances served the HE store, one served the incendiary store and one the detonator store. Ford's original entrances on the west side of the mine were retained as emergency exits and secured with locked steel gates, while Ford's Level was also secured by a gate that maintained security but also allowed the free flow of air for ventilation.

Due to the rising profile of the land and the gradual dip in the gypsum strata, the HE area at the innermost part of mine had an average overhead cover in excess of ninety feet which was more than adequate, but over the incendiary area there was only sixty feet, and the detonator store, the section of the mine containing the most sensitive of all components, was protected by scarcely more than forty feet of loose marl. To mitigate the risk of collapse due to heavy enemy bombardment and also to minimize the damage by blast to other sections of the mine should a catastrophic, accidental explosion occur within the incendiary or detonator stores, it was decided to strengthen the whole of these two areas with reinforced concrete. This was a major engineering task involving the construction of dozens of concrete support pillars carrying massive horizontal concrete roof beams and lining of the entire roof throughout the areas to be treated with a two-foot six-inch thick layer of reinforced concrete. It appears that corrugated steel sheeting was used to shutter the concrete used for the roof reinforcement, resulting in a curious, vaguely ecclesiastical vaulted appearance in many places. It was not at first thought necessary to extend this type of construction throughout the HE store, but in 1939 a small magazine area was formed by enclosing one bay in four-foot thick concrete walls and the following year parts of the HE section allocated to the storage of boxed TNT were also reconstructed in concrete.

Work also proceeded quickly on the surface camp site to the east of the mine. An examination compound was constructed immediately outside the HE mine entrance for the Ammunition Inspection Directorate, and beyond that was a comprehensive maintenance and workshop area with engine sheds for the narrow-gauge railways. Further east two groups of semi-underground pyrotechnic bunkers were under construction and between these and the station headquarters adjacent to the main Draycott to Tutbury road was a small communal site. Meanwhile, arrangements were being made for the establishment of an RAF rail interchange yard at Scropton on the former North Staffordshire Railway Burton to Uttoxeter line. Ford's already had facilities nearby, reached by a bridge carrying their narrow gauge railway across the river Dove, but this were quite inadequate for the needs of the RAF. Discreet discussions were held with Mr J.A. Dawson of Holly Bank farm resulting in the RAF taking possession, by informal consent, of several acres of land beside the railway line at Scropton on 14 September 1938, the deal being completed by the transfer of money in 1940. In an effort to maintain some air of secrecy about the new government works at Fauld, Mr Dawson was advised by the RAF to state, if asked, that his land had been requisitioned for the construction of a government oil depot. A two-foot-gauge railway was constructed heading east from the mine entrances to Scropton sidings, carried across the Dove by a new concrete bridge about half a mile downstream from the earlier

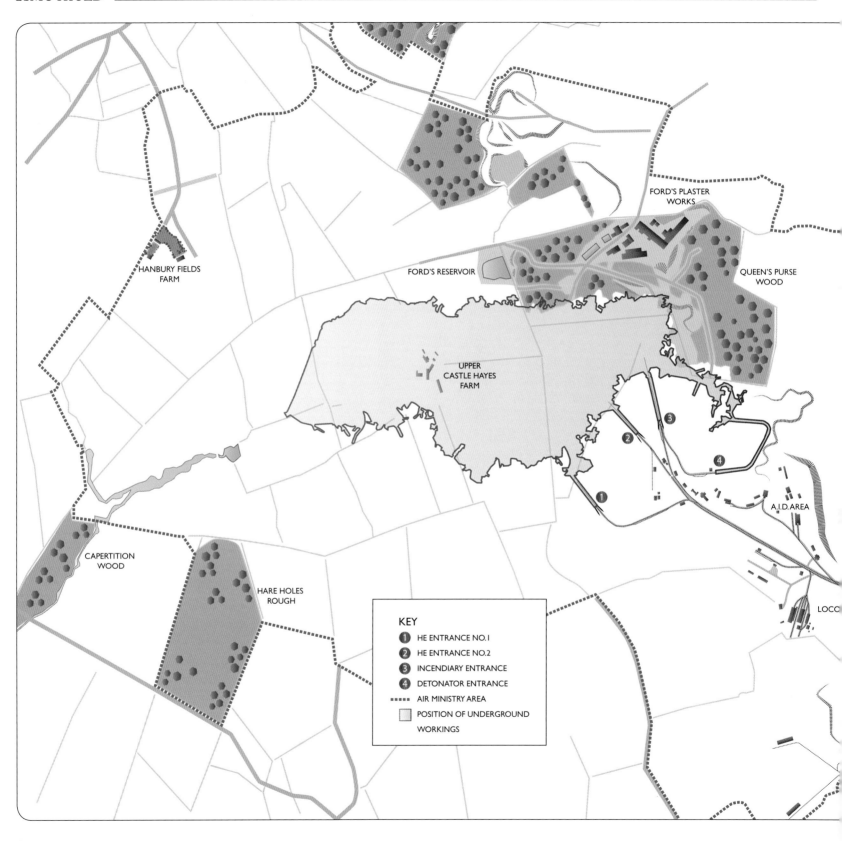

HANBURY FIELDS
FARM

FORD'S PLASTER
WORKS

FORD'S RESERVOIR

QUEEN'S PURSE
WOOD

UPPER
CASTLE HAYES
FARM

A.I.D. AREA

CAPERTITION
WOOD

HARE HOLES
ROUGH

LOCO

KEY

1 HE ENTRANCE NO.1
2 HE ENTRANCE NO.2
3 INCENDIARY ENTRANCE
4 DETONATOR ENTRANCE

▪▪▪ AIR MINISTRY AREA

POSITION OF UNDERGROUND
WORKINGS

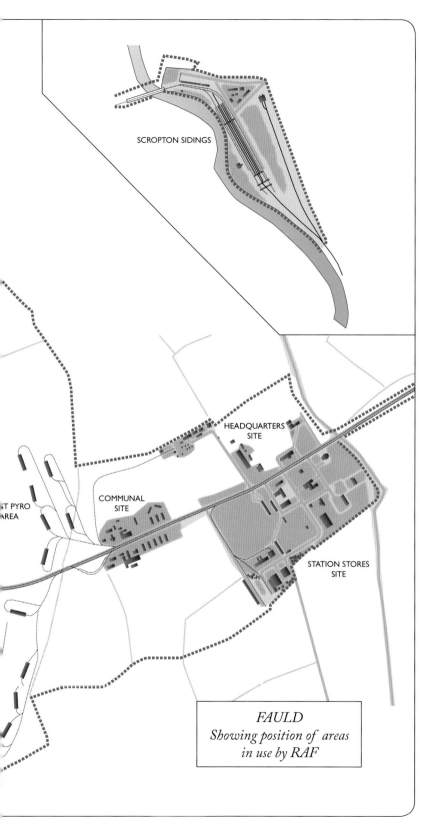

SCROPTON SIDINGS

HEADQUARTERS
SITE

COMMUNAL
SITE

T PYRO
AREA

STATION STORES
SITE

FAULD
Showing position of areas
in use by RAF

bridge built by the gypsum company.

While the remnants of the British Expeditionary Force were being evacuated from the beaches of Dunkirk in May 1940, at the moment when the future direction of the war was to turn to a more unpredictable and sinister direction, the initial phase of construction at Fauld was drawing to a close. The depot, by now the RAF's showpiece ammunition store, was already overflowing with high explosives, bombs, incendiaries, small arms and home defence ammunition of all kinds, and photographers from the Air Ministry Public Relations Branch had in February recorded scenes there for posterity. By early 1941 Fauld had established a number of satellite sites including a store for non-explosive materials at Flax Mill, two miles away, and had small arms ammunition stacked under field conditions at Hilton, three miles away from the main site and at Bagot's Wood twelve miles to the south. Additional space was desperately required for HE bombs at Fauld and at all the other reserve depots, and staff at No.42 Group headquarters were addressing this problem with some urgency. Two immediate plans were proposed: an extension to the underground store at Fauld, and the creation of a completely new, fifth underground reserve depot to store 20,000 tons of HE bombs.

Representatives from the Air Ministry held a meeting with the Directors of Peter Ford & Sons at the company's offices at Fauld on 25 June 1941 to discuss the possibility of the RAF extending their underground holding into the ten acres of abandoned mine workings west of the Castle Hayes Pillar. The directors did not immediately agree to this proposal, voicing concerns that the underground roadway to their currently active workings passed through this area and they were afraid that issues of security might prevent them from continuing operations there. The Air Ministry, however, pointed out that the roadway in question traversed the far western side of Ford's old workings and proposed that if a barrier, built at their expense, should be erected beside the road then the depot's integrity would be maintained and Ford's would still have use of the roadway. Only a very small area of Ford's old workings to the west of the roadway would be unavailable to the Air Ministry, although the option of later expansion into Staton's workings, which were further again to the west, would be lost. This plan was agreed and, following a survey, the Works Directorate estimated that fifty experienced labourers could transform the ten acres into first-class storage space for a further 5,000 tons of bombs in just six weeks. Conversion work included the construction of a blast-proof boundary wall nearly 1,000 feet in length and the boring of two tunnels to carry the narrow-gauge railway system into the new area, one through the Castle Hayes Pillar and one through a 150-foot wide rubble barrier to the south of the pillar. The blast-proof perimeter wall consisted of two brick walls on concrete foundations with the space between in-filled with rubble. Inevitably the conversion took much longer than anticipated and the new area was not available until October 1942, by which time the rules regarding safety distances within the mine had been relaxed, allowing the authorized capacity of the new area to be increased to 10,000 tons.

Linley Caverns

Meanwhile work was also advancing on the fifth reserve depot, a site for which had been selected at Linley near Walsall in Staffordshire. Linley Caverns had already been inspected and rejected by both the War Office and the Air Ministry some years earlier, but, despite warnings from its former owner about the quarry's instability and propensity for flooding, the RAF made a further inspection of the site on 30 April 1941 and took possession a few days later.

Limestone quarrying in the Walsall area, initially for building stone but later, and on a much larger scale, for lime for use in the iron and steel industries, began in the late eighteenth century. At first, quarrying was from surface outcrops, but as these reserves dwindled in the early nineteenth century the quarrymen followed the strata underground and by the middle of the century the subterranean workings covered an immense area and the worked-out areas were already something of a tourist attraction. William Hawkes Smith, writing of Linley Caverns in 1836, describes:

the silent forsaken caverns, exhausted of their stores, that are of considerable extent and very strong in their arrangement. The massive square columns, regularly disposed, give an Egyptian character to the labyrinthine halls and gloomy crypts of these once busy scenes.

Twenty years later Walsall's historian, E.L. Grew, gives a vivid description of the parties of summer visitors who flocked to the caverns which were brightly illuminated for the occasion:

In the limestone mines at Drew's End are caverns of immense extent which lead to a subterranean lake and are known by the name of Linley Caverns.

Below: Plan showing the location of Linley Caverns.

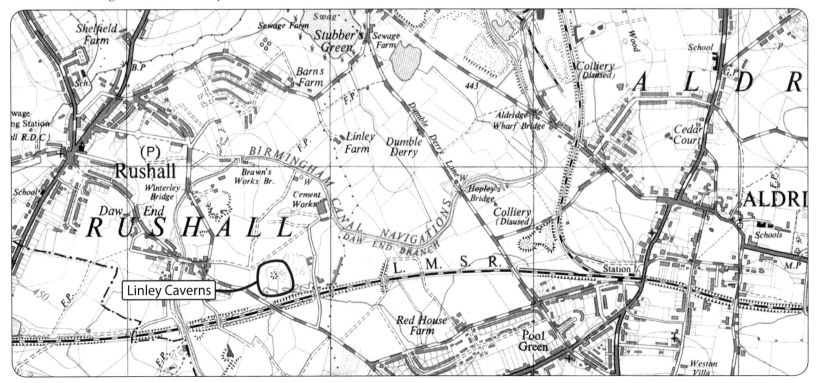

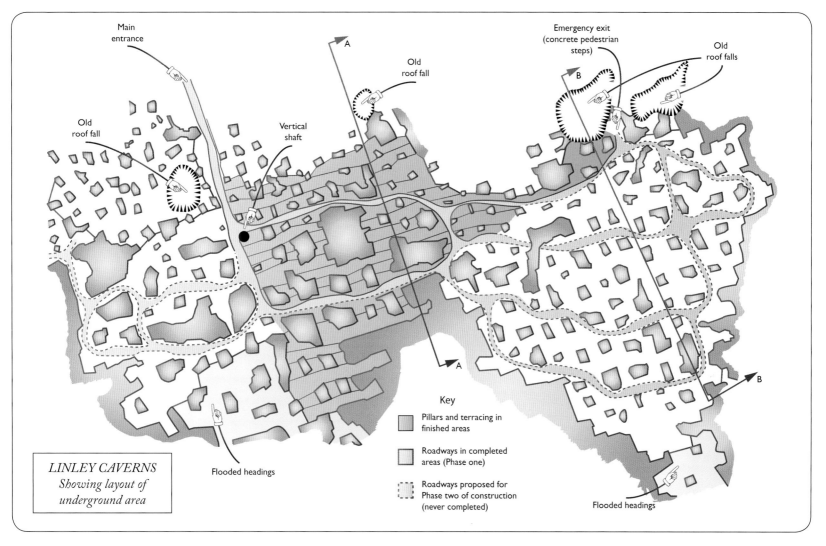

Main
entrance

Old
roof fall

Vertical
shaft

Old
roof fall

Emergency exit
(concrete pedestrian
steps)

Old
roof falls

Old
roof fall

A

A

B

B

Flooded headings

Flooded headings

Key

Pillars and terracing in
finished areas

Roadways in completed
areas (Phase one)

Roadways proposed for
Phase two of construction
(never completed)

LINLEY CAVERNS
Showing layout of
underground area

Above: Detailed plan showing the proposed layout of the bomb store in Linley Caverns and the extent of the work actually completed. Today the whole of the underground area is flooded.

Grew's underground lake was in fact the first indication of the rising water level within the mine which was one of the two natural features that were to be the undoing of the RAF at Linley Caverns a century later. The second and most serious problem was the instability of the quarry ceiling. Although parts of the quarry had become a tourist attraction in the Victorian era, mining continued in the deeper levels at Linley until the early 1930s. As they dug underground the quarrymen sought the Lower Wenlock Limestone strata which dipped at an angle of approximately ten degrees. Short, steep slope shafts intersected this strata at an initial depth of no more than fifteen or twenty feet but the natural slope of the quarry increased the headcover quickly so that a short distance into the quarry the cover was some forty feet, increasing, at the inner most and latest workings, to over 160 feet. For logistic and practical reasons the

RAF was compelled to use an area of the quarry, extending to about ten acres, that was within easy reach of the access shafts and thus had the shallowest of overburden. At depths of only twenty to forty feet the overhead protection was hardly adequate for safety and, to compound the difficulties, the structure of the roof in this area was very badly fractured and unstable.

The preliminary plans prepared in April 1941 were for a new, self-administering Reserve Ammunition Depot, provisionally numbered No. 68 MU, with an underground storage capacity of 20,000 tons of HE bombs, 5,000 tons of incendiaries and with a daily turnover of

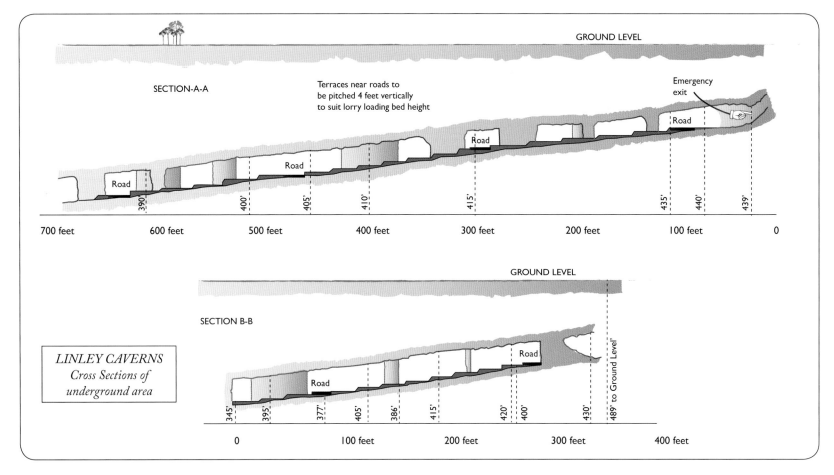

SECTION-A-A

Terraces near roads to
be pitched 4 feet vertically
to suit lorry loading bed height

GROUND LEVEL

Emergency
exit

Road

Road

Road

Road

390'   400'   405'   410'   415'   435'   440'   439'

700 feet   600 feet   500 feet   400 feet   300 feet   200 feet   100 feet   0

GROUND LEVEL

SECTION B-B

LINLEY CAVERNS
Cross Sections of
underground area

Road

Road

345'   395'   377'   405'   386'   415'   420'   400'   430'   489' to Ground Level'

0   100 feet   200 feet   300 feet   400 feet

600 tons. There was no immediate requirement for additional surface storage but land was acquired behind the Royal Oak public house for a camp for the 500-750 airmen who would staff the depot. A sketchy works programme was cobbled together early in July and, based upon this programme, an optimistic estimate of costs subsequently presented for Treasury approval. Unfortunately, the original survey had taken account of neither the terrible roof condition in the quarry nor the ten-degree slope of the floor, which necessitated the laying of costly concrete terraces to provide horizontal stacking areas. The extra £50,000 required for this, on top of the original £250,000 estimate, was just the first of a depressing series of budget over-runs. By 14 August costs were estimated to be in excess of £1,000,000, problems associated with frequent, random roof falls were mounting and a decision was taken to divide the project into several phases of construction. Initially only the first phase would be completed to provide 15,000 square yards of storage. The treacherous roof continued to be a cause of concern with regular huge falls of between five and 200 tons of rock collapsing without warning. Early in

Above: This cross-section drawing of the Linley depot clearly illustrates the problems created by the inclination of the original quarry workings.

October the Air Ministry issued a rather fatuous warning to staff at Linley that 'it is extremely advisable that no equipment or person is under even a small block during a collapse', and on 7 October Maintenance Command suggested to the Air Ministry that the expenditure to date should be written off and the site closed down. The Air Ministry was unwilling to abandon Linley, but agreed that no stocking should begin until building and reinforcement work in the whole quarry was completed, the hope being, presumably, that adequate engineering would satisfactorily stabilize the roof. This was not the case, however, for throughout the spring of 1942 a stream of adverse reports reached the Air Ministry concerning massive roof falls in the completed areas of the quarry.

On 5 March 1942 the Air Ministry finally ordered that those parts of Linley that were not yet completed should be abandoned, but that strenuous efforts should be made to ensure the safety of the completed sections. Furthermore it was stated that the depot would be downgraded to become No.21 MSU, a sub-unit of Fauld, used only for the storage of obsolete weapons and that, due to the continuing risk of roof falls, all HE bombs should be stored above ground. With the whole reserve depot concept turned on its head the situation at Linley was becoming farcical and became increasingly so in October when instructions were received that HE bombs, which had already been excluded from underground storage, should also not be stacked on the surface above the mine. It was feared that the shock wave from an accidental explosion on the surface would result in a general collapse underground, though how the ultimate consequence of this differed from that of an accidental underground explosion was not explained. Staff pointed out with some exasperation that there was no suitable surface stacking ground available at Linley that was not above the mine apart from the main quarry access road and that if this was used to stack bombs then the underground areas would be inaccessible and the problem would resolve itself, though in a rather obtuse way. As a codicil to these comments they also pointed out, darkly, that the road was itself collapsing into uncharted, ancient mine workings unconnected to the ammunition depot.

Linley Caverns was now a serious embarrassment to the RAF, but the arrival of the United States Army Air Force and its demand for bomb storage on a massive scale promised hope of resolution. Linley and the as-yet uncompleted surface depot at Wortley in Yorkshire were immediately offered to the Americans who, with uncanny prescience, just as immediately turned down the former and accepted the latter, at the same time also taking control of 11 MSU Grovely Wood in Wiltshire for good measure.

Seemingly saddled with the site in perpetuity, the Air Ministry convened a conference on 27 August to determine the future of Linley Caverns. The rate of roof falls had not abated and gave no indication of doing so in the near future, so a policy was formulated to somehow cope with this unfortunate fact. It was confirmed that the depot would operate as a satellite of Fauld and that all staffing and stock control would be accounted for at the parent depot. Thus, on 15 October 1942 the mine opened as a store 'for explosives for which there is no immediate demand.' In practice this meant small calibre and obsolete bombs, obsolete marks of larger bombs and empty bomb cases. Two six-ton diesel locomotives specially modified for work underground were transferred from Fauld and on 28 January 1943 the first consignment of obsolete 250 lb bombs were put in store. Throughout its relatively short working life Linley Caverns was

something of a backwater in the RAF's weapons storage programme. An apparent lack of discipline gradually developed; rules regulating what could or could not be stored underground were bent or broken and general safety precautions and examination procedures were systematically ignored. This lackadaisical attitude became endemic and its consequences at the parent depot proved catastrophic as the war drew to a close.

Fauld in action

During the build-up to D-Day and in the months that followed, Fauld, like all the other reserve ammunition depots, experienced activity at an unprecedented level, with monthly turnover approaching 20,000 tons and the transport and logistic organization stretched to its limit. The pressure was perhaps felt more keenly at Fauld than elsewhere because not only was it the largest of the underground depots by a considerable margin, it was also home to the headquarters of the Master Provisions Officer of No.42 Group. The task of the MPO, Wing Commander Kings, and his staff was to ensure that the daily ammunition and oxygen demands of all the operational RAF units were met and to ensure that ammunition supplies were routed to their destinations by the most efficient means. Requests from fighter and bomber stations were received each morning at the MPO's office and issuing instructions passed to the Chief Equipment Officer at Fauld or transmitted by teleprinter to the various ammunition depots throughout the country. The Master Provision Officer's organization, which was effectively a lodger unit at Fauld, was just one of three separate organizations at the station whose functions were closely interlocked, but each of which had its separate command structure and no immediate responsibility to the others.

Overall command of the station and its day-to-day running was in the hands of Group Captain Storrar, while management of the ammunition stocks was the responsibility of the Chief Equipment Officer who, until he retired in September 1944, was Wing Commander Agar Strath. Following his retirement Strath's deputy, Squadron Leader L.H. Anness, whom we have already met elsewhere in this narrative, took on the role of acting CEO until a suitable permanent replacement could be found. Responsibility for the mine area lay with a subordinate officer whose name has slipped from the record but whose title was the Commanding Officer 'A' Group.

Insinuated into this command structure was the third of Fauld's key organizations, the Aeronautical Inspection Department or

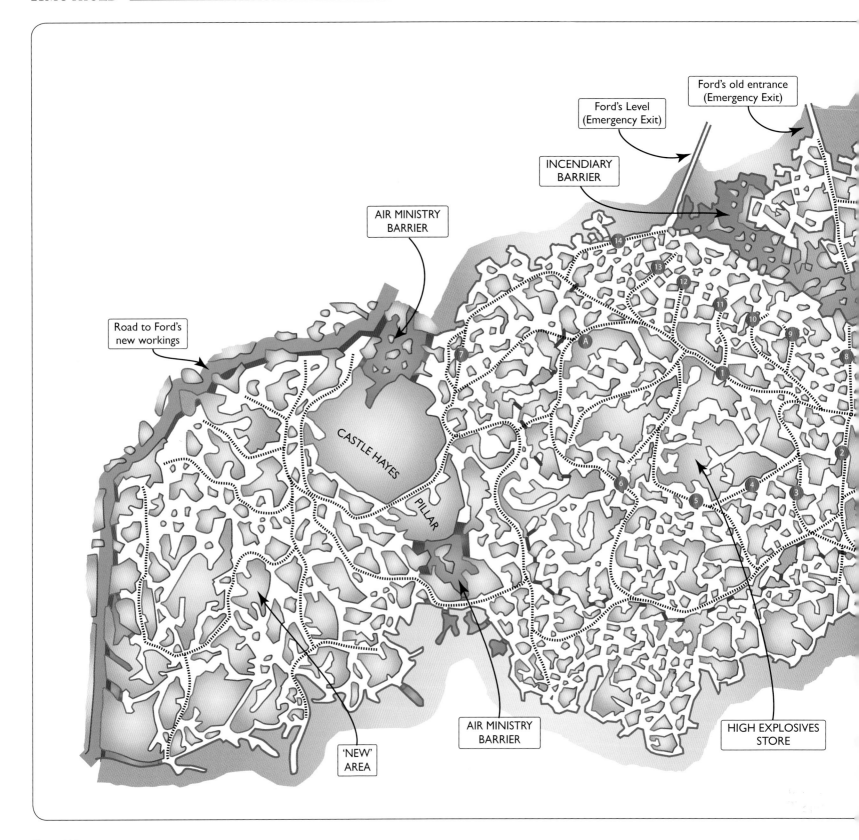

Ford's old entrance
(Emergency Exit)

Ford's Level
(Emergency Exit)

INCENDIARY
BARRIER

AIR MINISTRY
BARRIER

Road to Ford's
new workings

CASTLE HAYES

PILLAR

'NEW'
AREA

AIR MINISTRY
BARRIER

HIGH EXPLOSIVES
STORE

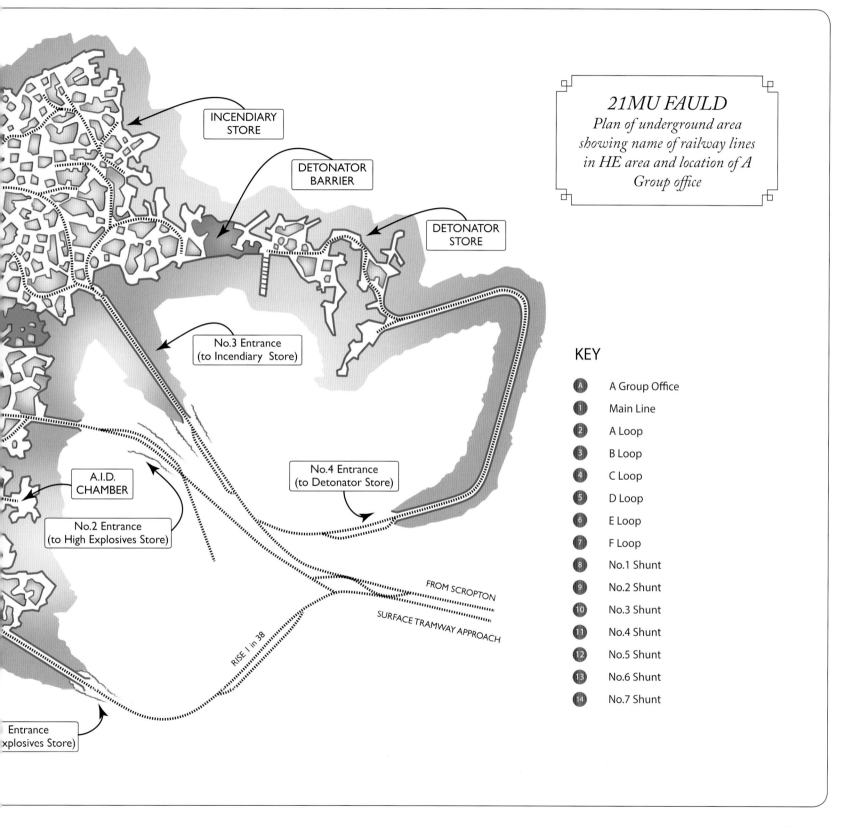

INCENDIARY STORE

DETONATOR BARRIER

DETONATOR STORE

21MU FAULD
Plan of underground area
showing name of railway lines
in HE area and location of A
Group office

No.3 Entrance
(to Incendiary Store)

A.I.D. CHAMBER

No.4 Entrance
(to Detonator Store)

No.2 Entrance
(to High Explosives Store)

FROM SCROPTON

SURFACE TRAMWAY APPROACH

RISE 1 in 38

Entrance
xplosives Store)

KEY

A — A Group Office
1 — Main Line
2 — A Loop
3 — B Loop
4 — C Loop
5 — D Loop
6 — E Loop
7 — F Loop
8 — No.1 Shunt
9 — No.2 Shunt
10 — No.3 Shunt
11 — No.4 Shunt
12 — No.5 Shunt
13 — No.6 Shunt
14 — No.7 Shunt

AID, a civilian department reporting to the Director General of Aeronautical Inspection at the Air Ministry and responsible for the inspection, examination and certification of ammunition and explosives. At the head of the AID hierarchy at Fauld was the Chief Inspecting Officer, James Edmund Pollard, and below him was a Chief Examiner, Mr Saunders, and a staff of Viewers. Of the RAF officers on site, those, including the Chief Equipment Officer, with direct responsibility for ammunition stocks were expected to be 'X' certified. This certification indicated that they had successfully completed a number of specialist courses and were qualified in the handing of ammunition and explosives. Nevertheless, on questions of

the safety of explosives in storage the AID Chief Inspecting Officer had the final word.

Demands for more labour to help fulfil the dramatic increase in turnover at Fauld through the autumn of 1944 resulted in an expansion of available manpower to almost 1,000 men by November. Included in this complement were 445 civilian labourers, a small but noisy USAAF detachment whose sole objective was to ensure that the three US bomb dumps at Market Stainton, Norton Disney and Brafferton received what was due to them in a timely fashion, and no less than 195 Italian prisoners-of-war from the nearby Hilton PoW camp who, since their country's capitulation in the previous year, had

Opposite: One of the depot's Ruston Hornsby diesel locomotives pulls a train loaded with 250lb bombs out of No.2 HE entrance.

Above: A train of 4-wheel bomb trucks en-route for Scropton Sidings having just exited the depot via No.2 HE entrance. Notice the brakesmen on the trucks, a necessary requirement to guard against breakaway wagons rolling back down the incline into the depot. The steeply inclined track to the upper left of this image leads to the long tunnel to the detonator store.

elected to work for the Allied cause as co-operators. These men were hard-working, conscientious and well liked by the RAF personnel who worked alongside them, but were, for the most part, thoroughly distrusted by local civilians outside the camp.

Even with the additional manpower the depot was becoming severely congested. Regular demands for increasingly large numbers of the hard-to-handle 4,000 lb HE bombs and inevitable shortages of trucks in which to despatch them tied up large numbers of men and caused numerous bottlenecks, while sudden changes in Bomber Command's requirements created regular shortages of some types of weapon and excess stockholdings of others. During November 1944, for example, incendiary bombs were building up at Fauld at an alarming rate and the Chief Equipment Officer found himself compelled to authorize the temporary stacking of many thousands of these in open storage close to the mine entrance until space could be found underground.

Opposite: In this view a train of loaded bogie wagons is seen in the cutting emerging from No.2 HE entrance with, in the background, a train of empties being shunted into No.1 entrance. A line of tipper trucks, used for building and maintenance work underground, stands on a spur to the right of No.2 line.

Right: A typical view of bombs stacked beside the line in the lower section of the depot near the Castle Hayes pillar.

Left: Members of the Ammunition Inspectorate staff at Fauld examining 250lb GP bombs stacked in the 'old' area of the depot. This photograph illustrates the density with which bombs were stored and the cramped conditions in the mine when it was full to capacity.

Chapter 7

MONDAY 27 NOVEMBER 1944

Monday, 27 November did not get off to an auspicious start. Group Captain Storrar, the station's Commanding Officer, had elected to go on leave that week so the depot was put instead under the temporary charge of Wing Commander Kings the Master Provisions Officer for No.42 Group, as he was the most senior officer on site. The Officer Commanding 'A' Group, responsible for the underground stores, had also gone on leave that morning, leaving the tunnels under the charge of his subordinate, Pilot Officer Rollo. Monday was Pilot Officer Rollo's rest day and he was not on site, so there was no officer with any experience in the mine that morning. Squadron Leader Anness - only a few weeks into the job of acting Chief Equipment Officer and more than a little upset that he had not been automatically offered the post on a permanent basis-was the last of the three officers, all inexperienced in their roles, upon whose shoulders lay the mine's destiny on that dreadful day.

Having completed his normal early morning administrative duties and cleared his desk of files from the day before, Squadron Leader Anness turned his mind to the niggling problems associated with the issue of a large consignment of 4,000 lb Mk IV bombs later that day. About 100 such bombs were due for despatch from Scropton sidings and there were not enough railway wagons available for the job. It was a bright, mild winter morning, so Anness decided that, rather than call for transport, he would walk the mile or so to Scropton where he intended to discuss the day's problems with Flight Lieutenant Coles, the transportation officer. Expecting him to be somewhere in the yard, Anness wandered around the loading ramps on a fruitless search for some time before heading for Coles' office where, at eight minutes past eleven, he found the transportation officer engulfed in a sea of paperwork.

Meanwhile, at nine minutes past eleven at Upper Castle Hayes Farm the owner, William Maurice Goodwin, and his wife Mary had just left home for the short car journey into Burton-upon-Trent on farm business. In the kitchen, with the master and mistress gone, three of the Goodwins' farm labourers, Steven West, Russell Miles and Bob Wagstaffe were settling in to a late breakfast along with the Goodwins' maid, Elizabeth Smith. This would be their last meal on earth. The track from Upper Castle Hayes Farm ran beside the high dam that held back Ford's reservoir and on past Purse Cottages, a pair of semi-detached dwellings in the shadow of the dam, before running through the factory yard to join the main road. As the Goodwins passed Purse Cottage at ten minutes past eleven that Monday morning Frederick Harrison, the local agent of the Prudential Assurance Company, was calling to collect the weekly premium from Sarah Hill. Within three minutes all four would be dead.

At eleven minutes past eleven, 140 feet below Hanbury Fields Farm in Peter Ford's gypsum quarry and three-quarters of a mile from the mine entrance, two gangs of quarrymen, twenty-one men in all, were well into their morning shift. They had already excavated four tons of gypsum which was loaded into one of the company's narrow-gauge trucks ready to be hauled to the surface. Two minutes later five of the nine men in Jack Gordon's gang would be dead.

It was a busy morning in the 'new area' of the Fauld bomb store. A large issue of 500 lb Mk IX HE bombs was imminent and twenty of these weapons had already been stacked beside the railway awaiting despatch. Briefly, though, the four civilian labourers detailed for this task and their charge-hand, Arthur Mellor, were called away for a more urgent job on 20 Road, loading four 4,000 lb bombs aboard a waiting train of narrow-gauge trucks. This job was delayed because the 'skids' — steel ramps to roll the bombs onto the wagons — could not be found and Foreman J.C. Salt, the sixth member of the gang, had gone off into the old area in search of them. Meanwhile two Air Ministry Works Directorate electricians, Mr Shipley and a young boy named Frew, were replacing blown light bulbs near the emergency exit into Ford's mine. In No. 28 Road AID examiners Nicklin and Brassington were inspecting a batch of type 28 pistols while examiner Thomas Sanders was on No. 27 Road with Leading Aircraftsman Fairbanks and Leading Aircraftsman Bailey. At twelve minutes past eleven Leading Aircraftsman Fairbanks reached for a brass hammer to remove a damaged exploder from a 1,000 lb MC bomb. This was one of a batch of three damaged bombs that had been jettisoned at West Freugh airfield some months earlier by a crippled bomber and returned to Fauld for repair. One minute later all these men would be dead.

At thirteen minutes past eleven, London time, seismographs at Casablanca, 1,500 miles from Fauld, recorded sudden and significant ground-waves, the instrument needles jumping high enough to raise alarm even in a period when, after five years of war, the world was somehow used to sudden trauma. Seconds earlier and just 120 miles away from Fauld at Weston-super-Mare on the north Somerset coast local inhabitants reported an eerie, ominous rumble carried by the light north-easterly breeze, while in Burton-on-Trent, just four miles from Fauld, a short, intense shock wave had already smashed windows, loosened slates and torn down tottering chimney stacks.

At that same moment, at Scropton Sidings, Squadron Leader Anness watched in awe from the doorway of the traffic office as, from where the hillside had sloped above his ammunition dump, with a shattering roar a great, black, rushing column of smoke and flame and debris a quarter of a mile in diameter tore upwards for three thousand feet to form a hideous searing mushroom cloud in

Below: 20 lb HE bombs undergoing examination by staff of the Ammunition Inspection Directorate underground at Fauld in the early years of the war. Lax oversight of the work of the Directorate was found to be a contributory factor to the disaster of November 1944.

the upper air. From within the mushroom cloud and from the sides of the pillar of fire black objects were seen to spiral out, exploding in the air or falling to the ground before detonating. Minutes later, it seemed, this mass of debris — later estimated at two million tons of earth, rock and boulders, smashed buildings, fragments of machinery, bombs, whole trees and dismembered cattle — rained down on the camp site, the surrounding fields, on Hanbury village and also on the small groups of men who were already rushing to the mine to rescue any survivors.

What had happened was obvious, but panic and confusion were absolute. For some reason nearly 4,000 tons of bombs stored in the new area had exploded en masse at 11.13 that morning, leaving an oval crater a quarter of a mile wide and 140 feet deep. Lower down the hillside injured men were stumbling from the two smoking entrances to the HE mine which were almost blocked by falling debris, but it seemed that the old part of the mine had survived at least partially intact. Concerned at first only with the rescue of survivors still trapped and quickly suffocating in the poisonous fume-laden air within the old mine, RAF staff were oblivious to the greater horrors that were unfolding on the far side of the hill.

On the hilltop where Upper Castle Hayes Farm once stood there was now just a blackened, smoking crater. The farmhouse along with its outbuildings, cattle and four tragic human actors had disappeared along with the mountain of solid rock, the upper section of the two-hundred-foot wide Castle Hayes Pillar, on which the farm had stood. No recognizable trace of the farm, not a brick nor fragment of tile or timber, was ever found, nor any trace of the inhabitants who, it was later assumed, were completely vapourized in the explosion.

But there was still worse. Shaken by the force of the blast, which was and still is the most powerful explosion ever to occur in the British Isles (by comparison, the atomic bomb dropped on the Japanese city of Hiroshima less than a year later was only four times as powerful) the dam holding back Ford's reservoir burst, releasing millions of gallons of water into the valley below. This immense torrent of water, mud, silt, boulders and uprooted trees first engulfed Purse Cottages, snuffing out the lives of Nellie Ford, Sarah and Harry Hill, and the insurance man, Frederick Harrison, along with William and Mary Goodwin, who were driving past in their car. Its energy hardly diminished, the raging mud-slide next tore through Ford's plaster works, destroying everything in its path that had not already been reduced to matchwood by the initial blast and falling debris. Twenty-four men died in the factory, crushed beneath collapsing buildings or

drowned in mud.

Below ground, blast from the explosion that had wiped out Goodwin's Farm and virtually destroyed the Upper Castle Hayes Pillar caused further carnage, both in the old bomb store and in Ford's mine to the west. The fifteen-foot barrier between the new area — the seat of the explosion — and Ford's underground roadway was ripped away by the blast and the roadway blocked by debris and massive roof falls. Nearer the surface mud, boulders and debris from the surface destruction were pouring into the shaft, blocking it completely and eventually burying it under some twenty feet of silt. Where the underground barrier was breached toxic gasses released by the explosion were seeping insidiously into Ford's workings to quickly claim the lives of five more men. The sequence of events that led to the loss of these men is vividly described in the evidence presented to the subsequent Court of Inquiry by Jack Gordon, Ford's underground foreman:

> *I was working in Ford's underground mine area when, just after 11 o'clock, I heard an explosion. This explosion was not sufficient to stop us working, but a second explosion occurred a few seconds after the first, which was very much greater and even lifted a wagon containing four tons of gypsum. During the second explosion the electric light went out and we were left to use the tallow candles which were normally carried as emergency lighting. The point where I and my party were working was about three-quarters of a mile to the south-east of the fan opening which exists between Ford's main-line and the 'New Area' of the HE Mine.*
>
> *I first sent one of my men forward towards the entrance to find out what was happening but he did not come back so I went forward myself. After passing the suction shaft which lies about a quarter of a mile south-east of the fan I came across gas and one unconscious man who was later rescued. The gas tasted like burnt sugar.*
>
> *I made a further trip forward to try to find out what was happening. I came across two dead men and then had to return as I was becoming overcome by fumes. We then decided to send two men up the suction shaft for help. They did not return but after about half an hour had elapsed two RAF men came down the shaft and managed to rescue me, by which time I had almost lost consciousness.*

The explosion also wreaked terrible destruction on the surrounding countryside as the millions of tons of debris and superheated bombs rained down from several thousand feet. The radius of destruction,

Above: Peter Ford's plaster works at Fauld in 1936. The isolated, twin-gabled buildings in the woods towards the right foreground are Purse Cottages. Ford's reservoir, which was to play a prominent role in the disaster, is in the centre foreground. The underground bomb store lies beneath the sloping hillside to the right of this photograph.

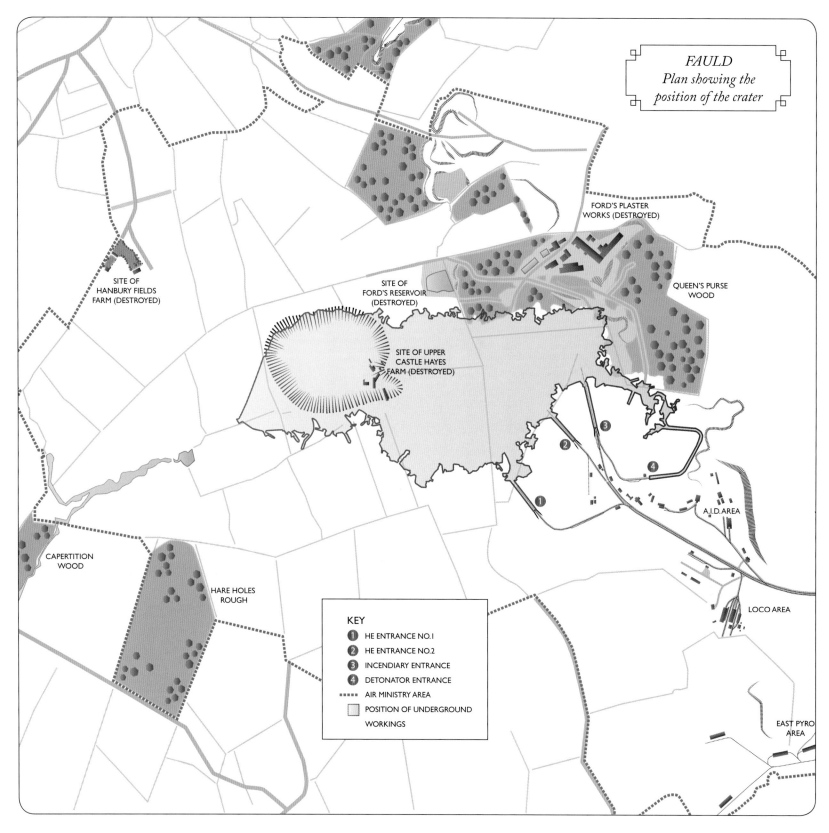

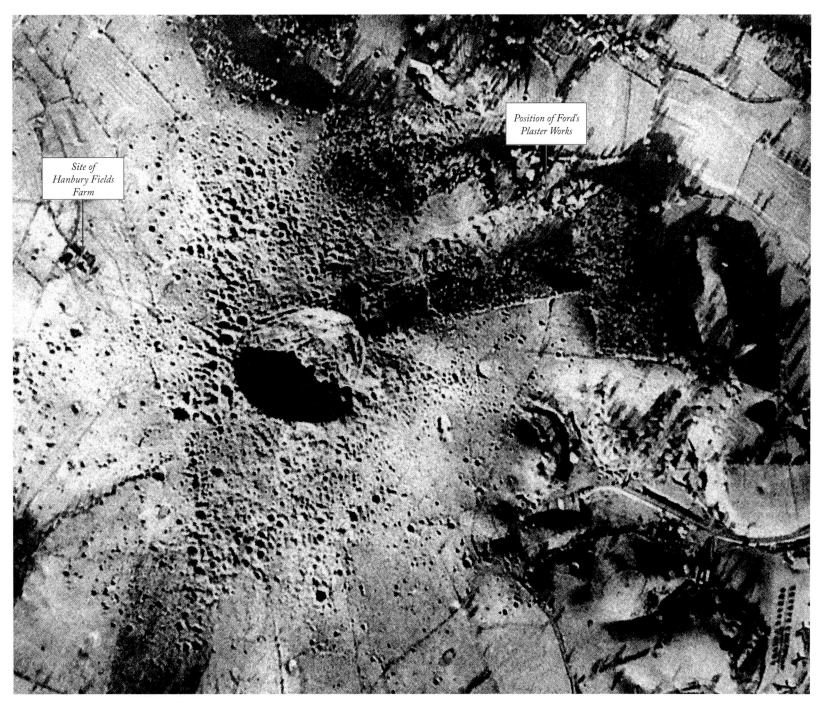

Site of Hanbury Fields Farm

Position of Ford's Plaster Works

Above: This aerial photograph, taken the day after the explosion, vividly illustrates the magnitude of the disaster. Ford's reservoir has completely disappeared and the factory has been engulfed by debris. It appears that the largest numbers of subsidiary craters (presumably from bombs ejected from the main crater then falling to earth and detonating on impact) are concentrated to the south and north-east of the main crater between Hare Holes Rough and Ford's factory. To the west and south-east the fall of bombs and debris has been numerous but more widespread. What is less evident in this photograph is the damage to buildings caused by blast rather than falling debris.

Below & opposite below: The remains of Peter Ford's plaster works, destroyed by the initial blast, battered by falling debris and then engulfed by mud from the breached dam.

Above: This panoramic photograph was taken less than twenty-four hours after the explosion and smoke can still be seen rising from the crater. The shattered remains of Hanbury Fields Farm can be seen on the horizon to the far left of the image.

though thankfully not of death, extended well beyond the factory and farms. In Hanbury village the Cock Inn was severely damaged with two wings completely destroyed by falling debris and the roof ripped off those parts that remained standing. The village hall, which served as the British Legion clubhouse, was blown to pieces by the blast, its fragments widely scattered across the fields and massive sections of brick and concrete footing thrown 700 feet from their original position. Elsewhere in the village and in the surrounding area dozens of houses, including Fauld Hall, suffered lesser damage, with roofs stripped, chimneys and ceilings brought down and windows smashed.

Despite stringent efforts by the Air Ministry Constabulary to contain intelligence about the incident, local press reporters were soon on the scene and the following day it was national news. The Daily Telegraph carried the headline:

90 Killed in RAF Dump Explosion. Midland Towns Rocked
People said that the explosion was 'like an earthquake'. The force was felt 45 miles away in Daventry, where women ran into the street thinking that a bomb had fallen when their windows and doors where violently rattled. In Coventry, 30 miles away, doors were blown open by the blast, and windows rattled. Houses were shaken in Leicester,

and the explosion was also felt in parts of Northampton. The shock was recorded on the instruments of Mr Shaw, the seismologist, at West Bromwich. 'In all my 36 years experience I have never known such a violent local disturbance,' he said.

At one farm I spoke to the farmer's wife, who said, 'It was terrible. I thought our last hour had come. The explosion killed nine or ten of our cows, and our whole flock of fifty sheep. The farm is ruined and there is no doubt that we shall have to leave.'

Mrs Weatherall, whose home is two miles away, had a miraculous escape when debris weighing several hundredweight crashed through the roof of her home. She said, 'When I heard the first explosion I ran to see that my 3-month-old baby was alright. As I left the room the debris fell through the ceiling. I picked up the baby and as I did so the bottom fell out of the pram.

Some idea of the force of the explosion is indicated by the experience of Miss P Hadley, who was driving a NAAFI mobile canteen some 12 miles away. Her vehicle was rocked from side to side, and when she stopped to see what was wrong she heard the explosion and saw a great cloud of smoke mushroom up.

One of two farm employees working in a cabbage field was blown to bits. His companion has not yet been accounted for.

Right: The bloated carcases of cattle killed in the meadows at Hanbury Fields Farm.

Opposite: Very serious damage was inflicted upon the Cock Inn at Hanbury, apparently by blast as there is little evidence from the aerial photographs of debris falling nearby. Two wings of the main building, seen here, were completely destroyed.

Hanbury Fields Farm

Much major damage was done to many buildings within a mile or more of the explosion; the tower of Hanbury church was cracked as was a gable wall, of Fauld Hall and roofs were blown from many smaller buildings. Hanbury Village Hall was completely destroyed, even its foundations being ripped from the ground. Hanbury Fields Farm, seen here, suffered such extensive damage that it was deemed irreparable and was subsequently demolished and the ground levelled. There is now no trace that it ever existed.

Destruction underground

The greater part of the old HE mine was saved from total destruction by the base of the Castle Hayes Pillar which was not breached by the explosion, although the initial shock wave and ground tremors caused widespread roof falls in the western end of the mine. The terrific blast wave created by the explosion was funnelled through the two rail headings that pierced the pillar, demolishing stacks of bombs and other ammunition over a wide area and propelling a complete train of loaded wagons out through one of the entrance tunnels. The situation within the mine at the moment of detonation is best described by Mr J.C. Salt, a civilian gang foreman, whose evidence at the Court of Inquiry was generally considered the most reliable. Salt stated that:

On 27 November 1944 I had to allocate work to about thirty civilian labourers through the leading store-man, Mr L. S. Alexander. The work consisted of loading and off-loading bombs and 60 lb SAP [rocket] heads. The off-loading of the 500 lb Mk VI bombs was taking place in 'C' loop and 17 shunt. All this work was in the old area of the

mine. The other gang was unloading 4000 lb HG Mk VI bombs on 20 road in the new area.

The first gang in 20 road had four empty trucks to load, of which only one could be loaded as that was the only truck that there were any skids for. I proceeded to the gang to help them to load that one truck and then sent the store-man into the old area to hurry the truck along with the skids on. He had been gone for about four minutes and I went after him myself. I arrived at the office on the main line facing Ford's level when the explosion occurred.

Salt went on to explain that he had just entered the office when he heard two distinct explosions, and that he thought they came from the direction of 'F' loop:

When the first explosion occurred the lights did not go out, I ran to the door to see which direction the explosion came from, looked down Ford's level then down 6 shunt, then up the main line, and then went back to my office to fetch my torch. I had just entered my office when the second explosion occurred and blew the lights out. It blew me out of the office with store-man Cresswell and Airman Still. I tried to find my

Left: No.1 entrance to the HE store suffered particularly severe damaged, inflicted both by falling debris and exploding bombs nearby on the surface and by the ferocious blast wave that traveled up the south side of the depot from the breached Air Ministry Barrier seeking to exhaust itself via the entrance tunnel.

Opposite: The remains of an entire train of wagons laden with small arms ammunition blown bodily by blast out of No.2 entrance tunnel.

way back in the dark. Civilians and Italians [co-operators, previously prisoners-of-war who volunteered to assist the Allies] were shouting find a light!'. I shouted to Cresswell to find my torch as he was nearer the office than I was. Cresswell came with my torch and I accompanied the personnel out to the mine entrance. As we were coming up the main line out of the mine we were almost carried off our feet by what seemed to be blast behind us, coming from the direction of the office. I got the civilians out of the mine entrance where Warder Simpson was lying injured on the bank. Someone pointed to the ground and we saw Warder Skellett under the rubble.

I went back into the mine with Flight Lieutenant Shuttleworth and two Mines Safety men. We proceeded to loop to see if we could get into the new area. We heard a sound on the side of 'F' loop and I called out to see if there was anyone there, and we found Mr. Woodhall the janitor.

By this time the National Fire Service Rescue Party arrived with oxygen masks and equipment and Wing Commander King and myself took the NFS party into the mine to make further attempts to get into the new area. We went along 'F' loop again and came to an impassable fall of roof. We went back down 'F' loop and around 'E2'loop in a further attempt to get into the new area. We ran into a fall of roof and proceeded to climb over the top but found the fumes were getting too bad and that three or four of the rescue party were overcome by them.

Questioned about the number of explosions he heard, Salt replied:

The first explosion was more of a bang, the second one sounded like thunder, that is, long and drawn out.

At the end of his evidence Foreman Salt told the court that in emergency exercises it took men working in the new area eight minutes to escape. All men working in the new area at the time of the explosion died.

Throughout the later inquiries into the cause of the accident much play was made of the multiple explosions that were reported by various witnesses. The consensus was that there were two detonations, a small one followed by a much larger explosion a few seconds later, although some less reliable accounts reported sequences of up to five explosions. In his evidence, Safetyman George Whittacker, who was working in the incendiary mine at the time of the explosion, stated that he:

heard a dull rumble and after a second or two the lights went out and there was another dull rumble. As we were making our way out of the mine we saw what appeared to be a shower of earth falling outside the mine entrance.'

Similarly, Ammunition Inspector Edgar Higgs reported that:

There was a crash, and a second later there was another crash and the lights went out.

Of the second explosion, Higgs said that:

It threw me to the ground. It was bigger than the first. The first crash made me stagger because of the shaking of the earth whereas with the second crash there was a rush of air which I think knocked me over.

Leading Aircraftsman Kenneth Macleod, who was banding boxes of 0.5 inch machine gun rounds in a bay off of 'F' loop at the time of the accident and who was one of the lucky men to escape from the mine that morning, told the court:

I was thrown against the wall by the first explosion. I went to make my way out of the mine and was thrown to the ground by the second explosion. The second explosion had a greater effect than the first, there was a terrific rush of wind and dust. On the way out I met Corporal Poynton at the junction of 'E' and 'F' loops at the Temple. Near the office a driver had left a locomotive with its lights on between 'D' loop and 5 shunt.

The immediate aftermath

Giving evidence at the Court of Inquiry, Squadron Leader Anness outlined his recollection of events at the moment of detonation. He explained that after a few minutes conversation with Flight Lieutenant Coles he was looking out of the office window when:

I heard a few dull thuds, approximately five, a pause of a few seconds, probably not more than three or four. Then a fresh series of explosions culminating in one vast rumble were heard and naturally my eyes were glued up towards the mine area.

Then I saw an enormous column of smoke shooting skywards for,

Above: Boxes of small arms ammunition, small calibre bombs and what appears in the foreground to be Smith gun ammunition, strewn about the main railway line in the northern section of the HE store.

I should imagine, two or three thousand feet and mushrooming out at the top. Black objects were coming out in this column and shooting out to either side. Visualizing the danger of falling objects reaching Scropton I shouted to everyone to stand up, thus offering a smaller objective.'

Some of Anness's subsequent actions appear in retrospect to be irrational and in his evidence he frankly admitted to a sense of panic, explaining that 'I can only put this down to the flurry of the moment'. He then explained that once he had judged that all the falling debris should have reached the ground:

I shouted for a railway train. After some delay this was obtained and we came along the track as fast as possible. While we were coming along the track Flight Lieutenant Coles passed us on his bicycle. By the time we got north of Spinney Ramp we found a lorry across the railway track so I jumped off and ran as fast as I could up to the Warders Lodge near the mine entrance, passing Flight Lieutenant Endersby.

Quickly observing among the smoke and confusion that several

of the stacks of incendiaries near the mine entrance were burning furiously, having been ignited by white-hot fragments raining down from the initial explosion, and satisfying himself as best he could that the mine itself was not alight, Anness began, somewhat ineffectually, to organize the fire-fighting squads:

I had noticed columns of white smoke coming up from the mine area during our journey and as soon as I arrived I shouted for the fire-master. As president of the Fire Committee of the unit all fire fighting naturally comes under my control. I asked the Warders where the fire was and whether the mine was on fire. They said 'no', so I went straight along to the incendiary stack which was on fire on the left.

I looked at the types of stores which were in stacks close to the burning stack and, thinking that some rocket heads were of an explosive nature, automatically called for volunteers to come and help remove them. If I had thought long enough I would have realized that I knew there were no explosive rocket heads there and that they were concrete ones, but can only put this down to the flurry of the moment.

Having found out my mistake I decided that the cluster bombs in the other stacks were too heavy to lift and presented no real danger

Left: A stack of 250lb HE bombs buried beneath a large section of roof, weighing probably in excess of five tons, that has fallen from a height of fifteen or twenty feet.

Opposite: 250lb HE bombs and boxes of 10lb HE bombs almost completely buried beneath a particularly serious roof fall. It was for planning and overseeing the safe extrication of bombs from conditions similar to this that Dr Rotter of the Air Ministry Ammunition Inspection Directorate was awarded the George Cross.

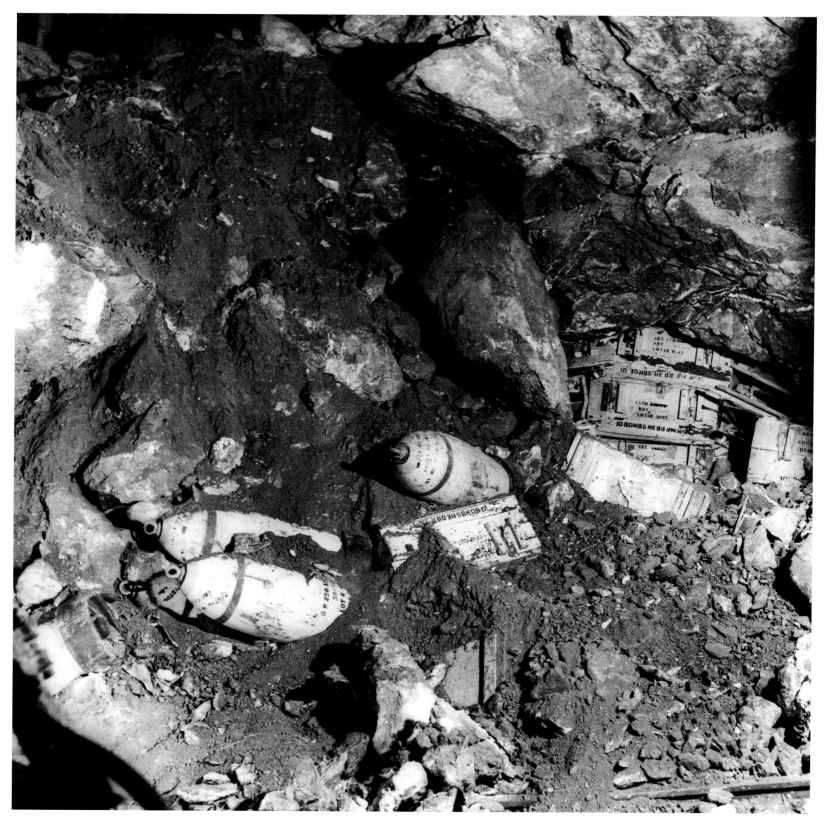

to personnel. The stacks were on the edge of a declivity and therefore I left that area and went across to the other burning stack near No.2 entrance to the mine, close to which was a large stack of boxes of ammunition type. When half-way across I suddenly remembered that they were all empties and again presented no danger. I then went along the cutting towards No.2 main entrance where a train full of SAA had been severely damaged and found the cutting deserted. I then returned to the Warder's Lodge and found Wing Commander Kings.

From this point Wing Commander Kings took effective control of the situation and the next part of this narrative is compiled from his account of events as presented to the Court of Inquiry. After explaining that his normal duties were concerned with the distribution of explosives to all units in No.42 Group and were not associated with any one particular unit, but that on the day of the explosion he had assumed command of No.21 MU because Group Captain Storrar was on leave, he continued:

I arrived at the unit at 09.00 hours and went straight to my office as I had intended that I would deal with my own immediate work first each day, and the arrangement was that if anyone at 21 MU wanted me for anything they could get me in the MPO office. The intention was that I would deal mainly with the administrative side and take any charges that would normally be taken by the Commanding Officer.

At approximately 11.10 hours on 27 November 1944 I heard a tremendous explosion. I was then in the MPO office facing the mine with a clear view right up to the mine. The ground shook violently and looking out of the window I saw a tremendous upheaval of smoke, rock and flames going up into the air. The explosion seemed to rumble as a continual roar for some time afterwards, I should say about twenty seconds.

I was standing in my office at the time with Flight Lieutenant Dawson and I said to him 'The mine!' We waited for a second or two wondering what was going to happen next and could hardly realize that the office was still standing with no windows broken. I then realized that as Commanding Officer I had better do something about it. My car was parked outside the office so I immediately proceeded to the mine. The fire picquet was going up immediately in front of the car.

When we arrived at the control point there were two incendiary fires burning and exploding fiercely. I told the fire picquet not to bother

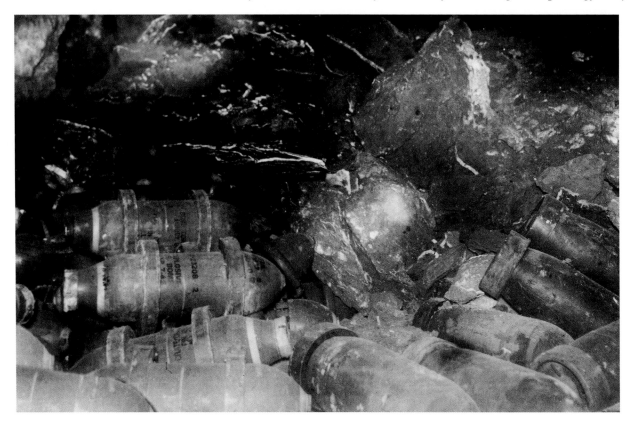

Left: More 250lb bombs trapped by a roof fall. This photograph, together with the one opposite and those on the previous page show something of the range of situations from which bombs and other ammunition had to be recovered. Some were almost completely engulfed in mud, some trapped by immense blocks of fallen stone and others buried and virtually invisible beneath mounds of finely granulated gypsum.

with the fires that had gone too far but to concentrate on nearby stacks.

I then made for the No.2 entrance to the mine. On the way I saw the body of a civilian who had been blown to pieces. I went into the mine which was, of course, in darkness. I was not familiar with the ways through the mine and had only been in it about twice before, but I knew that there were safety lamps at various places through the tunnels. I searched for a lamp but could not find one. I then realized that it was useless to continue without lights and without knowledge of the mine.

I cannot remember exactly what happened following this. I either came out of the mine and asked for a civilian volunteer with a lamp to guide me or else I met a civilian in the mine who volunteered to come on further into the mine. However, store-man Mylotte with a lamp and I made a further search of deeper regions of the mine. The lamp was very poor for two people in the blackness of the mine and I decided to search for a further lamp which was eventually found but would not work.

To the best of my knowledge we proceeded to the area of 'E' loop and 'F' loop where there were fumes. Mr Mylotte complained of the effects of the fumes and, as it seemed impossible to get enough light and the fumes appeared dangerous, I decided to abandon the search and to organize a better equipped search party.

I should have mentioned that when we entered the mine I saw the civilians coming out with lamps, several of them suffering from shock and minor injuries and they were helping each other along. On our way out it seemed that most of the civilians had got out of the mine as we had not met any more. On the way out we met a party consisting of Flight Lieutenant Shuttleworth, Foreman Salt and two or three airmen going in. The time was then approximately 11:45 hours. The bodies of Mr Paterson, Constable Skellett and another constable who was seriously injured had all been removed and, I believe, the injured constable was already on his way to hospital.

Considering that there was little more he could do for the time being, Wing Commander Kings returned to his office to telephone Group Captain Honey at No.42 Group headquarters to report the incident. Honey suggested that on account of the obvious danger from fumes in the mine the local Mines Rescue organization should be contacted immediately. Kings called both the Mansfield and Ilkeston Mines Rescue Organizations at 1.30 pm, but due to some

Left: When this photograph was taken in June 1945 recovery of trapped bombs must have been well in hand. This view appears to show temporary timbering in place to support an area of poor roof while the bombs trapped beneath were dug out.

misunderstanding the emergency units were not despatched until 4.30 pm, arriving three quarters of an hour later. In the meantime several National Fire Service units had arrived with one-hour breathing apparatus and were probing into the deeper recesses of the mine, but with little success due to the short duration of the equipment. Wing Commander Kings led the first search party using NFS breathing apparatus:

I decided to search the mine again and asked for a volunteer to act as a guide. Foreman Salt volunteered and, together with four NFS men, all of us wearing gas masks, we proceeded into the mine. Some airmen also volunteered to come in to act as a message chain, spaced at audible distances from one another. I instructed these airmen to keep in conversation and to come out at the least sign of fume effects. After proceeding two or three hundred yards the leading airman proved a casualty and had to be helped out by one of the NFS oxygen squad. We proceeded to the extremity of 'F' loop where a solid block fall had taken place. We decided to try to get round behind this fall and Mr Salt got us around to 'E' loop, I believe on 'E2' road, and then to roads 14 and 21. Fumes were very intense and we were all feeling the effects.

Many falls of rock had occurred and ammunition and bombs were strewn all over the place. We came to a further heavy fall which was almost blocking the way. Mr Salt and I tried to get through here but the lights were very poor, our eyes were badly affected despite wearing goggles, and we could not see clearly. One of the remaining NFS firemen then complained of dizziness and it was decided to abandon the search as Mr Salt was the only one who knew the way out. We returned to the surface forty minutes after entering the mine.

Wing Commander Kings then immediately returned to his office to make arrangements for a roll-call of all personnel on the site, instructing Flying Officer Clements to take the roll of service personnel and two civilian foremen to count the civilian workers. Lieutenant Sylvestry, the senior Italian officer, was detailed to round up all the Italian co-operators. These men were then sent back to Hilton PoW camp under guard for their own protection because, according to Wing Commander Kings' account, 'one or two people were making unpleasant remarks about having Italians on the unit'.

A little later in the afternoon it was discovered that a press reporter from a local newspaper had got into the unit among the confusion on the back of a fire tender but had been apprehended and detained by Flight Lieutenant Shuttleworth pending a decision on what to do with him. Acting upon advice from Wing Commander Kings, Shuttleworth instructed the reporter, in the severest terms, not to make any statement of the accident until the news was officially released by the Ministry of Information. To avoid further similar problems the local press agency representative was contacted and instructed to circulate a general warning against publishing any stories or speculation about the explosion. This instruction, though, as we have already seen, was largely ignored.

Having done all he could for the time being to organize his men, Wing Commander Kings returned to the mine area to see what progress was being made against the incendiary fires near the mine entrance which had by now been burning for several hours:

I proceeded to No.1 entrance where a fifty-ton dump consisting of about 250 incendiary clusters containing 19,000 four-pound incendiary bombs and about 5,000 type 'X' bombs, was exploding and burning fiercely. There was another similar dump about twelve yards away. I went around this dump and found that the boxes were in flames from the heat of the burning dump. I directed a hose which was too short to get round the front on to the top of the front row of clusters. This had some effect. I then went round to the second fire which appeared to be safe. I then returned to the first fire and found that two NFS men with a hose extension had managed to get round to the front of the dump where the heat was most intense and had succeeded in putting out the burning boxes. This undoubtedly saved the second dump from going up.

Someone pointed out that there was a further dump on the far side of the fire. I went round to this dump and with the help of two or three airmen removed the tarpaulins which were burning. Boxes in the centre of this dump were also in flames but the NFS extinguished these with a hose.

I then rang Group Captain Honey and reported that the fires were under control and that as far as I could tell the explosion had probably occurred in the new part of the mine which had completely disappeared.

It was now 5.15 pm and the first Mines Rescue teams had arrived from Ilkeston and Mansfield led by Mr Robertson who was chairman of the local rescue organization and also a colliery company director. Robertson was immediately put in charge of the rescue operation and Wing Commander Kings placed guards at each entrance to the mine with instructions to allow only properly organized rescue squads with gas masks and breathing apparatus to enter. Although almost exhausted, Foreman Salt once again volunteered to take the first

Above: A roof fall at this location has upturned one of the narrow-gauge ammunition trucks, shearing off one of the wheels. A pile of 250lb bombs is visible in the background and there is a stack of boxed 303 rifle rounds behind the standing figure awaiting recovery.

rescue party down into the mine, leading them to the underground air-raid shelter where a fresh-air base was established. Meanwhile more military police and warders were put on traffic control duty on the surface where the roads were becoming congested with ambulances, fire appliances and rescue organization vehicles.

By early evening five specialist mines rescue teams were searching underground with the help of the NFS firemen who had being working since midday and who had agreed to co-ordinate their efforts with the mines rescue men and to put themselves under the control of Mr Robertson. Two or three more bodies were found and mobile fans were installed in an ineffective attempt to clear the fumes, but as the day drew to a close it was obvious that no more survivors would be found and the search was abandoned. Tragically, the fruitless search had already cost the life of James Beard, one of the mines rescue volunteers, who became detached from his mates and, unable to find his way out of the mine, was overcome by fumes as his air supply expired.

Seventeen people known to have been working in the mine at the time of the explosion were still missing. Three bodies were located late on Monday trapped beneath fallen rock and dislodged bombs, but it was impossible to recover these until Thursday 30 November when the fumes had abated. The search for the remaining bodies was then abandoned until the mine and its precarious contents were declared safe.

Chapter 8

THE CIVILIAN TRAGEDY

Within an hour of the incident news had reached the Regional Civil Defence Headquarters and by mid-afternoon a major Civil Defence rescue operation was under way at the drowned plasterboard factory with units from all over the north and east Midlands in attendance. Units from Leicester and Burton-on-Trent were on the scene quickly, but initial progress at Ford's works was hopelessly slow as the available equipment, principally picks, spades and shovels, were useless in the muddy quagmire that had engulfed the factory. Later that day more Civil Defence personnel from Impney Court training centre arrived together with thirty soldiers from Branston Ordnance Depot, but without adequate equipment they too could make no headway against the all pervading mud. In frustration, both Major Dennison, the Deputy Regional Commissioner, and Captain Simmonds, staff officer of the Lichfield sub-area, railed against the futility and disorganization of the rescue effort, demanding that one person and one organization, preferably the Civil Defence Corps, should be put in overall charge of the various Civil Defence, police and military units that were currently working ineffectually and with a marked absence of direction.

Following a heated discussion it was agreed on Tuesday 28 November that control of the unified forces should he vested in Captain Simmonds with Mr Rose, the Impney Court training officer, as his technical advisor. Simmonds' first act in his new role was to contact a nearby United States Army unit with a request for mechanical earth-moving equipment. The Americans immediately agreed to provide whatever assistance they could and despatched a squad of engineers with a bulldozer and dragline, neither of which, unfortunately, proved to be of much use. Two days later, following a site visit, Major Dennison reported that:

the American troops had provided a bulldozer which had broken down before the work had commenced. A mechanical grab was on the site but out of action and practically nothing had been done in the way of using mechanical equipment up until 4.00 pm [on 30 November] when the Americans brought another machine to the site which was only capable of pushing the mud before it.

By this time Police Divisional Superintendent Heath was becoming concerned about the health risk posed by the carcases of the two hundred or so cattle that had been killed by the initial explosion and which were now putrefying among the other carnage. The previous day his men had been busy destroying dozens of other animals that survived the blast but were horribly mutilated. Now, with their equipment ineffectual against the mud and with nothing better to do with their machinery, the Americans were put to work burying the animal carcases in mass graves.

A Ministry of Home Security investigation into the deaths of so many cattle, which may have seemed something of a trivial issue at the time, given the magnitude of the human disaster, nevertheless provided an interesting insight into bovine psychology. After explaining that most of the cattle that had perished instantly had died because the blast completely collapsed their lungs, the MoHS report went on to say that:

Several cows which found their way back to the various farms were found to be suffering from shock, damage from flying stones which were in some cases embedded in the animals, and severe bruising as though large pieces of debris had hit them. Five cows that were taken off the fields belonging to Fauld Manor Farm on the night following the incident were found to be in a dazed state and the following morning were found to be dead.

By Friday 1 December the situation was becoming desperate. No more bodies had been recovered and little visible progress had been made with the clearance of debris. The previous evening the Regional Civil Defence Corps headquarters had despatched telegrams to the Air Ministry and the Ministry of Home Security admitting that 'Civil Defence resources had become unequal to the task'. At an emergency meeting on Friday attended by all the senior Civil Defence staff including the Regional Commissioner, Lord Dudley; the Regional Air Liaison Officer, Group Captain Thomson; senior police officers; Colonel Whitehouse, commanding officer of 874 Mechanical

Equipment Company; representatives from the Ministry of Works and Robert Murt, the Staffordshire County Surveyor together with Mr. Binns, the director of R.M. Douglas Ltd, the county's preferred civil engineering contractor, a determined effort was made to get things on a proper footing.

Major Dennison, the Deputy Regional Commissioner, opened the meeting by pointing out that they must better direct the work of recovering bodies and that there might be political repercussions 'if there should be any doubt in the minds of the public that the utmost efforts were not being exerted to recover these bodies'. It was obvious, he said, that the present arrangements were inadequate and called upon the County Surveyor to take over the task, using all the available resources of his department. Murt agreed to this proposal on the condition that he be allowed to employ the contractors R.M. Douglas Ltd 'as the department has neither the equipment nor labour'. This created an immediate and unexpected sticking point over the question of finance and a protracted argument ensued over which department would ultimately foot the bill. The problem was the extraordinariness of the situation. There had been expensive accidents at military establishments before and the services had always picked up the bill; similarly, the cost of clearing up after enemy action was always paid from the pocket of the Ministry of Home Security. At Fauld the explosion had occurred on a military site but its effects were predominantly the destruction of civil lives and property. To complicate things further the event was not the result of enemy action and there was simply no precedent for a financial resolution. The Civil Defence opinion was that the procedure should be no different from when an RAF aircraft crashes on civilian property; in those cases the Air Ministry always paid compensation. The Air Ministry disagreed vigorously, however, and subsequently the Ministry of Home Security confirmed that it would pick up the bill in the first instance, but hinted darkly that it would, by hook or by crook, recover the money from the Air Ministry after the war.

With the financial position established, a contract could be let and work commence. It was agreed that a Royal Engineers unit of twenty-five men in two shifts would work day and night for the next seven days, allowing the County Council and its contractor time to organize plant and equipment, after which the latter would take over the whole task. One more body was discovered at Ford's on Wednesday 2 December, after which it was agreed by Lord Dudley that night work would cease because it was 'quite impossible for any of the missing to be still alive'. Armed with a plan of the factory provided by Ford's plant manager and information regarding the likely whereabouts of the missing workers at the time of the incident, Robert Murt, the County Surveyor, drew up a scheme that entailed digging two roadways through the accumulated mud, one towards a section of the main building that had not been completely destroyed and another towards the carpenters shop. The contractors R.M. Douglas Ltd had assembled a prodigious amount of plant at Fauld, including three dragline diggers, three sixteen-ton skimmers, three bulldozers, nine dumper trucks and a host of lighter plant, and, despite the dreadful conditions, was making satisfactory progress.

Priority was given to the cutting of a route to the main office building because it was thought that at least five bodies still lay there, but it was reported on 16 December:

It is quite possible that some of these bodies may be recovered before we reach the offices as some days ago a safe which was in the far office was recovered approximately 130 feet below its original position which illustrates, I think, the intensity of the avalanche of clay, trees and water.

It is interesting to note that a wheel of the motor car owned by Mr Goodwin of Upper Castle Hayes Farm was recovered as well as an overcoat which it is believed was his property. It may be assumed that when the explosion occurred he was making his way through the works in his car and therefore it is likely that his body may be recovered during the excavation leading to the offices.

Despite all the effort, progress was still painfully slow. Eight more bodies were recovered from the factory site on 13 January and, although there were many more still to find there, disquiet was voiced publicly about the authority's apparent indifference to the fate of the occupants of Botham's Farm and Upper Castle Hayes Farm. A week later, to pacify the complainants, Robert Murt issued a report outlining progress to date. Referring to the two farms, he stated that :

The sides of the crater had, in places, since the explosion fallen in and it is anticipated that such slips will continue for a considerable period to a varying degree according to climatic conditions until the soil takes up its natural angle of repose.

One can estimate that at least 3,000,000 cubic yards of material has been deposited upon the fields of Upper Castle Hayes Farm and Hanbury Fields. At Botham's Farm one man is still missing. Farmhands heard him talking ten minutes before the explosion. Another labourer on this farm was killed and his body, minus legs, was found completely buried, head down, and it is generally felt that the missing man may have suffered a similar fate.

At Goodwin's Farm four people are missing, three men and one woman, who were presumed to be taking a meal in the farm at the time of the explosion. It is generally felt that the four missing persons must have been blown to bits with the rest of the farm at the time of the explosion and no search has revealed any of the bodies. In support of this theory a lower leg with kneecap attached and some fragments off flesh severed at the ankle have been found near the site of the offices at Peter Ford's and it is assumed that this fragment probably reached the spot in the condition it was found in by the force of considerable explosion.

It might be mentioned that the Vicar of the parish and the chairman of Hanbury Parish Council have been contacted and both endorse the opinion that no useful purpose will be served by further search.

The difficulties surrounding Upper Castle Hayes Farm hinged upon the fact that so absolute was the destruction that no one could say exactly where the farm had been. Aerial photographs of the crater were taken by an Air Ministry unit from Fradley and an attempt made to correlate these with large-scale maps of the area, but even this was inconclusive. A report from the Regional Civil Defence Commissioner concluded that:

The house and most of the buildings on the farm were in the crater. I was informed by my Intelligence Officer that even if the buildings were not in the crater but on the lip nothing would be found of the occupants.

My conclusion will be further checked on the ground and a report submitted on my final conclusion, and instructions obtained as to whether any attempt whatever shall be made on this site to locate the bodies.

This view was later reinforced at the Coroner's Inquiry into the deaths held on 10 February. The inquiry was attended by Mr A.G. Newman, an Assistant Treasury Solicitor who recorded in his departmental record that:

The whole farm has disappeared (and the writer may add that in private conversation the Coroner informed him that local inhabitants who had lived in the district all their lives are unable to say even

where the farm originally stood, so completely has the terrain altered.)

It had long been obvious that no useful work could be done at either Botham's Farm or Goodwin's Farm and on 27 January the Ministry of Home Security transmitted a final recommendation to the Regional Commissioner and to Air Marshal Donald, Air Officer Commander-in-Chief of Maintenance Command, that the searches there should be abandoned. Following this decision the task of recovery was ended. Douglas's final bill to the County Council amounted to £14,815.

There were two other concerns that surfaced among the locals in the immediate aftermath of the disaster. Within a few hours of the explosion rumour of the event had spread around numerous RAF aerodromes in the midland area and by the following day the sky above the crater was frequently filled with low-flying aircraft, their pilots either sightseeing or taking unauthorized photographs. Many residents of Hanbury who were relatives of the dead and missing found this somewhat insensitive and complaints were voiced to Police Superintendent Heath who immediately reported the matter to the Air Ministry and to Major Dennison at Civil Defence headquarters, to whom he wrote:

During the afternoon of Wednesday it was reported to me that an abnormal number of aircraft were continually flying low over the scene of the incident, causing distress to the families who had suffered. At my request the Air Ministry agreed to place Fauld and five miles around it out of bounds to aircraft flying. Unfortunately an authorized low-flying route passes within two miles of the locality. In addition to my action with the Air Ministry I have arranged to have personnel posted at the site to observe and report on low flying aircraft.

One of those pilots who might have been guilty of this offence, his identity is unknown, was a test pilot from RAF Tattenhill who later published an account of his experience which gives a graphic picture of the immediate aftermath of the disaster:

I was sitting in my office attending to the paper-work on an aeroplane I had just test flown when it happened. There was a sudden distant roar, windows rattled, the metal office walls creaked and shook and a door opened. I ran outside and saw a huge mushroom-like form rising slowly into the air until it had assumed the shape of a giant umbrella. It seemed to remain there for a minute or two before falling steadily in streaks, back to earth. There were many speculations amongst those of us who saw it, the most popular being that it was a V2 rocket.

Three-quarters of an hour later I test flew another aircraft and flew over the site.

Not a blade of grass could be seen, for the entire area had been completely covered by the thousands of tons of earth blown into the air and broadcast over a wide area. A few tree stumps protruded grotesquely from the reddish-brown soil, and the ruins of one or two farms were dotted about in the shapeless heaps of smouldering bricks and rubbish.

Houses a mile or two away from the explosion were burning and many buildings showed signs of having been badly damaged. On the outskirts of this picture of desolation, I noticed a wood — or what had once been a wood — of about five acres in extent. Huge trees had been snapped off at the roots like match sticks, and only a few at the far end were left standing; the remainder were lying about and twisted in all directions. Another copse of evergreen trees which seemed to have escaped the full force of the blast was plastered with earth, giving the trees the appearance of having been made of plasticine and producing a most weird effect.

On the occasion of this first flight I was not aware of what had caused it, but that a disaster of appalling magnitude had taken place was obvious. As I flew round at a height of 1,000 feet the whole thing seemed unreal and reminded me of some fantastic illustration of the Moon or Mars, from one of Jules Verne's books, and indeed, the groups of people I could see working knee-deep in mud might well have been Martians going about their daily tasks in some strange land instead of rescue squads intent on the grim business of searching for the many unfortunate victims of this awful tragedy.

The second cause of friction was the RAF's apparent indifference to the civilian hardship beyond its boundary fences in the days and weeks that followed the disaster. While this may have held true in subsequent days and weeks as the focus of activity turned from rescue and recovery to the apportionment and avoidance of blame, it was not the case in the first few hours after the blast, as Wing Commander Kings' testimony makes plain. What is obvious is that until some time after 12.30 pm no one from RAF Fauld had gone to the top of the hill overlooking the site; staff there were oblivious of the enormous damage that had been done to Ford's works and Hanbury village and were equally unaware of the magnitude of the crater. Until that time all effort had been concentrated on recovering the dead and

injured from the mine entrances simply because these were the only locations where such efforts had any hope of success. It was not until after the first NFS unit arrived with breathing apparatus at 12.15 that Wing Commander Kings first looked beyond the immediate scene of devastation. Kings explained that after dealing with the NFS and instructing Squadron Leader Anness to arrange the delivery of four mobile canteens from a nearby airfield he went up the bank at the back of the mine and,

in view of the many craters around I instructed Flying Officer Amberton to call in a bomb disposal squad immediately. I then went over to the main crater which from my viewpoint looked nearly half a mile across, and decided that in view of the number of small craters all over the place that bombs must have been thrown out of the mine, probably at great temperature, and must have exploded in the air and on the ground when landing from the great heat.

I sent a party of a Warrant Officer and fifty airmen with spades and shovels, who had come over from Church Broughton, round to Ford's works to assist at that site as I heard that they had suffered extensive damage and casualties. During the afternoon I directed many offers of assistance to Ford's works and Hanbury.

Nevertheless, word of the rumours about RAF indifference soon reached the Assistant Under-Secretary at the Air Ministry who, realizing the potential political consequences, minuted his Minister that:

There is a certain feeling that the RAF might take a more direct interest in the proceedings relating to damage outside RAF property.

In response, during early January Squadron Leader Catford from No.42 Group and Mr Hawkins from the Ministry of Home Security visited practically all the people concerned in connection with compensation matters. The Minister was subsequently informed that:

Squadron Leader Catford, a specialist on house damage, has been sent by the Air Ministry to handle civilian damage. All these facts have been broadcast in the district by loudspeaker vans and assistance in cash and otherwise is proceeding. The Air Ministry is in touch with the local Assistance Boards and Mr Green from the Burton-on-Trent Assistance Board has set up an office in Hanbury.

Similar concerns were raised by A.P. Hughes at the Ministry of Home Security who wrote to the Air Minister advising him that:

I saw our Principal Officer in Birmingham recently and he said that he thought it would be very much appreciated by those who suffered from the explosion if before work ceased an officer from the RAF could pay a visit and perhaps see some of the people most directly affected.

It was then suggested that the AOC No.42 Group should 'arrange for further visits for RAF officers in order to remove any suggestion of lack of interest, and he agreed that this should be done', but the problem was to persist throughout the prolonged period of recovery and inquiry and soured relations between the RAF and residents of Hanbury and Fauld for many years.

The Court of Inquiry

A Court of Inquiry was convened on 5 December 1944 by Air Marshal Sir Grahame Donald, KCB, the Air Officer Commanding No.42 Group, to determine the cause of the disaster at 21 MU Fauld. Air Vice Marshal A. Lees, CBE, DSO sat as Presiding Officer.

Intelligence gathered during the previous week pointed to seven possible causes, most of which could be discounted immediately. Even before the Court convened three other rumoured causes achieved brief notoriety, were investigated, disproved and quickly quashed. Within minutes of the explosion stories were circulating that three German aircraft were seen diving low over the depot; several individuals reported sightings to the police, but investigations proved that none of these people had witnessed the event first-hand and were just reporting what they had been told. Later it transpired that one man had been the source of all these reports, but his identity was never discovered. Rumours that four recently escaped German prisoners-of-war from a nearby PoW camp had been seen lurking around the perimeter of the depot the previous day were similarly proved to be spurious in origin, but there seemed to be less willingness, among local civilians at least, to exonerate the Italian PoWs who worked in the mine and who, it was rumoured, were guilty of sabotage. This despite the fact that nine of their number were killed in the disaster.

The seven possible causes of the explosion pinpointed by the Court of Inquiry were:
- A catastrophic roof fall
- Spontaneous ignition

- Electrical fault
- Defective plant or equipment
- Presence of explosive gasses
- Rough handling of sensitive weapons in the mine
- Incorrect practice.

We have already seen much of the earlier evidence taken from Wing Commander Kings, Squadron Leader Anness and Foreman of Stores J.C. Salt, all of which described the explosion and the events immediately before and after in some detail, but threw little light on the cause. Their statements, and those of other witnesses, tended to agree (with the exception of Squadron Leader Anness, whose evidence was on this matter as on several others less reliable than the majority) that there were two distinct explosions, a relatively small initial detonation followed by a second, catastrophic explosion some seconds later. Estimates of the interval between the two explosions varied from three to twenty or more seconds.

Evidence from Eric Bryant, the Air Ministry Works Directorate engineer who had overseen the construction and maintenance of the depot since 1936, comprehensively discounted the possibility that either a roof fall, spontaneous ignition or naturally occurring explosive gas had caused the blast, and evidence from other AMWD staff indicated quite conclusively that neither an electrical fault or defective machinery was the source of ignition. The only AMWD plant within the mine at the time of the explosion were two electric locomotives and forensic examination of these after the event found no faults that could have contributed to the disaster. There was no air-conditioning equipment in the mine and all the lighting apparatus was in good order up until the time of the explosion.

There remained, then, the possibilities of rough handling or incorrect practice and the focus of the inquiry turned upon the weapons that were stored in the new area at the time of the blast, and upon the men whose lives ended there. Leading Aircraftsman Michael Watson, who was the last man to leave the new area alive and whom fate had spared that Monday morning as he went off in search of skids to load the 4000 lb bombs awaiting despatch there, explained that five minutes before the explosion twenty 500 lb Mk IX bombs were positioned by the rails awaiting transport, and equipment was being got ready to load four 4000 lb bombs on to railway trucks. Asked whether he was aware of any 500 lb cluster bombs stored in the new area (this was a class of weapon that was known to be of dubious stability and an early candidate for responsibility for the disaster), Watson confirmed that there were in excess of 600 boxes of such bombs in one bay and that many of them were cracked and, in his opinion, dangerous. Watson's reply immediately prompted the Court to ask whether or not the AMWD electricians ever climbed on stacks of cluster bombs to change light bulbs. Both Watson and a later witness, Corporal Lionel Poynton, replied quite categorically that this was never done.

Questioned about the condition of the electric lighting in the new area and the process by which dead lamps were replaced, Poynton replied that normally there were two lamp boys whose sole task was the replacement of blown bulbs. The lamp boys, he said, had a reputation for making nuisances of themselves with their ladders and staging. Watson and Poynton were then asked whether they were aware of Smith gun ammunition stored in the mine. The high explosive round for this weapon, as we have seen earlier, was probably the most dangerously unstable item of ordnance ever produced in the United Kingdom and was vilified by all who came in contact with it. More Home Guard volunteers were killed by Smith gun misfires than by enemy action and, as we saw in the introduction to this book, in a post-war memoir one west country Home Guard officer described at length the Smith gun's 'terrifying reputation for killing its crew'. Some 30,000 rounds were later recovered intact from the old area, but neither witness could recall there having been further stocks in the destroyed section of the mine.

Finally, Corporal Poynton was asked about the presence of American bombs in the new area. Among the more conservative British ordnance officers and armourers there was a longstanding scepticism about the safety of much of the output of the American armament industry, and faulty American-made projectiles were thought to have been responsible for a number of relatively minor accidents at British Army field storage depots. It was said, for instance (and not without a grain of truth) that the British would design a safe fuse and then spend ten years trying to make it work, whereas the Americans designed fuses that worked and then spent ten years trying to make them safe. Poynton replied that to his knowledge there were two American-made 4,000 lb bombs in the new area on Ford's Level, one with its damaged exploder partially removed. He went on to state that this bomb had been there for at least twelve months, had not been worked on for several months and further work on it was not scheduled for the immediate future.

Reviewing the evidence thus far, the Court agreed that, whilst there were items of ammunition stored underground that perhaps should

not have been there, it was considered unlikely that mishandling of these stores was the cause of the accident. It seemed increasingly likely, therefore, that the accident resulted from a catastrophic blunder by one or more of the men who died in the crater. Given the nature of their last known tasks the inquiry was now focused on the last few minutes on earth of five men: AID inspectors Nicklin, Saunders and Brassington, and Bomb Armourers Fairbanks and Bailey.

The first of the most pivotal witnesses to give evidence was James Edmund Pollard, the Chief Inspecting Officer. Asked to explain the jobs the men of his department were engaged upon on the morning of the incident, he replied:

I detailed Mr Saunders, the Examiner, to carry on the inspection of two jobs that were going on in the High Explosives area. He was assisted by Viewers Nicklin, Brassington, Higgs and Cox. Nicklin and Brassington were employed on inspecting No.28 Pistols in Road 26 in the new area, Higgs and Cox on external inspection of 1,000 lb MC bombs on 'D' Loop in the old area. Saunders would walk around the two jobs. Higgs stated that he had seen him about five minutes before the explosion going down 27 Road.

Suspicion had by now fallen upon the increasingly large numbers of unit-return bombs that were accumulating in the depot, i.e bombs that had been returned from airfield dumps because of faults or damage, or bombs that had been jettisoned by aircraft forced to return to their home bases with their weapons still aboard. Asked about the procedure for dealing with such bombs at Fauld, Pollard replied:

All returned bombs are inspected at Scropton Sidings for the presence of detonators. Since July 1945 only one bomb has been discovered with a detonator in place: a 500 lb GP MkV containing a 45 grain detonator.

In order that it should fully understand the relevance of the more technical evidence yet to come, it was explained to the Court how the various components of a typical high explosive bomb were assembled to form a complete round. It was explained that a bomb usually consisted of a thin outer case containing a large quantity of relatively stable high explosive, usually TNT/RDX, which is quite difficult to detonate. Running through the middle of this filling is a steel exploder tube which contains a material known as Composition Explosive or 'CE', which acts as an intermediate between the detonator attached to the bomb's fuse and the main filling and which, in effect, amplifies the small explosion of the fuse and ensures the complete detonation of the main filling. Bombs held in store were invariably un-fused and blanking plugs were screwed into the fuse pockets at each end of the exploder tube.

Asked what repairs would be undertaken underground, Pollard told the Court that the work would include:

replacing transit bases, pistols, suspension lugs, etc. but no internal repairs. Bombs with broken exploders are taken into the surface AID compounds for extraction.

This statement was of vital importance in the light of later evidence placed before the Court. Pollard was next asked about the recovered jettisoned bombs that were stored in the mine at the time of the explosion. He explained that:

They were 500 lb and 1,000 lb MC bombs and we inspected them in the surface AID compound. They had broken plugs, no pistols, plugs both ends and some of them had no exploder tubes. None of them were cracked nor was the main filling exposed, but they were distorted. They were re-plugged and marked up for return to factory for washing out.

Next to appear was Leading Aircraftsman Michael Watson and his evidence was in damning contradiction to Chief Inspecting Officer Pollard. Watson explained that he had been employed underground examining and replacing exploders in bombs and then went on:

I think they [Nicklin and Brassington, the dead AID Viewers] have done such work both in the surface AID compound and in the mine. I do know they were employed, together with myself, on examining and replacing where necessary exploders in the mine at 21 MSU Linley. This task took place in August 1944.

On the day of the explosion Nicklin and Brassington were not working on HE bombs, so no blame could be apportioned to them, but Watson's evidence so alarmed the Court that Group Captain Storrar was next called to explain the alleged practices at 21 MSU Linley. When questioned, Storrar stated:

I was aware that exploders of 500 lb GP bombs had been changed in the mine at Linley. This work was either in progress when I arrived

or started very shortly afterwards. I do not think that this should have been done underground, neither did Group Captain Honey, HQ 42 Group, who visited Linley in company with me. I discussed the matter with the Chief Inspecting Officer and Chief Equipment Officer and was assured that in the special circumstances the work ought to continue underground.

The special circumstances were:
• The mine was in the process of being emptied and the remaining HE content was very small.
• There was no surface AID compound at the unit.
• There was no suitable surface area at the mine where such work could be carried out other than the main access road.
• The roof of the mine was so weak that an explosion on the surface could cause a total collapse of the structure.
• Work on the exploders was conducted in an otherwise empty bay.
• Bombs were being made serviceable to meet a most urgent requirement for Bomber Command.

The most conclusive and damning evidence was that of Armourer Corporal Lionel Poynton who had been in the new area with storeman Salt, just a few minutes before the blast. He stated:

We proceeded into the new area to No.27 Road where Leading Aircraftsman Fairbanks and Leading Aircraftsman Bailey were working on 1,000 lb MC bombs which, I believe, were Unit Returns, having been jettisoned. This work consisted of removing nose and tail plugs where possible and removing the exploder container complete, or where this was not possible, removing the CE from the exploder pocket and collecting it in an ammunition box.

While I was there I saw a bomb with the transit plug in the tail removed set up horizontally on some form of batten about a foot from the floor. Leading Aircraftsman Bailey was chiselling out the CE from the exploder pocket. He was using a brass chisel and a hammer. I do not remember if the hammer was steel or brass.

As I have done this quite often previously in connection with similar work in the AID compound I warned Leading Aircraftsman Fairbanks and Leading Aircraftsman Bailey to take care as this is a dangerous job. It was the first instance, to my knowledge, of this kind of work being done in the HE mine.

The Court then asked: *Do you remember whether the bomb they were working on was lying alongside other bombs?* to which Poynton replied:

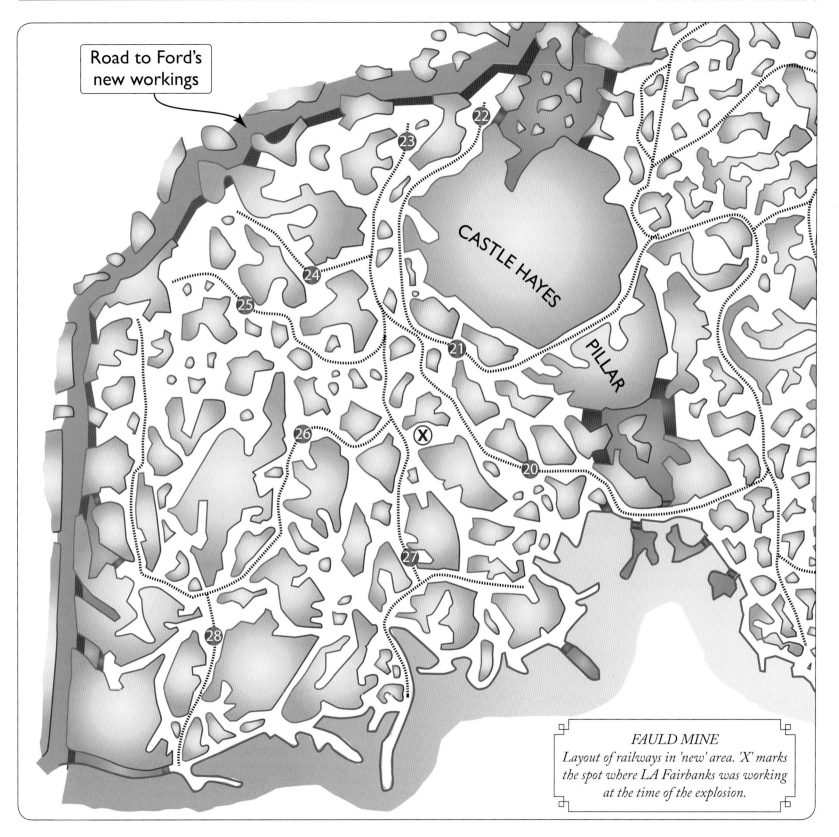

Road to Ford's new workings

CASTLE HAYES

PILLAR

FAULD MINE
Layout of railways in 'new' area. 'X' marks
the spot where LA Fairbanks was working
at the time of the explosion.

Yes, it was one of a row of about ten bombs. Some of these bombs had been completed.

Storeman Salt was then recalled and, when questioned, stated that: *On one occasion, only about a month ago, I saw an airman who might have been Leading Aircraftsman Bailey, who had been removing an exploder pocket from a 4,000 lb bomb in 'G' Loop on Ford's Level.*

The Court asked: *What action did you take?* to which Salt replied: *I asked him if he knew such work must not be carried out in the mine. He replied 'I am working for the AID,' but he stopped this work after I had spoken to him and as far as I know no further work was done on this bomb.*

Giving further evidence about repairs undertaken underground, Leading Aircraftsman Kenneth Macleod stated: *About a week previous to the explosion I was talking to Leading Aircraftsman Fairbanks. He told me that he was working in the new area on No.26 Road at 'the same old job'. I took 'the same old job' to mean removing exploders from bombs.*

Other witnesses confirmed that Bailey was often seconded to the AID and was quite 'cocky' about it; there was a certain amount of kudos associated with the job and he rather relished saying to RAF NCOs: *Sorry, you have no authority over me, I am working for the AID.*

Further investigation revealed that the bombs mentioned by Armourer Corporal Poynton included three 1,000 lb MC Mk1 bombs, filled with RDX/TNT, that had been jettisoned and returned from West Freugh. These were among eight similar bombs sentenced on 19 May 1944 as: *unserviceable and recommended for return to filling factory for boiling-out.*

By now the Court of Inquiry had heard enough evidence to come to a conclusion.

Findings of the Court of Inquiry

The Court finds that in all probability the work of chipping out the CE (Composition Explosive) of a 1,000 lb MC bomb using a brass chisel was the cause of the initial explosion. It is known that CE will explode easily if struck between brass and steel surfaces.

This bomb was one of a row of 1,000 lb MC bombs that were presumably exploded by sympathetic detonation or by fragments.

The Court concluded that the Explosives Regulations had not been adhered to and recorded that:

There are obviously mitigating circumstances during wartime when urgency is a keynote, manpower is of poorer quality and quantity, and more work is expected of a unit than that for which it is designed. Some relaxations can be made with safety and there must have been a tendency to extend relaxation locally owing to 'familiarity breeding contempt'.

There was negligence on the part of AID supervising staff present in the mine, due either to lack of knowledge, lack of a proper sense of responsibility, or lack of proper direction from senior authority.

Neither the Chief Inspecting Officer (AID) nor the Acting Chief Equipment Officer can be entirely absolved from all responsibility.

The Court was disturbed at the standard of AID Viewers, commenting that:

This may be due to manpower shortages, but is more likely to be caused by inadequate wages. It is recommended that this responsible work be rewarded by a more appropriate rate of pay.

It is also recommended that Viewers should be qualified by a Course of Instruction before taking up such work and be kept up to date by subsequent refresher courses.

Finding that Group Captain Storrar, the Commanding Officer, should be absolved of all responsibility for the accident, the Chairman of the Inquiry recorded that:

According to regulations the Chief Inspection Officer is responsible to the Commanding Officer for inspecting repairable items, for saying what work is to be undertaken, and for supervising the work; he is not responsible for effecting the repair. In practice, however, there have been occasions when, owing to urgent operational requirements and shortage of labour, a Commanding Officer has asked a CIO and his staff to do the repair work. In this circumstance it is clear that the actual work of repair should have been the responsibility of the Chief Equipment Officer and should have been supervised by the CIO or his staff. Both of these officers should have been aware of the incorrect practice.

Some members of the Court questioned the competence of Group Captain Storrar, pointing out the fact that he was not 'X' certified, and recommended that he should be replaced as Commanding Officer of the Fauld depot. This was not accepted by Air Marshal Sir Grahame Donald who stated:

I am not convinced that the Commanding Officer should hold 'X' certification, as I feel that a good, experienced Chief Equipment Officer who is 'X' qualified and a good Chief Inspection Officer should be fully capable of commanding a large explosives unit such as 21 MU Fauld, where there are seventeen 'X' qualified officers on establishment.

He continued:

I have a very high opinion of the ability of the present Commanding Officer, Group Captain Storrar, and I submit most strongly that this recommendation should not be allowed to result in his posting away from 21 MU.

Consequences

The Court had found quite conclusively that, beyond all reasonable doubt, the action of striking a brass chisel by Leading Aircraftsman Fairbanks had initiated the explosion, but ultimate responsibility did not lay there. Some person or persons had to take the blame, and those persons were James Edmund Pollard and Squadron Leader Anness. In arriving at this conclusion the Court took into account the fact that much of James Pollard's evidence was less than forthright. The problem now was what disciplinary measures, if any, should be taken against these men. The power to make recommendations on this matter lay in the hands of Air Marshal Sir Grahame Donald, Commander in Chief of Maintenance Command, and he made his opinion known to the Air Council in a letter dated 23 June 1945:

My considered opinion, formed after interviewing Squadron Leader Anness and discussions with the AOC No.42 Group, is that he failed, as Acting Chief Equipment Officer of No.21 MU, to exercise the control required of an officer of his seniority in an explosives unit, since he was not sufficiently aware of the work being undertaken in the unit. I hesitate, however, to suggest any disciplinary action which will connect too closely with the explosion on 27 November 1944 and the consequent loss of sixty lives.

As regards Mr Pollard, the Chief Inspecting Officer, the view of the AOC No.42 Group, who knows him better than I do, is that Mr Pollard is a knowledgeable and efficient AID officer in whom he had complete confidence until November last, but it seems that there was work being undertaken at Fauld of which he should have been

but was not aware. The AOC also reports a 'lack of frankness' on the part of the CIO in the subsequent inquiry. Mr Pollard has since been posted by the Director General of Aeronautical Inspection to an appointment outside No. 42 Group and I do not wish to submit any special recommendation.

The final decision was outlined three months later in a minute prepared by the Secretary of State for Air on 17 September, in which it was stated that:

In view of the findings of the Court and the recommendation of the Commander in Chief of Maintenance Command, I feel that an Air Council Letter of Displeasure is warranted in this case. Squadron Leader Anness is at present the holder of an 'X' symbol, but this will be withdrawn under the provisions of King's Regulations, Clause 3, Paragraph 386.

Squadron Leader Anness felt he had been unfairly treated in so far as the Court of Inquiry, which had been convened simply to determine the cause of the explosion, had become, in his opinion, a trial of his own culpability at which he was not permitted to defend himself. He made repeated representations to his senior officers and eventually, exercising his prerogative as a commissioned officer, asked leave for his case to be brought before the King. Anness was interviewed many times in connection with his claim and to aid his interviewers his curriculum vitae was widely circulated:

December 1925 - Commissioned from Cranwell
July 1927 - Promoted to Flying Officer
December 1927 - Completed a short armament course
April 1929 - Following a car accident in Iraq, Anness lost the sight in his right eye and was declared unfit as a pilot
January 1931 - Transferred to Stores Branch
July 1933 - Completed 'X' course
January 1937 - Promoted to Flight Lieutenant
August 1939 - Promoted to Squadron Leader

Despite all his representations his claim was ultimately rejected, the clear implication in the correspondence relating to his case being that, following the accident in 1929 after which he was declared unfit to fly, he was insufficiently motivated to carry out the ground duties that were available to him.

The Coroner's Inquest

Partly in reaction to the dearth of detailed information about the accident released by the Air Ministry, partly in an effort to quell the increasing public disquiet, but more importantly because the large number of civilian deaths caused by the incident were not the result of enemy action, it was felt inevitable that a Coroner's Inquest would be required. Consequently, a jury was assembled and, in the first week of February 1945, a Coroner's Inquest was opened at Burton-upon-Trent. As to the cause of those deaths its remit was a broad one; unlike the RAF Court of Inquiry it did not need to determine the detailed cause of the explosion, but only to decide upon one of four possibilities put before it:

- That the explosion was due to the activity of the Irish Republican Army.
- That the explosion was caused by sabotage by the Italian co-operators.
- That it was caused by a blast within Ford's gypsum mine.
- That it was caused by a technical mistake by the RAF.

Additionally, the jurors were asked to establish whether or not the missing, whose bodies were unlikely ever to be found, had in fact died in the explosion. Dismissing the first three possibilities, the Coroner issued a public apology to the Italians, who in his opinion had been harshly treated by the local population subsequent to the explosion. Opening the inquest, the Coroner stated that, in his view,

the verdict should be one of accidental death caused by an explosion on government property. We need not say why. So much for the bodies that have been found. We now come to the missing, which is a more difficult matter. I have to get sufficient evidence to present to the Ministry of Home Security in order to obtain authority to presume death.

The circumstances here are almost unprecedented and I have little beyond the Gresford Colliery disaster of some years ago to guide me. In that disaster, eventually, however, certain seams were bricked-up, death having been presumed. And here there are dead in the Dump of whom there is no hope of recovering and you will see from the evidence that the search is being abandoned because of that reason.

A detailed record of the proceedings was kept by Mr A.G. Newman, an Assistant Treasury Solicitor, who attended the whole inquiry on behalf of the government. Newman's notes are comprehensive and often poignant, as in the following extract, recording the closing stages of the case:

In his closing address to the jury the Coroner paid tribute to the work done by May Elizabeth Cooper, a local woman. He stated that a school had been turned into a mortuary and for seventy-two days this woman had attended there and received and dealt with all the bodies and portions of bodies brought in, had acted as caretaker and cleaner and had never faltered.

The significance of this is the fact that her own husband was one of the missing and in point of fact his body was recovered only the day before the inquest took place. At any time during the period of seventy-two days therefore, any one of the bodies brought in might have proved to be that of her own husband.

The jury delivered its verdict late on the afternoon of Saturday, 10 February and it was, in the absence of any of the findings of the RAF Court of Inquiry, broadly in line with the Coroner's recommendation. It stated:

We find that all the victims named by the Coroner died accidentally as the result of an explosion at the RAF dump, the causes of which are at the moment unknown. It does not appear to be sabotage or anything at Ford's. The deaths of the missing can be presumed. We desire to commend in particular Mrs Cooper and Police Constable McKay, and desire to express condolences generally.

So that was the end of the matter. With the Inquest and Inquiry out of the way, all that remained was to clear up the mess.

Bravery awards

❧

George Medal:
Squadron Leader Kings, Flight Lieutenant Lewin
Foreman of Stores Mr J.C. Salt

❧

British Empire Medal:
Corporal S.B. Rock, Corporal J.S. Peters
Foreman of Stores H. Coker

❧

Commendation: Welfare Assistant Mrs M.E.Degg

Chapter 9

RECOVERY & RECONSTRUCTION

By mid-January 1945 the first thoughts were being directed towards the reconstruction of the depot and very rough costings prepared. Apart from the partial destruction of several of the mine entrances and the total loss of the new area, which had been built very cheaply at a cost of less than £27,000, damage to RAF property was relatively insignificant. In a letter to Burke Trend at the Treasury, dated 19 January, Squadron Leader Kitts estimated that the total reparation bill might be in the region of £80,000, including £30,000 to make a barrier between the old mine and the base of the crater. £13,000 had already been spent on the task of recovery. The problem posed by the three hundred acres of agricultural land surrounding the depot, not owned by the RAF but laid waste by falling debris, was a thorny one. Initially it was thought that it was so badly disturbed that it could never again be made suitable for agriculture and that the only option might be for the government to purchase it and leave it to weather, possibly for decades. Eventually, perhaps, it might be handed over to the Forestry Commission.

Meanwhile, while the RAF was engrossed in its own problems, British Gypsum was pressing the Air Ministry with regard to the reinstatement of Ford's mine, where vast reserves of gypsum essential to the post-war reconstruction effort were now quarantined due to the destruction of the entrance shaft on the Ford's factory site. Initially the RAF proposed to pay a capital sum in compensation to British Gypsum for the land and wrecked factory and for the value of the outstanding twenty-one-year lease of minerals that the company held from the Duchy of Lancaster. Neither the Duchy nor the company was, however, prepared to accept this proposal.

The first concerns were to make some estimate of the amount of ammunition lost in the explosion and still trapped underground and then to organize its recovery. Detailed records of current stockholding were lost in the explosion as the only complete schedule was held in the foreman's office in the new area which was destroyed. Separate lists had previously been kept above ground, but this practice had ceased due to labour shortages.

Estimates were prepared by comparing dockets for receipts and issues kept at Scropton sidings and, once account had been taken of all the recoverable stores in the old area, it was found that 3,522 tons of high explosive bombs had been lost in the new area.

Following a preliminary examination a rather pessimistic report on the condition of the mine was sent to the Air Ministry with a request that Dr Rotter, whose expertise had enabled the recovery of all the trapped explosives following the collapse at Llanberis in 1942, should take charge of the recovery operation at Fauld.

Perturbed, despite Rotter's willingness to undertake the task, the Under-Secretary of State for Air replied:

I am sorry to hear that the damage is so much worse than we feared at first. Before Dr Rotter is requested to undertake the dangerous work for which he has volunteered I should be obliged if you would carefully consider other alternatives and send me an appreciation of the risks involved. Might it not, for example, be better to blow up

Fauld Bombs Destroyed In The New Area	
4000 lb HC MkV	630
4000 lb HC MkIV	753
4000 lb HC MkII	201
4000 lb GP MkI	1
2000 lb MC MkII	7
2000 lb MC MkIII	8
1900 lb GP	9
1000 lb US type 59	15
1000 lb US type 65	3
1000 lb MC MkI & Mk II	90
500 lb GP Mk IV	80
500 lb GP type 64	23
500 lb AS MkIII	500
500 lb SAP MkIV	180
500 lb MC MkIV	250
500 lb MC MkIX	20
500 lb HE Cluster	630 boxes
250 lb GP MkIV	96
250 lb GP MkIV	125
250 lb US	560
250 lb GP MkIIIC	983
23 lb fragmentation	500
500 lb incendiary clusters	680 boxes (150 tones)

Above: Several tons of rock loosened by the explosion are propped precariously by timber beams above two 4,000lb HE bombs. The boxes nearby contain American manufactured 23lb fragmentation bombs which were regarded by staff at Fauld to be the most unstable items of ordnance stored there.

the remaining explosives rather than risk precious lives in trying to retrieve them? Would not the work of retrieving them involve an immense expenditure of skill, labour, time and material. If the roofs are in some cases partly supported by stacks of explosive will they not have to be shored up before the explosives are recovered?

What is the final estimate of the loss we shall have suffered through this explosion? Does it dangerously effect our reserves of any particular bomb or explosive?

Adamant that the recovery should go ahead, Maintenance Command dismissed the Air Ministry concerns. In reply to the second point in the Under-Secretary's note, it was stated that the most serious loss was that of the 1,585 4,000 lb bombs, which represented about one month's industrial production.

4,000 tons of bombs and explosives were trapped in the mine and in places the ceiling was supported by the trapped material. One-fifth of the mine was affected by damage. The remaining undamaged portion amounted to about 40,000 square yards and contained some 19,000 tons of ammunition which was gradually removed and transferred to RAF Tatenhill where it was maintained in open storage.

By 20 September 1945 nearly 23,000 tons of bombs had been recovered from the old HE area, including the 4,000 tons that had to be extracted under extremely hazardous conditions from beneath fallen rock debris. In several cases it was found that stacks of ammunition, including American-made cluster bombs, the most sensitive type stored underground, were actually supporting areas of fallen roof and their extrication was fraught with danger. Writing to the Under-Secretary of State for Air on 11 September, the Commanding Officer of Maintenance Command could report that:

With the exception of one cavern, which is believed to contain only SAP bombs not exceeding seventy tons, all explosive stores have now been removed front the mine. The only cavern which remains is filled with mud which has entered from above; its complete clearance will not be effected for some weeks. Apart from the somewhat improbable presence of a cluster bomb which may have been deposited there by a freak blast, the handling of SAP bombs should not entail any abnormal risk. The principal risks to be encountered are those normal to quarrying in unsound rock and to the mud.

The last bombs were finally removed on 27 November 1945, a year to the day after the explosion.

Meanwhile a 'Special Air Ministry Panel' was convened to look into the future of the Fauld site with the object of developing four specific proposals:

- To review the options available to construct a new tunnel for the British Gypsum Company in order for the company to access the gypsum reserves isolated by the destruction of the shaft at Ford's works.
- To draw up plans for the reconstruction of the HE mine at minimal expense to provide storage for 4,000 tons of explosives.
- To produce plans for the extensive reconstruction of the mine, including the construction of new underground barriers and traverses, to provide storage for 12,000 tons of explosives under the more stringent peacetime safety regulations.
- To find a means to drain the crater which had partially filled with water that was slowly draining through fissures in its base and threatening to flood the adjacent gypsum workings and the surviving sections of the RAF bomb store.

After protracted negotiations the Air Ministry finally agreed to meet the cost of sinking a new access shaft, laying narrow-gauge tracks to link this to the existing British Gypsum system and to erect a new locomotive shed, weighbridge and canteen to replace the facilities destroyed at Ford's works. Construction of the new adit was delayed due to indecision regarding its best location, the eventual choice being a point midway between the now buried Ford's shaft and the existing Staton's shaft half a mile or so to the west. Work was under way, however, by 9 October 1945 and was expected to be complete by 30 June the following year.

Both the Duchy of Lancaster and British Gypsum were keen that an inscription recording the names of those who died at Ford's works and the circumstances of their deaths should be carved into the stone lintel over the new mine entrance, but the Air Ministry consistently refused to endorse this scheme, which they thought inappropriate, despite representations from a broad range of pressure groups.

Tragically, during the sinking of this shaft the Fauld mine disaster claimed its last victim. As work neared completion on 9 January 1947 at the inward end of the new 600-yard-long underground link road that joins the new shaft to Ford's heading, a group of labourers accompanied by two roof inspectors were erecting the last of a series of support girders under an area of unstable roof. That morning George Astle, Staton's under-manager, accompanied by Eric Bryant, who had previously been the Air Ministry engineer in charge of the construction of the Fauld bomb store but who left the Air Ministry to work for Statons in December 1946 at the age of thirty-six, decided to inspect the work in progress. As they approached the area where roof strengthening was under way they met quarry safety-men Utting and Foster and were assured by them that the roadway ahead was secure. Bryant and Astle proceeded on their way walking just three feet apart when almost immediately a two-ton block of stone fell from the roof, killing George Astle immediately and missing Eric Bryant by a hair's breadth.

Reconstructing the bomb store

Even before the last bodies had been recovered from the mine, Maintenance Command was looking at the possibility of reconstructing those parts that remained standing and putting the depot back into use. Asked to prepare a rough costing, the resident engineer, Mr Eric Bryant stated:

There are about 50,000 square yards of stacking area in the 'old' mine not including railways. About 15,000 square yards are to some extent damaged. Clearing, timbering and gobbing will cost about £1 per square yard (i.e about £15,000). Most of the necessary material is on site and the job will employ fifty men for six months. The 'new' area (of 10,000 square yards) is completely written off. It had cost £27,000 to develop (a very low price due to the extremely good roof conditions encountered). The Incendiary mine was intact except for the entrance which would cost about £1,000 to clear. Likewise the Detonator area was undamaged except for the entrance which would cost £500 to repair.

By the time the old area had been completely cleared of trapped bombs and explosives, however, the war had ended and different, more stringent, peacetime criteria were applied to the storage of ammunition. The magazine regulations which stipulated specific safety distances that must be maintained between certain volumes of explosive materials and civilian habitations were strictly applied and it was found that, if the mine was rebuilt to its existing wartime

Right: Reconstruction work using brickwork and rolled steel joists well under way in the north-west corner of the depot. It was hoped that by using this form of construction the greater part of the damaged area to the east of the Castle Hayes pillar could be recovered but, as will be shown in the pages that follow, much of this effort was largely unsuccessful.

Above: Another view of the reconstruction work in progress showing extensive temporary timber roof supports in place prior to the construction of new brick and concrete walls. Because many of the railway lines were realigned during the rebuilding it is difficult to locate this photograph with precision, but it appears to be in the vicinity of 'A' Group office with the Main Line in the foreground, 'F' Loop to the left, with No.6 Shunt turning north from it, and a temporary construction line from the emergency exit in the centre of the picture.

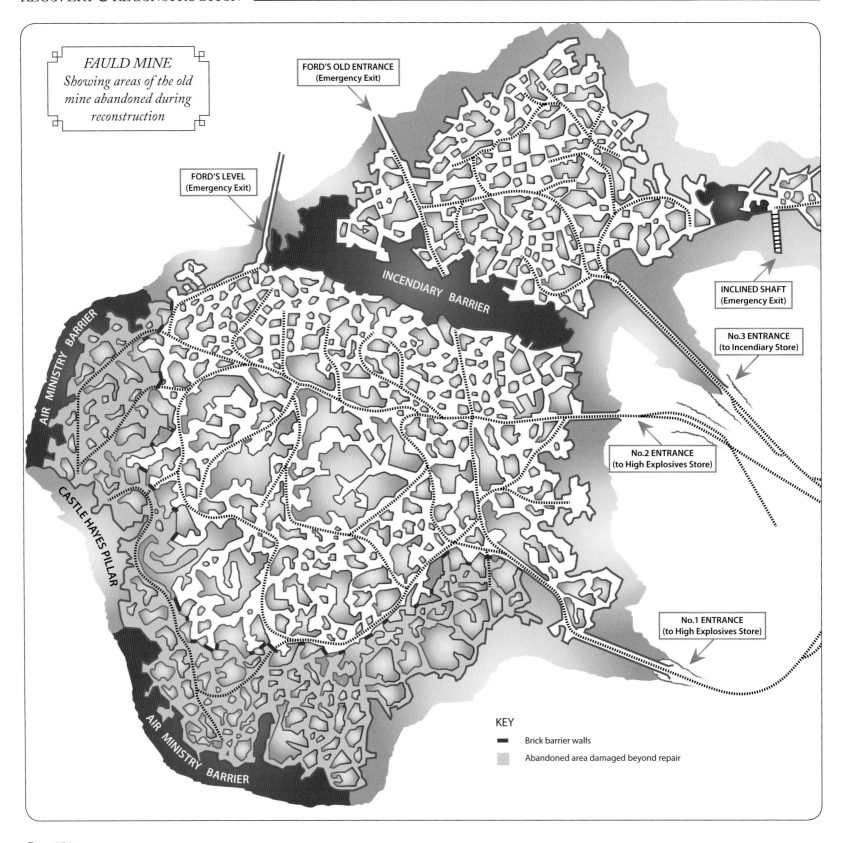

FAULD MINE
Showing areas of the old mine abandoned during reconstruction

FORD'S OLD ENTRANCE
(Emergency Exit)

FORD'S LEVEL
(Emergency Exit)

INCENDIARY BARRIER

AIR MINISTRY BARRIER

CASTLE HAYES PILLAR

AIR MINISTRY BARRIER

INCLINED SHAFT
(Emergency Exit)

No.3 ENTRANCE
(to Incendiary Store)

No.2 ENTRANCE
(to High Explosives Store)

No.1 ENTRANCE
(to High Explosives Store)

KEY

Brick barrier walls

Abandoned area damaged beyond repair

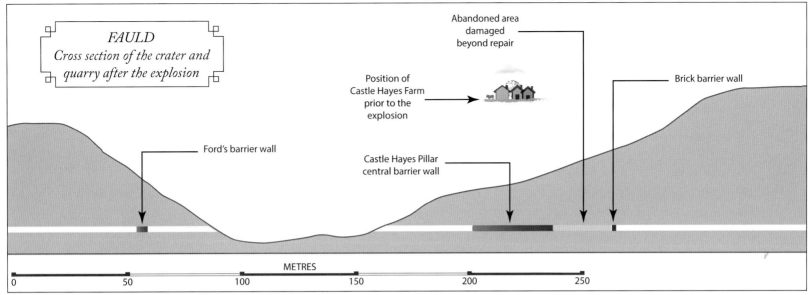

FAULD
Cross section of the crater and
quarry after the explosion

Abandoned area
damaged
beyond repair

Position of
Castle Hayes Farm
prior to the
explosion

Brick barrier wall

Ford's barrier wall

Castle Hayes Pillar
central barrier wall

METRES

0   50   100   150   200   250

Above: West-east cross section of the crater.

standard, then the maximum allowable content would be no more than 4,000 tons of high explosive.

The options then were to rebuild to the original specification, which would provide capacity for an uneconomically small weight of ammunition, or to thoroughly redesign the structure incorporating massive blast walls and traverses to absorb the detonation wave of an accidental internal explosion.

The latter plan was the most attractive, so plans were prepared to re-organize the underground storage into four or five districts each with a capacity of approximately 2,000 tons of HE or a gross weight of weapons of 4,000 tons. The areas were to be sub-divided to ensure that there were no distances greater than 150 feet that were not protected by blast barriers, and full advantage was to be taken of the natural rock formation to form these barriers. There were to be no straight gangways between areas without rock or concrete blast-obstruction. It was thought that the mine could provide adequate storage for 16,000 – 20,000 tons of bombs with a maximum net content of 12,000 tons of high explosive under these conditions. The anticipated cost of this, however, promised to be prohibitive and early in 1947 the Air Ministry recommended that

Plans for traversing the Fauld depot to the specification of the special panel should be drawn up but should not be implemented

Opposite: A post-reconstruction plan of the High Explosive store. The pink shading indicates the damaged areas which it had been hoped to reconstruct but which were eventually abandoned.

until a further emergency arises. It will then be for the authorities then responsible to decide whether traversing will be put into effect and the High Explosive content raised, or whether the emergency is such as to justify an increased risk of increasing the holdings without traversing.

Ultimately only minimal reconstruction was undertaken, the most important works being the construction of walls and backfill blocks to stem the flow of mud and water from the crater area. Shattered pillars in the area of the Castle Hayes Pillar were supported by brickwork and concrete shuttering, and elsewhere mining arches were erected to support weakened areas of roof.

It had initially been hoped that most of the Old Area to within close proximity of the Castle Hayes Pillar could be recovered and, indeed, at early stage reclamation work was started in the area to the north of the pillar approaching Ford's Level and the emergency exit. It was found, however, that the continued ingress of mud from the crater could not be stemmed and this work was abandoned in a partially finished state. Similarly, a large area running along the entire southern boundary of the Old Area, from the now destroyed tunnel through the Air Ministry Barrier to No.1 entrance was also abandoned. The main lateral force of the explosion seems to have completely destroyed the barrier adjacent to the tunnel allowing the blast wave to exert its full destructive effect throughout this area of the mine before venting itself through No.1 entrance. Lightweight brick walls were constructed around the damaged and abandoned areas leaving a buffer zone approximately one hundred feet in depth between the original perimeter of the mine and the area that was eventually recovered and re-commissioned.

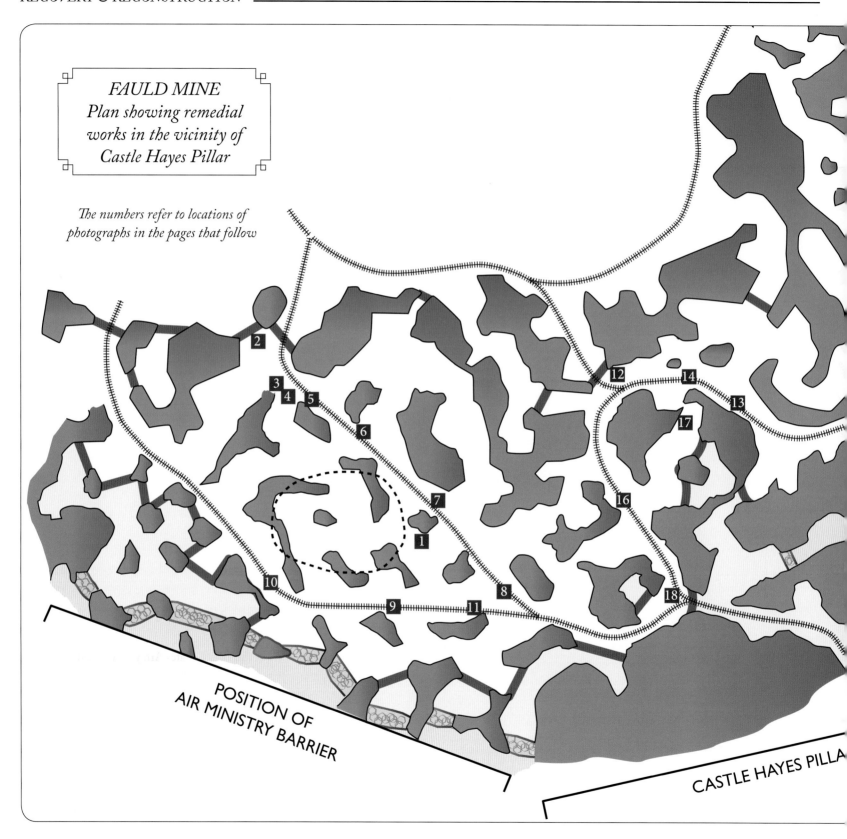

FAULD MINE
Plan showing remedial
works in the vicinity of
Castle Hayes Pillar

The numbers refer to locations of
photographs in the pages that follow

POSITION OF
AIR MINISTRY BARRIER

CASTLE HAYES PILLA

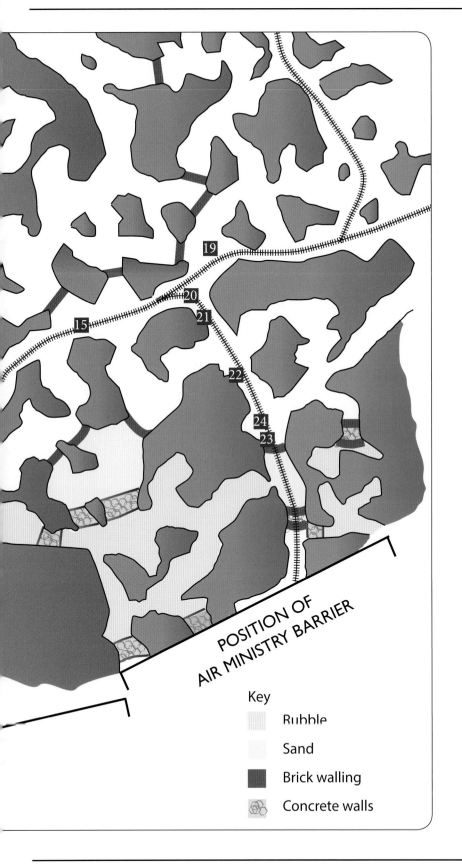

Key

Rubble

Sand

Brick walling

Concrete walls

POSITION OF
AIR MINISTRY BARRIER

Left: This detailed plan of the pillars and walls in the vicinity of the Castle Hayes pillar illustrates the various remedial measures undertaken by the Air Ministry Works Department to stabilise the most badly damaged area of the HE mine.

The first task, other than ensure the stability of the roof where it had been badly shaken by the blast, was to stem the inflow of mud and debris from the crater. It was initially hoped that this could be accomplished by reconstructing the pre-disaster barriers to the north and south of the Castle Hayes pillar, a task that was completed by filling the voids between pillars created by the blast with rock and debris and containing this with a facing wall of either battered concrete or cemented block wall.

Although the Air Ministry was confident that all the accessible munitions buried beneath roof falls and collapsed pillars had been recovered by Dr Rotter and his team, it was felt that there was a remaining risk that some unexploded bombs may have fallen back into the crater and be deeply and undetectably buried there. To obviate any future risk to the depot from such munitions spontaneously detonating, thousands of tons of sand were brought into the mine to create a shock absorbing barrier. The sand barrier was contained behind brick curtain walls built, in most places, some forty feet out from the concrete or cemented stone block walls. As the photographs on the pages that follow illustrate, none of this work proved wholly effective and mud from the crater continued to overwhelm the barriers and flow into the areas it had been hoped to reconstruct.

Eventually almost the whole of the damaged area with the exception of that between the lower section of 'F' Loop and the emergency exit was abandoned and a brick perimeter wall built, leaving a deep 'buffer-zone' between the crater perimeter and the surviving parts of the depot. At first a number of inspection doorways were left into this area together with several grilled sections to allow for the circulation of air, but later, probably when the United States Army moved in during the 1960s, the whole area was completely sealed.

The numerals in red rectangles on this plan denote the locations of the photographs on the pages that follow.

1 *Above:* In this area, to the north of the Castle Hayes pillar work had started on the strengthening of a damaged pillar but was then abandoned as the new works were overwhelmed by the inflow of mud. Notice the steel reinforcing bars protruding from the partially completed brickwork, which seems to be bulging slightly under pressure from the roof. There appears to have been a relatively recent roof fall to the left of the pillar.

2 The walls in the background are part of the boundary between the recovered area of the old HE store and the section abandoned due to damage sustained in the explosion of 1944. It had been hoped, ultimately in vain, that much of this area north of the Castle Hayes pillar could be recovered. The railway line to the right of the picture is the old main line, known as Ford's Level and later re-designated 'F' Loop when the original reconstruction plans were drawn up. In the end only a short stub-end of this line was brought back into use.

3   *Opposite:* In the background there is an almost completed new concrete pillar which, like much of the concrete work in Fauld, has been constructed using vertical corrugated steel sheeting as external shuttering. At first sight it appeared that the green-painted corrugated steel in the middle distance was shuttering that had been left in place around another uncompleted pillar, but further investigation showed that it was, in fact, a courtesy wall around a workmen's urinal. There have been a number of roof falls since work was abandoned in this area. Notice the yellow line marked on the ceiling – in most quarries adapted for military purposes during the Second World War this was marked-out by the surveyors and usually denoted the centre-line of proposed railways. The white line to the right of it appears to be an older marking that has been chiselled away. In this case neither line seems to correspond with the existing line of rails, so their meanings remain something of a mystery.

4   *Above:* The rather crude arrangement inside the workmen's urinal provides an interesting study in concrete hydrodynamics. Where the buckets were tipped once filled is anyone's guess.

5 *Above:* In this area known as the 'Frying Pan', a short distance to the south of the picture opposite, a substantial new brick reinforcement has been constructed, but next to it there has been a substantial roof fall. Behind the concrete platform in the foreground, which is an original bomb loading area adjacent to the narrow-gauge railway, there is an area supported by temporary wooden props awaiting more permanent works to be put in place. However, debris from the crater has broken through to the right of the propped area curtailing work there.

6 *Opposite:* The glazed, bull-nosed bricks used on the corners of many of the walls are a curious feature of the building work in this area.

7 *Above:* To the left can be seen a new brick wall, representing some half-completed repair works using as a foundation a former raised loading platform beside the un-named loop of railway track between the main line and 'F' Loop. Notice the yellow line on the ceiling above the line of rails. Although damage looks relatively light here, with just a minor roof fall, there is a substantial inflow of mud visible in the background.

8 *Opposite:* A little further towards the Castle Hayes pillar the route of the un-named loop is filled to the roof with mud and slurry and is quite impassable. The heavy wooden timbers to the right of this view are temporary support put in when it was hoped this area could be salvaged. Graffiti on the left-hand wall dates from 1941, when the depot was in active use.

9

Above: This photograph, taken on an abandoned section of 'F' Loop, indicates the scale of remedial work undertaken before the area was completely abandoned. The new wall to the left of the central pillar appears to have been partially demolished by a roof fall. The cost of producing the curved steel beams to the right, which are probably the first of a series that would have extended the whole length of the wall, must have been out of all proportion to the value of the storage space they facilitated.

10

Right: The openings in this brick support wall beside 'F' Loop appear at first sight to be doorways into offices but are, in fact, just blind arches built, one must assume, to economise on the use of bricks. Notice the section of wall loosened and dislodged by movement of the rock ceiling above.

11

Right: A little further towards the Castle Hayes pillar the route of 'F' Loop is completely blocked by a thick gypsum slurry. Here the rolled steel mining arches and the junction of the un-named loop have partially disappeared beneath the ingress from the crater. The photograph on page 167 shows the route of the loop line on the far side of the left-hand pillar.

12 *Above:* Here, just inside the boundary wall where the old main line joins the line through the Castle Hayes pillar, the timbering above the rolled steel arches has given way and the roadway is partially blocked by a substantial roof fall. The rails to the left continue in a curve before entering the tunnel through the Castle Hayes pillar joining the old and new areas of the mine.

13 *Above:* On the old main line, a pair of mining arches bent over by the force of the blast.

14 *Above:* Mining arches partially warped by the heat generated by the explosion and subsequent blast wave. Although the heat must have been quite intense, if brief, and the timbers used as packing above the arches appear scorched, there is only a minor amount of smoke-blackening to the walls and ceiling compared with nearby areas. Notice the greenish-blue colouring of the early installation of copper sheathed 'pyro' fireproof cabling on the ceiling, a result of chemical reaction resulting from the brief exposure to high temperature and a cocktail of chemicals from the explosion. It appears that the rails have been removed in this passageway, probably for reuse elsewhere to assist with moving sand or other materials to reconstruct the barrier.

15 *Above:* A section of the main line close to the Air Ministry Barrier, near to its junction with the line through the barrier. The overhead cover in this area was already unstable (hence the numerous steel arch supports), and the explosion has brought down large areas of roof. Its proximity to the main pathway of the blast wave through the destroyed barrier has resulted in considerable contamination by smoke and soot.

16 *Above*: This view shows the old main line in close proximity to the tunnel through the Castle Hayes pillar, which is just a few metres from the right-hand edge of this photograph. The short railway branch to the right, heading into a pile of sand, is not a feature of the original railway layout but is one of a number of short shunting spurs put in to handle the many wagon-loads of bricks, sand and other building materials required to shore up the damaged area. Note the density of the soot from the explosion and subsequent fire, blackening the walls and ceiling. The concrete arch visible through the right-hand opening can be seen in more detail opposite.

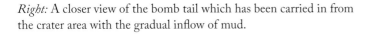

17 *Above*: One of the few sections of concrete reinforcement constructed at the inward end of the depot, close to the tunnel leading through the Castle Hayes pillar to the new area. Notice the crack in the left-hand wall caused by ground movement at the time of the explosion, and the heavy wooden door which was probably one of a pair securing the end of the tunnel to the new area. Note, too, the bomb-tail protruding from the mud close to the right-hand wall.

Right: A closer view of the bomb tail which has been carried in from the crater area with the gradual inflow of mud.

18 *Above:* The blocked entrance to the tunnel through the Castle Hayes pillar. Behind the hard-packed rubble wall the entire accessible length of the tunnel has been filled to the roof with sand to form a shock-absorbing barrier.

19 *Above*: This smoke-blackened pillar is typical of the area near the severely damaged Air Ministry Barrier which suffered the brunt of the blast.

20 *Above:* No. 20 Road (the railway link to the new area via the tunnel through the Air Ministry Barrier), near its junction with the old main line.

21 *Right:* A little to the west of the image above, this view of No.20 Road shows evidence of roof falls that have occurred since the explosion. A very large slab of rock has fallen against the right-hand side of the mining arches while another fall of smaller boulders has partially blocked the rails in the foreground.

22 *Overleaf:* The intensity of the explosion and fire can be gauged from the density of soot visible in this photograph of No.20 Road close to the partially demolished Air Ministry Barrier. The railway line branching off to the left is another of the temporary spurs laid in to facilitate the transport of building materials. The old ammunition box seen nearby contains fishplates and bolts used to assemble this track.

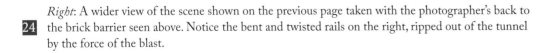

23 *Above*: The securely bricked-up entrance to the tunnel through the Air Ministry Barrier. The lettering incised into the brickwork reads DANGER RUNNING SAND BEHIND BARRIER 1946'.

24 *Right*: A wider view of the scene shown on the previous page taken with the photographer's back to the brick barrier seen above. Notice the bent and twisted rails on the right, ripped out of the tunnel by the force of the blast.

Crater

Ford's factory (rebuilt)

FAULD MINE
Crater and mine entrances in 1946 following reconstruction

Rebuilt HE Entrance No.2

Rebuilt HE Entrance No.1

Rebuilt Detonator Entrance

Temporary HE stores
(Nissen huts on east pyro site)

Temporary HE stores
(Nissen huts on west pyro site)

Reclamation of land

The problem of what to do with the contaminated surface land became critical because it was realized that if it was left unmanaged the derelict area would soon become a liability to the surrounding cultivated land by harbouring- weeds and vermin. Eventually the RAF found it necessary to purchase 273 acres of the most badly disturbed agricultural land which it was thought could never be brought back into profitable use. Initially the RAF saw little prospect of improving the land, due to the limited availability of labour, but in June 1945 a novel regeneration scheme presented itself.

As a matter of expediency immediately after the explosion, an arrangement had been made for prisoners from Stafford jail to assist with the clearance work, but following a meeting between the prison governor and representatives of Maintenance Command, a longer-term solution was proposed. The prison governor suggested on 27 June that he should become a contractor to the RAF for the partial reinstatement of the damaged land, providing labour free of charge, if the RAF could cover the cost of transportation and domestic facilities for the prisoners when on site. It was suggested that a joint representation by the Air Ministry and the Prison Commissioners should be made to the Treasury for funding this scheme, the RAF staff suggesting that the Prison Commissioners would represent the case to the Treasury more as a scheme for the reclamation of criminals than the reclamation of damaged land and, with the Air Ministry making an initial issue of plant, lorries, huts etc, the Commissioners would accept liability for the replacement of them as necessary and for their continued maintenance, recouping themselves as far as possible from the sale of produce. In effect the Commissioners would become tenants of the land at Fauld and would work it for what they could get from it.

The general principles of this plan were quickly agreed, but there was some contention regarding the time scale over which the RAF would provide transportation and other services free of charge. The Commissioners considered that if the majority of the land was eventually restored to agricultural rather than forestry use (the former being the more potentially profitable option) then a period of three years would be appropriate, for by 1948 it should have become a viable economic proposition. The RAF thought eight or nine months a more attractive period but eventually gave way.

It was finally agreed that the Air Ministry would provide the necessary services until 1948 on a sliding scale, but insisted that as certain areas were reinstated those suitable for agricultural use should be let to commercial farmers, and unviable areas like the crater should be planted with trees and eventually transferred to the Forestry Commission. Over 34,000 trees, principally ash, spruce and poplar, were planted on the worst affected land at Hanbury Fields Farm alone. To accommodate the prison workforce the RAF refurbished a couple of huts at the domestic camp on the old USAAF searchlight site at Draycott-in-the-Clay and provided in addition 'a marquee, a few tables and chairs and barrack stores'.

Conscious always of the need to minimize costs, an internal Air Ministry memorandum, dated May 1946 noted:

Where we can now arrange agricultural lettings to farmers as the land becomes cleared or can get it planted with trees, we must do this rather than leave the Prison Governor to cultivate the land at any cost to us.

On the same theme, the author continued:

Now that the area remaining for reclamation has so sensibly diminished we assume that steps will be taken to reduce the numbers of transport, civil engineering and agricultural vehicles to a minimum and that succeeding returns will show appreciable reductions in both the extent of plant and operating expenditure.

With much of the day-to-day responsibility transferred to the Agricultural Executive Committee, the reclamation programme ran on until 1949 and was an unqualified success, as was made clear in a letter from Mr L. Kins, chairman of the committee, to the Air Ministry in April, just before the scheme was wound up:

I thank you very much for your kind letter of 22 instant and beg to assure you that it has been a most interesting experience to be associated with the work of reinstatement of lands damaged by the explosion at Fauld in November 1944.

The success of the restoration has been achieved, primarily in my opinion, through the smooth and excellent co-operation there has always been between the parties mainly concerned, namely your Ministry, the Prison Authorities and my Committee, through the whole period that the work has been in progress.

Closure of the depot

For a short time from 1966 the depot was leased to the American Army to house ammunition expelled from France following de

Gaulle's decision to withdraw his country from NATO. Due to operational problems (including technical difficulties raised by the proposed introduction by British Railways of colour-light signalling on the main line adjacent to Scropton Sidings) and other safety considerations, the RAF decided in October 1967 that the Fauld depot and its associated sidings were no longer viable. The United States Army were offered and accepted the recently decommissioned Royal Navy Cordite Factory site at Caerwent in South Wales as an alternative and a two-year evacuation programme was subsequently drawn up. Closure had been on the cards for several years before this, however, and arrangements were already in hand for the disposal of much of the peripheral land, including the two hundred acres of recovered agricultural land blighted by the explosion.

The RAF had been negotiating with various parties for some years in an effort to generate a commercial return from the crater and its surrounding land, but had had to proceed with caution in order to avoid upsetting local sensibilities. Discussions had continued since 1960 with the Central Electricity Generating Board, which proposed filling the crater with fly-ash from its generating stations, but this proposal was finally withdrawn on the basis of scientific advice in 1964. Calculations had indicated that the fly-ash would have absorbed huge volumes of rainwater which would have put an intolerable load on the still-active underground gypsum quarry galleries nearby and would also have caused mud seepage and flooding of the bomb store in winter. A later scheme to sell the crater to the local authority for use as a refuse dump was met with a local furore and the threat of a national outcry, as the following report from the Air Officer Commanding in Chief to the Ministry of Defence indicates:

The Commanding Officer, RAF Fauld, has had further discussions with the Chief Public Health Inspector of the Tutbury Rural District Council who is of the opinion that a refusal of his request to use the Fauld crater for rubbish disposal will result in a great deal of local, if not national, press comment and perhaps Parliamentary questions when the matter is reported to the council.

The crater remains today and will now do so in perpetuity. A rough cross of white alabaster in its base commemorates those whose bodies remain buried there, while a granite memorial put up by Hanbury Parish Council stands on its western edge.

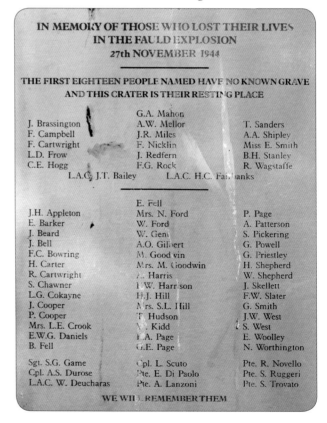

Chapter 10

SURVIVING SURFACE FEATURES

The history of the depot from its reconstruction in the late 1940s, through its continued use by the RAF up until 1966 and its brief period of American occupation prior to final closure in 1967 is not well documented. Despite the obvious contrary evidence there appears to have been a general public assumption that following the explosion the underground storage area was almost completely destroyed and that the little that remained was abandoned and sealed-up as kind of war grave. This assumption seems to persist still today. However, as we have seen in the previous chapter, such is not the case. Almost the whole of the 'old' High Explosives mine except for the area immediately adjacent to the Castle Hayes pillar and the Air Ministry barrier was recovered and put back into service and the incendiary mine was largely undamaged apart from the entrance which was quickly repaired. Similarly, the detonator store seems to have sustained no immediate internal damage, although the long entrance tunnel required substantial rebuilding.

One aspect of the reconstruction task that is not fully recorded is how much of the concrete reinforcement in the eastern section of the HE mine is a feature of the original design and how much is new work resulting from the post-war reconstruction to comply with peacetime safety distances. The majority of the work appears to be original and is of a very different standard to the recorded new work near the Castle Hayes pillar which has been completed in red brick rather than concrete. Another chronological problem concerns several areas of the floor in the detonator store which are badly distorted, possibly as an immediate result of the explosion (the ground cover in this area being much less than elsewhere and thus offering less resistance to movement), or, probably more likely, as a result of gradual settlement of the disturbed land above over many decades.

For twenty years after closure little seemed to change at Fauld. When visited in 1987 most of the buildings on the main camp site and at the mine entrances were intact, as were the east and west incendiary areas, the bunkers in the latter area being used for storage by a fireworks company. Some of the larger buildings in the administration area were in use as storage or for light industry while others lay intact but derelict. The locomotive sheds and the area immediately adjacent to the mine entrance were occupied by British Gas who had established an experimental and research facility there. At Scropton Sidings the bridge over the river Dove had been demolished and the standard gauge track in the yard had been removed. Most of the buildings were demolished although the standard-gauge locomotive shed survived and much of the narrow gauge rail network was still intact on the platforms. All the mine entrances were clearly visible although sealed by concrete-block walls.

At the time of writing, in July 2014, the scene has changed substantially. A small number of original buildings survive at the camp site although most have been demolished to make way for a modern industrial estate. The incendiary bunkers still survive, as do the majority of the buildings in the locomotive area together with those near the mine entrance, although these are being gradually swamped by a vast and growing mountain of waste timber, for the site is now occupied by a waste disposal company. The cuttings leading to the mine entrances have recently been completely backfilled with earth and debris and their locations are now difficult to identify.

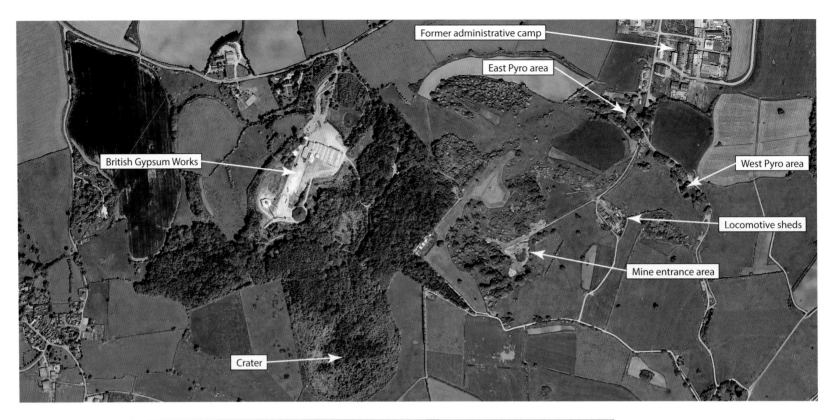

Former administrative camp

East Pyro area

British Gypsum Works

West Pyro area

Locomotive sheds

Mine entrance area

Crater

FIRE ALARM

IN THE EVENT OF FIRE
* BREAK GLASS *
TELEPHONE EXCHANGE
GIVING EXACT LOCATION
OF THE FIRE

Above: A contemporary aerial view of the RAF Fauld camp site. The overgrown crater, although still easily discernable, is not as prominent as it was just a decade or so earlier. The current British Gypsum works stands a short distance to the north-west of the site of Ford's destroyed factory. Buildings in the locomotive maintenance area and both groups of pyrotechnic magazines have survived largely intact. To the north, the majority of the buildings on the administrative site have been demolished to make way for a small industrial estate.

Left: This building, identified on the Air Ministry site plan simply as 'Timber Building (used as garden shed)', appears to have been moved from its original position but has retained its former function. Notice the fire-alarm break-glass push button and adjacent sign.

Above left: This substantial, windowless structure is marked on the official plan as the telephonic communications building.
Below: Nearby, this other monolithic structure is the depot's main electricity substation, surrounded by a substantial protective blast wall. When this photograph was taken in 1987 the substation was still in use providing power to a number of houses locally and to the industrial estate, which was then in the early stages of development.

Above right: This group of buildings in the camp's communal area, still standing in 1987, included the civilian workers canteen, adapted for use at that time as a community centre.
Right: This building, somewhat whimsically labelled on the door 'Bomb Disposal' was in fact the communal site's vegetable preparation and storage building.
Below right: This unidentified building on the headquarters site, possibly the Officers' Mess, appears to have been in the process of demolition when this photograph was taken in 1987.

Above: Building No. 304 on the station stores site, identified on the official plan as a Type 'P' storage building.

Above: Remains of the narrow-gauge railway from Scropton Sidings run along both sides of the main road through the surface camp towards the mine entrances.

Opposite below: The narrow-gauge locomotive sheds and maintenance facility in 1987, at which time the site was utilized as a research facility by British Gas. Notice the surviving camouflage paintwork on the end of the electric loco shed on the right. The left-hand building was the diesel loco shed. Original a third building, used for locomotive maintenance, stood between them.

Right: The small warden's hut at the entrance to the east pyrotechnics area.

Below: The more substantial police lodge guarding the west pyrotechnics area.

Above left: The entrance to one of the six large semi-underground bunkers on the west pyrotechnics site.

Above: This view, looking west from the railway incline leading up to the detonator store, shows the rebuilt transformer house supplying power to the Incendiary store, with the start of the railway cutting leading to No.2 entrance to the HE store in the background.

Left: The top of the emergency exit shaft from Ford's workings, which also acted indirectly as a ventilation suction shaft for the new area of the bomb store. It was via this shaft that Ford's underground foreman, Jack Gordon, and two of his men managed to escape after the explosion.

Above: The mine entrance area during the period of British Gas occupancy. The building to the right with the bricked-up window is the Air Ministry police lodge. The grey building to the left is the time-checker's office and the red brick building beyond is a latrine block. The shadowy area beyond the latrine is the cutting to No.2 HE entrance.

Right: The bricked-up entrance to the incendiary store. This is located to the right of the HE entrance and is one hundred feet or so behind the latrine block.

Right: Slightly to the east of the mine entrance area on the north side of the main access road there is a narrow, steep-sided, flat bottomed valley in which the Air Ministry established an Ammunition Inspection Department examination compound. Amongst the buildings in this compound were a boilerhouse and boiling-out plant, a detonator exploding bay, a proofing tunnel, and, this, a bomb-test building.

Below: Built into the hillside, it is constructed of massive timbers and is surrounded by a blast wall with the intervening space filled with sand. The single-storey test chamber has a flat, steel-plate ceiling overtopped by a pitched-roof second story filled with several feet of aggregate. This view shows the entrance end, the doorway partially obscured by collapsed timber.

Left: A view of the bomb-test building from above. The whole of the above ground section is the upper floor which was filled with loose aggregate to dissipate some of the blast in the event of an accidental explosion.

Right: On the hillside edge above the bomb-test building stands this splinter-proof aircraft-spotter's shelter which has extensive clear views over the countryside to the south of the depot. Unusually, much of the internal timber work has survived.

Below left: One of several concrete air-raid shelters in the communal site. Originally these were all buried under substantial mounds of earth. Most have been demolished and this one, which is in an area scheduled for industrial redevelopment, has had its earth mound removed in preparation for demolition.

Below: A pillbox, located in close proximity to the spotter's shelter overlooking the mine entrances. Notice the angle-iron supports that once supported camouflage material, possibly a pitched roof to make it look like a small domestic building.

Chapter 11

UNDERGROUND TOUR

Above: The heavily overgrown cutting heading towards No.2 High Explosives entrance. The barred gates securing the entrance can just be seen through the nettles and fallen tree. Before the explosion the banks on either side of the cutting were sloped but during the rebuild these brick retaining walls were constructed.

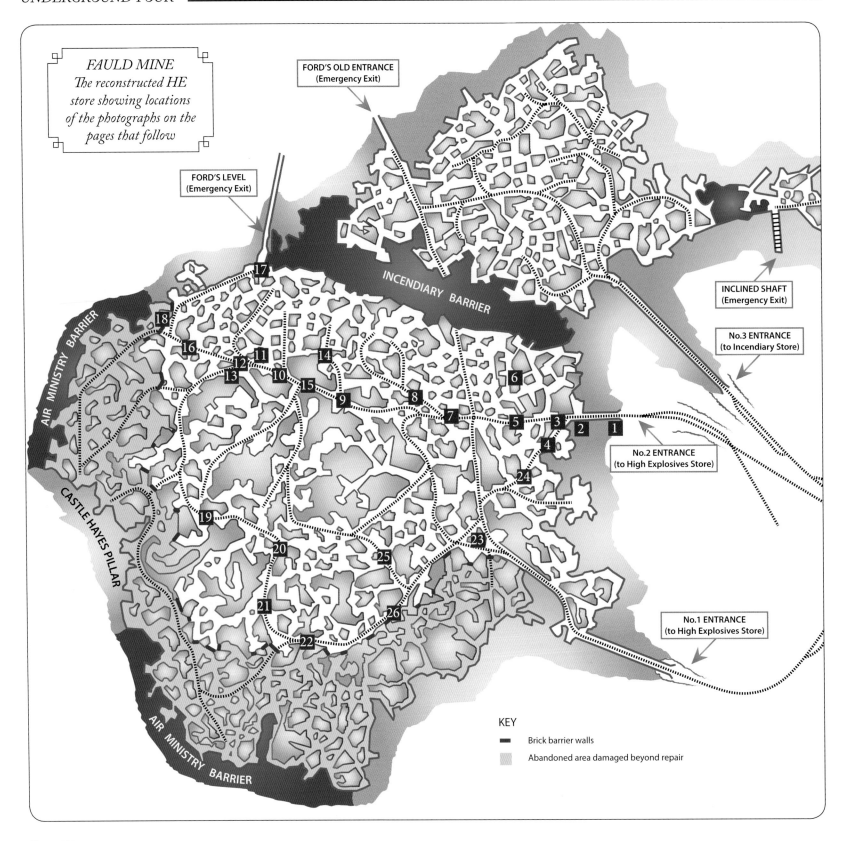

FAULD MINE
The reconstructed HE
store showing locations
of the photographs on the
pages that follow

FORD'S OLD ENTRANCE
(Emergency Exit)

FORD'S LEVEL
(Emergency Exit)

INCENDIARY BARRIER

INCLINED SHAFT
(Emergency Exit)

No.3 ENTRANCE
(to Incendiary Store)

No.2 ENTRANCE
(to High Explosives Store)

No.1 ENTRANCE
(to High Explosives Store)

AIR MINISTRY BARRIER

CASTLE HAYES PILLAR

AIR MINISTRY BARRIER

KEY

Brick barrier walls

Abandoned area damaged beyond repair

1 *Above:* Immediately inside the gates this long, concrete-lined rectangular tunnel leads into the main High Explosives area of the depot. The danger sign refers to the massive 'up-and-over' blast door at the end of this tunnel, a photograph of which can be seen overleaf. The angled steel plate seen behind the danger sign is to protect from the risk of damage by a derailed truck the large number of power cables that emerge from an underground duct at this point. The cables are then supported on high level hangers up to the blast door where they are carried down again into under-floor ducts.

2 *Opposite:* The up-and-over blast door protecting the HE store from a nearby external blast. The door is rather like a standard garage door except that it weighs several tons. The danger referred to by the sign at the entrance is recognition of the fact that it is suspended overhead by a pair of distinctly corroded steel cables.

2 *Right:* The counterweight and winding mechanism for the blast door. The door could be raised or lowered by pressing push-buttons on the wall on either side. As an emergency measure it was possible to hand-crank the door from the outside by means of a removable handle on the end of the motor shaft, which protruded through the wall. Electrical interlocking between the door and external gates ensured that only one could be open at any time.

3 *Below:* Just beyond the blast door the main line heads west towards the inner-most end of the mine while a branch to the left passes the carpenter's workshop and heads towards the Triangle, the route to No.1 entrance and the return leg of the main line running up the south side of the depot.

4 *Above:* A view towards the Triangle with the carpenter's shop and store on the left, together with some damaged switchgear. A great deal of damage to the electrical equipment appears to have been caused when scrap metal thieves broke into the depot in the early 1980s.

5 *Right:* A view looking up the main line, under the blast door and towards the entrance tunnel. The railway spur to the left leads to the bulk explosives magazine.

Right: The two-road standard-gauge locomotive shed at Scropton sidings.

Below left: Narrow-gauge rails still in situ at Scropton sidings in 1987.

Below right: The raised concrete structures are the edges of the loading platforms at Scropton. The now empty trackbed of the yard's two standard gauge sidings run between them. The square concrete blocks are the bases for the girders which once supported an overall canopy above the full length of the loading bays. In the right-hand distance can be seen the red brick Transportation Office.

6 *Right:* Inside the magazine area the single line spur branches into two loading sidings. The explosives storage area is on the far side of the left-hand wall and from the railway sidings is accessible only through the green-painted hatch visible in the middle distance. The magazine could hold up to 20,000 tons of raw TNT in boxes.

6 *Below left:* a view through the hatch into the storage area.

6 *Below right:* Throughout the TNT storage bays the floors are covered with an inch-thick layer of spark-proof bituminous composition.

7 *Right:* The two images on this page show the junction of the Main Line and No.1 Shunt. This view is looking east on the Main Line towards No.2 entrance, with 'A' Loop on the right heading towards the Triangle and No.1 entrance. No.1 Shunt merges with the Main Line to the left of this photograph.

7 *Below:* This view, looking west towards the crater, shows 'A' Loop merging with the Main Line on the left-hand side and No.1 shunt curving off into the storage areas to the right. The high-level pipeline carries fire-fighting water; the yellow-painted pipe-junction is a fire hose connection point.

8 *Above:* A view along No.1 Shunt showing the district toilet block on the left. Lavatory facilities in the depot were fairly primate, employing Elsan chemical toilets rather than flush toilets and a proper sewage system. Notice that off the main railway lines the level of roof supports is somewhat less monumental.

9 *Above:* The cathedral like architecture at the junction of the Main Line with No.2 Shunt on the right (which subsequently branches to form No.3 Shunt). A little further down the Main Line 'B' Loop diverges to the left.

10 *Opposite:* In this view we see the Main Line disappearing east through the arches in the centre background, heading towards No.2 entrance. No.5 Shunt can be seen merging from the left and 'D' Loop branches from the Main Line in the background and runs behind the pillar carrying the warning sign. This loop passes through the middle of the depot and eventually re-joins the Main Line on its outward leg towards No.1 entrance.

11

Left: This image shows one of the most important junctions in the HE store, where traffic destined for the New Area would be separated from that either heading into storage or routed for despatch via No.1 entrance. 'A' Group office, where all the administration for the Old Area was done and where stockholding records were kept, is accessed by a door in the left-hand wall. The left-hand railway line is the new Main Line, formerly known as 'E' Loop before the explosion obliterated the lower section of the old main line. The route diverging to the right of the new Main Line in front of the office is 'F' Loop, previously known as Ford's Level, which now terminates at the barrier wall although it had been hoped, until the area adjacent to the Castle Hayes pillar was abandoned, that following repairs this would have continued through the recovered area as the main line. Finally, the right-hand line is No.6 shunt, heading towards storage bays near the emergency exit.

12 *Above:* A closer view of the junction of the new Main Line and 'F' Loop, which passes through the only area seriously damaged by the explosion that was successfully repaired. The start of an extensive area of new brickwork can be seen here on both sides of the railway.

13 *Opposite:* The entrance to 'A' Group office. It was from here that Civilian Foreman J.C. Salt ventured forth to look down No.6 Shunt, Ford's Level and the Main Line after he heard the first explosion.

13 *Left:* A closer view of the front of 'A' Group office.

13 *Below left:* The view from inside the office looking out with the start of Ford's Level visible in the background. Foreman Salt had just walked in through this doorway to fetch his torch when the blast wave from the explosion struck, blowing both he and Storeman Cresswell and Airman Still, who were completing some record-keeping in the office at the time, bodily out through the door onto the railway line.

13 *Below right:* The interior of 'A' Group office showing the rear pedestrian exit which gives direct access to the storage areas in the heart of the depot.

14

Left: A typical storage area on the north side of the depot in the vicinity of No.4 Shunt.

15 *Right:* The junction of No.4 Shunt, curving away to the bottom left of this view, and the Main Line, looking north. The derelict state of the wagon chassis standing on the main line is not due to blast damage but is a result of timber decay caused by almost fifty years' incarceration in a damp and unventilated mine. The green door partly concealed behind a pillar gives access to a small toilet block.

16 *Above:* Major reconstruction work is evident here in the north-west corner of the depot, close to the damaged section of the Air Ministry Barrier north of the Castle Hayes pillar. The extensive use of brickwork and heavy rolled steel joists in this post-war reconstruction is quite unlike the engineering elsewhere in the depot.

16 *Above opposite:* More post-war reconstruction in a storage bay to the north of the photograph seen above.

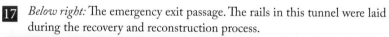
17 *Below left:* Blast doors at the inward end of the emergency exit.

17 *Below right:* The emergency exit passage. The rails in this tunnel were laid during the recovery and reconstruction process.

18

The end of the surviving section of 'F' Loop, with No.7 Shunt branching to the right. The tank wagon was part of the depot's fire brigade train. The brick wall in the background is the barrier sealing off the damaged area below the rim of the crater.

18 *Above:* The end of 'F' loop, looking in the opposite direction to the photograph on the previous page. The decaying ammunition truck is standing at the start of No.7 Shunt .

18

Left: A short rake of derelict wagons standing on 'F' Loop just to the west of the rebuilt area shown on page 214, near the concrete-lined tunnel at the junction with No.7 Shunt.

18

Below: Another view of the accumulation of wagons at the inner-most extremity of the depot, showing the proximity of the 'F' Loop and No.7 Shunt junction to the post-restoration perimeter wall on the right-hand side of this view.

18 *Above:* Detailed view of one of the derelict wagons at the end of 'F' Loop, showing the construction of the wooden superstructure and the arrangement of the brakesman's handle and platform. Individual braking of these wagons was important due to the relatively steep inclines inside the depot and on the surface route to Scropton Sidings.

19 *Above:* This location, in the south west corner of the new area, marks the transition between the area of the mine, adjacent to the Castle Hayes pillar, brought into use prematurely in 1938 to satisfy urgent RAF storage requirements, and the more heavily engineered area to the east. The main line curves away to the east through the green doors, with the stub-end of No.8 shunt cut short at the barrier wall. The green doors control airflow at the innermost end of the depot.

20 *Left:* A typical view along the Main Line at the innermost end of the depot; the absence of significant engineering works is a feature of this area. The section of the mine close to the Castle Hayes pillar was the first to be brought into use, towards the end of 1938, and in order to commission this area as quickly as possible the work undertaken there was necessarily minimal. The walls and ceiling here are noticeably smoke-blackened as a consequence of the explosion.

21 *Above:* A raised stacking area to the right of the picture opposite with some concrete roof support pillars visible in the background.

22

Left & above: An example of one of the new, steel-bodied double-bogie ammunition wagons bought in the post-war years as replacements for those lost in the explosion of 1944. The location is on the outward leg of the Main Line in the south-west corner of the depot at the point where the steel arched and concrete lined tunnels run out, giving way to the more lightly engineered structure seen on the previous page. This wagon appears to have been last used by the Works Department to remove stone waste from the depot, probably from the roof fall, evidence of which can be seen in the foreground of the image opposite.

22 *Right:* The brass maker's plate from the wagon indicates that it was built by Hudson's in 1955 and that its Air Ministry serial number was 226. I believe the number '263' painted on the end was a lot number put on when all the rolling stock was put up for auction when the depot closed.

23

Above: A 270-degree panoramic view of the Triangle showing, from left to right, the line coming into the depot from No.1 entrance, the Main Line heading south-west towards the wagon shown on the previous page, and the northward run of the Main Line towards No.2 entrance. The branch to the right goes into the Ammunition Inspection Chamber.

24

Opposite: Several bays to the east of the line linking No.1 entrance and No.2 entrance were made inaccessible from the railway line by these steel grilles. Access could, however, be gained from the route into the Ammunition Inspection Chamber and it is possible that these bays were dedicated to ammunition awaiting inspection.

25

Right: The wide expanse of 'D' Loop, illustrating the flattened arches and steel-shuttered concrete construction widely used in the central area of the HE store.

26 *Above:* This view of the Main Line shows a typical example of the steel and concrete reinforcement constructed above most of the railway routes in the depot. It forms, essentially, a canopy protecting both trains and personnel from the risk of roof falls.

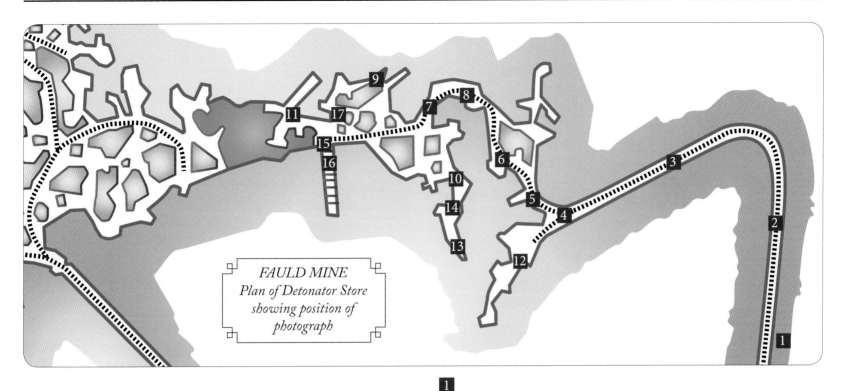

FAULD MINE
Plan of Detonator Store
showing position of
photograph

The Detonator Store

1

Below: An exterior view of the 'artificial' access tunnel that curves around the hillside edge before entering the detonator store. The large concrete block is a plug that once blocked an opening in the side of the tunnel, possibly an abandoned emergency exit, but that has slipped out of position due to subsidence on the hillside.

The detonator store (sometimes referred to as the fuse store) is a relatively small area of the mine separated from the adjacent incendiary store by a fifty-foot wide rubble barrier. The entrance was badly damaged in the explosion of 1944 and, as no pre-explosion photographs of the area have been discovered, there is no positive evidence that the rebuilt entrance was similar to that which it replaced. The new entrance is inordinately long, consisting of a 500-foot long tunnel that turns through 180 degrees to face back towards the No.2 HE entrance. Much of this is built on the cut-and-cover principle along the edge of a natural precipice. It is possible that the original entrances consisted of just the first short leg of this tunnel.

The detonator store has a somewhat shallower overburden than the rest of the depot and appears to be constructed within a more irregular stratum of rock. Various areas are on different levels which are joined either by sloping passageways or long flights of steps. Although it is recorded that the entrance and the storage areas were reconstructed and re-commissioned after the explosion there is much evidence of severe ground movement, manifesting itself in cracked walls and pillars and in some locations significant upheavals of the floor. It is possible, however, that this damage is the result of ground pressure or settlement that has occurred in the fifty years or so since the depot closed.

2

Above left: Inside the approach tunnel to the detonator store.

3

Above right: Debris from the surface at the location of the guillotine blast door, blocking access to the storage areas. This view is from the outer section of the tunnel.

4

Right: The blockage viewed from the inside of the detonator store. At the time these photographs were taken a small hole enabled access, but once inside a fall of debris completely blocked the only means of egress, precipitating something of a frantic dig through jagged concrete and tangled reinforcing bars to get out again.

5

Above: A view from the first railway junction inside the detonator store out along
the access tunnel with the blockage in the background.

6

Above: The start of the northern branch of the detonator store's railway system, which leads into the main section of the storage area. The stepped passageway to the right lead to a semi-isolated group of chambers including a bay known as the 'museum', which is assumed to have been an exhibition bay in which examples of all the munitions stored at Fauld was kept for reference purposes.

7

Right: A view up the main northern railway line with Bay No.10 on the left and the switchgear for the area lighting in the distance.

8 *Above:* In the middle of the main area of the detonator store the railway line branches into two, the right-hand branch heads west towards the emergency exit and ventilation plant, while the left-hand branch heads south towards a dead-end bay terminating in a roof-fall that predates the construction of the depot.

9 *Above:* Bay No.13 beside the northern main line, also known as the 'Yankee' bay, presumably because American made detonators and fuses were stored there. Notice the grooves and ducts in the floor to drain away seepage water.

10 *Below:* A typical storage area remote from the railway system.

11 *Above:* The southbound branch from the main line, looking north towards the junction. Notice the switchgear for the lighting in this more-or-less self-contained area, and the cracks in the walls and floor the result, it is believed, of ground settlement in the decades since the depot closed.

12 *Above:* Towards the western extremity of the detonator store the upheaval of the floor becomes increasingly pronounced. It is probable that immense stresses were generated at the time of the explosion and that over the subsequent decades this has resulted in structural instability. The shallow ground cover (in places less than thirty-feet), and the proximity of the detonator store to the hillside edge, has rendered it more susceptible to settlement than other areas of the depot.

13 *Right:* Storage bays in the short storage heading near the entrance tunnel. Notice the stepped terracing, necessary on account of the inclination of the stratum at this point.

14 & 15

Right & below: Further examples of structural damage due to ground movement at the innermost end of the depot. Notice the extensive use of guttering and drainage ducts required to cope with seepage water. This indicates that the ground above the mine is badly fractured, allowing water to percolate through. The seepage water is collected in a number of drainage sumps which are fitted with pumps to the surface for use if the natural drainage proves inadequate.

16 *Above:* A typical view in the wet area of the depot. The rails are severely corroded, there are calcite straws (stalactites) hanging from the ceiling and cracks are apparent in the floor and walls on the right hand side of the passageway.

17

Opposite: On the southern perimeter of the innermost end of the detonator store an inclined shaft acts as both a ventilation air shaft and an emergency exit. The emergency exit stairway can be seen behind the two ventilation fans at the bottom of the inclined shaft. The doorway to the right of the fans gives access to a drainage sump and pumping chamber.

18

Right: A view up the emergency exit shaft.

19

Below: Other than the two fans mounted at the bottom of the inclined shaft there is very little ventilation plant in the detonator store. This auxiliary fan, located a short distance from the main pair, ensures that air circulates adequately around the bays on the north side of the depot. Notice the splendid array of calcite stalactites, one of which appears to stretch from floor to ceiling and has formed its own mini-stalagmite.

BIBLIOGRAPHY

For detailed, definitive accounts of the construction and operation of all the underground factories and storage facilities in the Corsham area, see:
N J McCamley, *Secret Underground Cities*, 2014, Folly Books
Nick McCamley, *Second World War Secret Bunkers Second Edition*, 2014, Folly Books

Additional information regarding RAF ammunition storage policy, particularly relating to chemical munitions, can be found in:
N J McCamley, *Disasters Underground*, 2003, Pen & Sword

The complete history of chemical warfare, with special reference to the UK mustard gas factories and underground storage facilities, can be found in:
N J McCamley, *The Secret History of Chemical Warfare*, 2006, Pen & Sword